'Getting to grips with t[h] e our
priority, if we say we're [...] the
world is unravelling ar[c] [...]her
Kingdom's drum becom [...]ess
in to authentic relationsh [...]ce
life throws at us. How el[s] [...]mer True
surrender means that "feas[...] [...], as Jenny points out, will
be a daring, dangerous, e[...]ung adventure. Break out of your
comfort zones and enjoy something far more effective and fruitful;
I dare you!'
Simon Guillebaud, author, speaker, founder of Great Lakes Outreach, Burundi

'This book is inspired, accessible and immediately draws you in.
You could choose to nibble at the edges, but I urge you to tuck
wholeheartedly into this sumptuous feast. Deeply moving at times,
it is challenging and thought-provoking in equal measure. It's also
the sort of book you want to come back to regularly, for digesting
alone or chewing over within church groups.'
Dr David Simmons, Cinnamon Network

'This book is the overflow of the passion of the author. Her words
will inspire you to feast on the goodness of the love of the Father
who has spread a table before you! Pull up a chair and feast!'
Tony Fitzgerald, Apostolic Team Leader, Church of the Nations

'Jenny Sanders takes us on an inspirational journey through the
feast that God lays before us, as we learn to follow Him. *Spiritual
Feasting* is essential reading for anyone who yearns for more than
either bland and stodgy religion or superficially appealing spiritual
bling. Jenny describes how we are invited into deeper intimacy with
the One who is not only the Bridegroom and giver of the feast, but
is Himself the very Bread of Life.
  'This is a book you will want to return to again and again.'
Giles D Lascelle, psychotherapist; author of Breakthrough: The Art of
Surviving

'A friend once suggested that the problem with many followers of
Jesus is that they get stuck at the cross. It's an endless cycle of sin
management and nothing beyond it, never becoming free indeed.

Jenny Sanders has given us the meat of the fuller journey, dispelling the shallow pursuit of happiness, and instead providing the keys for experiencing life, life to the full!'
Ian Hatton, facilitator, speaker, writer, creator of 'Morpheus Genius', South Africa

'This is a book which I recommend for anyone who is serious about following Jesus. It will encourage and challenge you as Jenny unpacks the mystery of the two sides of the cross. On one side is suffering, which we still encounter in many forms; on the other we celebrate the victory of Jesus and the thrill of a new joy-filled life of feasting with Him at the table He has prepared for us, whatever unappealing "menu" we may face.'
Florian Bärtsch (MTh), Chairman of Kingdom Ministries, Switzerland

'There are two things to consider when purchasing a book: the message in the book and the messenger who wrote it. In *Spiritual Feasting*, the messenger and author is Jenny Sanders. I have known her for more than twenty-five years. She is creative, intelligent, witty, sensitive, loyal to God and her family, and an experienced writer. In this book, Jenny reminds us that it's not what you're eating that determines your health; it's what's eating you that determines your health.

'This book will inspire and empower you to move from surviving to thriving in the midst of the storms of life. I encourage you to read and apply it.'
Dr Ed Delph, NATIONStrategy, Phoenix, Arizona; author; Dean of Faith in Culture at Primus University, Phoenix

'Jenny Sanders makes her proclamation, as did the psalmist of old, that, "As for God, his way is perfect" (Psalm 18:30). The words in this book are not merely theoretical truths. Because the author has lived in the good of them for many years, they come across imbued with clarity and power.

'We all need to learn to look beyond secondary causes and third parties, knowing when to echo the words of the Saviour, "Shall I not drink the cup the Father has given me?" (John 18:11). There are situations in which to simply respond with the two words, "Yes

Father." It is called "the grace of acceptance", and it has the power to change and enrich our lives.'
John Sutton-Smith, retired English teacher and deputy headmaster, Scarisbrick Hall, Lancashire

'I have had the great privilege of knowing Jenny for many years. Her gift of teaching and her ability to communicate profound truth with wisdom, tenderness, humour and scriptural clarity is infused with her utter dependence on, and pursuit of, God.

'In this outstanding book, Jenny urges us, with brilliant insight, to engage in this journey of true discipleship, whatever life may throw at us, and teaches us to drink deeply and eat lavishly, for the Father offers a sumptuous feast and a brimming cup. This book is an invitation, written with wit, profound honesty and deep love. So why wait – tuck right in!'
Rev Tim Buckley, Vicar of St Matts & St Thomas à Becket Church, Assistant Area Dean for Bath

'This book is a great resource for any Christian believer, whether you have been following Jesus for a few days or for many years. Read it alone or as part of a group study. Read it with an open heart and expect to come away changed. It will challenge you to take your faith seriously while exposing you to God's heart of love for you and His desire to help you become more like Jesus.

'But be warned: this is not a book for the faint-hearted. This book exposes the scandal of looking good on the outside while actually being disconnected from the authentic spiritual life that God offers us. It tackles the challenging reality of following Jesus in a fallen world, not shying away from honest disappointments and real-life experience.'
Steve Petch, Lead Pastor, Welcome Church, Woking, UK

'Jenny Sanders is a wise and witty woman, who's poured her reflections into this unusual book. You may think you know all there is to know about feasting, but think again. Every chapter offers new insights that help us reflect on our daily lives, as Jenny opens up the Bible to us in new and interesting ways.'
Hazel Southam, journalist, author of My Year with a Horse: Feeling the Fear but Doing it Anyway

'Jenny writes as she lives: eloquently, full of faith and with integrity. Within the pages of *Spiritual Feasting*, her recipe of solid biblical insight, encouragement, admonition and humour combine to present a book of substance that will radically change your perspective on how to keep on living in the fullness of God's love when life doesn't deliver what you expected it to.'

'*Spiritual Feasting* is worthy of a Michelin star!'
Allison Todd, Co-Founder & CEO of Mercy in Action, UK

'Jenny, from her own place at God's table and with a heart leaning in to the Lord, has drawn out some of the mysteries of the nature of the Father and brought them to life in this book. As you read, you will recognise again an invitation to know the love of the Father and the opportunity to enter into intimacy with Christ that is available in the midst of the realities of life.
Pastor Joshua Churchyard, Church of the Way, Benoni, Johannesburg, South Africa

'This book definitely gives food for thought. Having worked in the same town as Jenny for nearly ten years in Hampshire, we so valued her friendship, fellowship and insights. In this book, Jenny wrestles honestly with the universal issues of suffering and feasting which are challenging, refreshing and much needed.

'I believe this is a timely book and hope many will welcome the invitation to engage more fully with the "art of savouring God". The beauty of the Christian faith is that the unmerited grace of God is given freely to all who believe. May we take our places at His table as we respond to His invitation: "If anyone hears my voice and opens the door, I will come in and eat with that person, and they with me" (Rev 3:20).'
Rev David G Williams, Team Rector of Princes Risborough, Diocese of Oxford, Area Dean of Aylesbury and Team Leader

'So often we settle for less than the best God has for us. In Jenny's engaging book we are encouraged to come to the table and experience more! As we do, even in the hard places, our souls can be satisfied with the richest of foods. I'm delighted this book is now out there.'
Rev Andy Percey, Manvers Street Baptist Church, Bath

SPIRITUAL FEASTING

Jenny Sanders

instant
apostle

First published in Great Britain in 2020

Instant Apostle
The Barn
1 Watford House Lane
Watford
Herts
WD17 1BJ

Some content taken from *Dirty Glory*, by Pete Greig. Copyright © 2016. Used by permission of NavPress. All rights reserved. Represented by Tyndale House Publishers, a Division of Tyndale House Ministries.

Thanks to Astrablu Media, Inc for references to Babette's Feast.

British Library Cataloguing-in-Publication Data

A catalogue record for this book is available from the British Library.

This book and all other Instant Apostle books are available from Instant Apostle:

Website: www.instantapostle.com

Email: info@instantapostle.com

ISBN 978-1-912726-22-6

Printed in Great Britain.

Acknowledgements

My friends have told their stories in their own words but, with their permission, I have also edited them and occasionally added a detail which I knew and felt was relevant to include. I'd like to thank all of them for their willingness and vulnerability in agreeing to share their stories here. I am deeply grateful and know that my readers will be too.

'Sally' and 'Mike' are pseudonyms. I have told Uncle Rob's story myself, with both his and Lesley Oake-Judkins' permission, and included the additional facts which came to light after the event from various sources. You can read his detailed account in *Father Forgive: The Forgotten 'F' Word* by Robin Oake (Milton Keynes: Authentic, 2008). I hope you do.

Thanks

I am so grateful for the fellow 'diners' who have come on this feasting journey with me and who have helped shape, hone and enhance the work to make it all that it is, especially the magnificent team at Instant Apostle, as well as those who have encouraged me along the way, often holding up my arms when they became weary…

Specifically, but not exclusively: Florian & Anni Bärtsch, Louise Donoghue, Hilary Evans, Carrie May, Jane McNally, Charlotte Osborn, Carol Peel, Ian & Jessica Rowlands, Judy Scott, Caroline Tysoe, Leslie Ward, Sue Wakely, Raoul Witherall.

And, of course, my family who champion me consistently: Elspeth, Rhiannon, Callum, and Kirsty & Matthew Race. To Bernard, my long-time feasting partner, cheerleader, adventurer, warrior, companion and friend; thank you for always believing in me. You guys rock.

For DAD, who's exhortation to 'Keep on keeping on' has been the drumbeat of my life.

Thank you.

We miss you.

Menu

Foreword

'You are what you eat', as the saying goes. It's true – what we consume shapes us, for better or for worse! Well, the good news is that this book is seriously good for your health. If you're tired of snacking on sound bites in your faith and long for truth that will really sustain you, this book is just what you need.

Allow me to tantalise your taste buds a little. Jenny is a cordon bleu writer who invites us to explore what it means to feast on God's goodness, even when life doesn't serve everything we'd hoped for. Her wisdom matters. So many of us will be tempted to walk away from our faith when life doesn't taste sweet, assuming that a good God wouldn't allow us to be served anything sour or difficult to swallow. But my experience, through many trials, tells me that it is sitting next to Jesus at the table that makes contentment possible, even when circumstances are not palatable. Jenny reminds us that God's invitation of grace is everything we need.

Now, anyone who knows me will tell you – I'm no chef. My children used to tell guests that they'd know when dinner was ready because the smoke alarm would go off. Charming! When my children were small, our family would often spend time with Jenny and her family. Here is a woman who knows how to calmly rustle up food for a crowd. But as good as her baking might have been, it was Jenny's welcome, her advice, insight and care of others that kept us coming back for more. Her table was always a place of acceptance and authenticity. I'm delighted that this atmosphere also permeates these pages. You'll enjoy her gift of hospitality.

I must add, despite my lack of enthusiasm for cooking, I do love great food. I just prefer somebody else to cook it! And when I am fortunate enough to eat out, it's not just the quality of the meal that matters to me, it's the presentation that really makes the difference. *Spiritual Feasting* is a great meal; it is nutritious and delicious. But what makes it memorable and special is how it is served to you. Jenny is a really good writer. It's a delight to read words crafted so beautifully. This is fine dining indeed.

So, allow me to encourage you – this is not a meal to rush through. It's not fast food. Savour each course. Allow the flavours to permeate your mind and soul. Let the truth of how good God is soak in. Do linger over the questions and take your time at the table of God's goodness as you read.

If, like me, you are hungry for more of God, pull up a chair. You'll love *Spiritual Feasting*.

Cathy Madavan
Speaker, writer, coach and author of Digging for Diamonds *and* Irrepressible

Aperitif

Introduction

When he was at the table with them, he took bread, gave thanks,
broke it and began to give it to them.
(Luke 24:30)

A few months ago, one of those videos of military personnel being reunited with their families crossed my social media screen. There's no shortage of them; usually it's Dad coming home unexpectedly at Christmas or on someone's birthday and the inevitable tears, hugs and general celebration that follows. I feel rather awkward as a detached voyeur who has no connection with any of the protagonists, even though I want to rejoice and cheer with them as they reconnect, so I tend to scroll over them these days.

However, this one seemed a little different. It featured a mum who had returned from service and came into her son's school hall during the lunch period dressed in a tiger mascot outfit, complete with 'head'; no one could see who was inside the suit. Catering assistants smiled, the kids giggled as she high-fived and sashayed her way to a bench opposite her son, who was probably about ten years old. He was messing about with his friend, enjoying the chance to hang out with his buddies, completely unaware of the true identity of this unexpected guest. There was horsing around and banter going on; he laughingly offered the tiger visitor his friend's lunch until the point where Mum felt it was time to remove her disguise. For a moment nothing happened at all; you could almost see the mental wheels of recognition turning. Then with a strangled shout, this wonderful son threw down his food and ran, as though his life depended on it, around the table and threw himself into his mother's arms. His unbridled joy and unrestrained love for her may not have taken her by surprise, but it did me.

The presence of so many onlookers mattered not one bit to him; there was no embarrassment, no awkward self-conscious greeting; just a wholehearted giddy delight. I was quite unprepared for what happened next. Something in my own spirit responded, and with a lurching sob I found myself completely undone, reeling away from the screen and dissolving into a wailing heap, bawling my eyes out like a baby.

How embarrassing; thank goodness I was alone. What was that all about? Gradually, I realised that the action on the screen had somehow connected and resonated with my own spirit, powerfully illustrating what it will be like for the children of God when they finally meet Jesus face to face.

So much of life can be ho-hum routine even for His followers. In fact, He's sitting with us the whole time, but we don't always recognise Him (remember the disciples on the road to Emmaus?), or engage with Him much beyond the superficial, let alone at a level of genuine, joy-filled intimacy. Sure, we know He's with us because the Bible, preachers and our mind tell us that's *academically* true; but it doesn't always *feel* true. Yet there are moments when Jesus, like that mum, kindly reveals Himself to us more clearly. One minute we are sitting comfortably at the tasks of our life then, suddenly, He breaks in and reminds us of His tangible presence, His power, might, grace and love. Our spirit leaps; a spiritual veil is briefly lifted and we experience a few moments of revitalising clarity. It's truly marvellous; but it can also be overwhelming.

The son in the video responded beautifully, honestly and enthusiastically. I felt a tremor in my own heart – an echo of the child's yearning – a deep longing to throw myself into Jesus' arms of acceptance, safety and strength. From there, my perspective on the world, my immediate context of geography, relationships and work all look tangibly different.

I don't want to merely visit that place for an emotional boost or spiritual top-up; no, with all my heart I want to live there.

The mum at the school lunch table turned what was an ordinary occasion for her son into a celebratory feast, just by her presence. His sandwiches didn't become any more exotic or the lunch a gourmet meal; it was her company which made the seismic difference. Jesus does that for us, all day, every day, when we accept His invitation to 'feast' at the table set before us. Yes, it's about embracing the 'menu' we are served each day, but primarily, it's about enjoying His company in fresh, exhilarating ways while we tackle that 'menu'. Whatever my changing circumstances, or yours – those myriad events which unfold in every rhythmical twenty-four-hour cycle – God always gives us a choice in how we react to them. I don't always choose well. Often I have no natural inclination to 'feast' and consequently miss out on 'eating' and fellowshipping with Him in that place. How about you?

A crucial time

In this book, I want to invite you to come with me to take a fresh look at the last part of Psalm 23. The passage is familiar, but this message about feasting with Him is one you may never have heard before. It's important and timely.

Many see the twenty-first century stretching bleakly before us in a time of spiritual famine and confusion, of unprecedented challenge and change in the world. It's true that, more than ever in our lifetimes, nations are fragmenting, interpersonal and international hostility is increasing; the gap between rich and poor is growing ever wider and the anger of younger generations at the economic and climatic world they are inheriting is increasing. At times, you can almost smell the

21

despair. The temptation for the people of God to retreat and withdraw into spiritual ghettos is strong; it feels as though defeat may be at our door.

However, that is not the whole picture; God has very different plans and purposes, and those who follow Him and name Him as Lord are privileged to be part of those. We are commissioned as the hope-carriers, the life-bringers, the good-news people in the midst of these turbulent times.

We cannot be salt and light if we are hidden away. Somehow, we must engage with *real* people with their *real* challenges in the *real* world. In order to do that effectively we need a new maturity and an authentic, robust, living faith of a calibre far greater and deeper than we have probably known before. We need to respond to every season of life by staying in step with our heavenly Father, clothed in Jesus' robes of salvation and drenched in the Holy Spirit. Thus equipped, we will be prepared not only to tuck into whatever is 'served' to us today – appetising or not – but also to enjoy the exquisite privilege of dining with the One our hearts truly yearn for.

Our faith *must* have its source in a genuine, vibrant, growing, intimate relationship with Jesus and be radically empowered by the Holy Spirit. Fair-weather believers will fall by the wayside. We need to do much more than simply survive; there is much at stake.

In recent days, the people of God have enjoyed revelations about the nature of God as Father in new and refreshing ways. Discovering that God is approachable, accessible, tender, loving, kind, gentle and forgiving has been a defining moment for many whose own fathers were the opposite, or worse. Men and women, in church and out, carry the wounds of absent, disengaged and/or cruel and abusive fathers. Acknowledging and addressing these realities has lifted the lid on a huge spectrum of hurt, pain and disappointment. Where such emotional injuries have been gently and patiently unpacked, and a healing process walked through with understanding, compassion and wisdom, there has been a new lease of physical, emotional and spiritual life for individuals eager to take hold of the truths of God's fatherhood, unfettered by their own pasts. It's a delight to see the fruit of such change in many lives around the world.

Amid all this burgeoning life, however, there is a nagging possibility that we could inadvertently become irrelevant, disempowered infants whose world doesn't extend far beyond our own perceived needs if we settle in this place. Spiritual babies, much like physical ones, are sources of enormous joy; but of course, we expect them to grow. Babies who don't reach their developmental milestones are a source of concern. Maturity is part of life spiritually just as much as it is physically.

I don't believe that we can flourish in these increasingly demanding times unless we do mature and learn to 'feast' on the things God has entrusted us with in the present. There is no Jesus-follower who isn't consistently challenged to focus on Him, His character, His goodness and His promises. These deep, immoveable foundations are able to anchor us through every twist and turn of the roads we all travel or, using a paraphrase of David's metaphor, will allow us to feast at the table set for us.

His 'Shepherd Psalm' is, perhaps, the most well-known portion of Scripture. The familiar words of comfort and encouragement have lifted the head of many a weary traveller through life and at journey's end. Usually, the focus is on the first part of David's sheep-related words, but in this book we're going to focus on the closing verses: the challenging dinner-related part.

Let's remind ourselves at the outset of what Psalm 23 says, emphasising our focus:

> The Lord is my shepherd, I lack nothing.
> He makes me lie down in green pastures,
> he leads me beside quiet waters,
> he refreshes my soul.
> He guides me along the right paths

for his name's sake.
Even though I walk through the darkest valley,
I will fear no evil,
for you are with me;
your rod and your staff,
they comfort me.
You prepare a table before me in the presence of my enemies.
You anoint my head with oil; my cup overflows.
Surely your goodness and love will follow me all the days of my life,
and I will dwell in the house of the LORD forever.
(italics added)

Using this book

However familiar you are with this passage, let me invite you to approach it again with open ears, fresh eyes and a willing heart as the divine Host of the feast draws you in to His banqueting house.

This is not designed as a book to be read at one sitting. I recommend that you 'chew over' each chapter well so that you can really digest it and receive maximum spiritual nutrition from it. Each one closes with a few reflective questions to contemplate, either alone or with others. During the writing process I have been privileged to glean from the wisdom, experience and stories of other 'diners' who have written over a span of more than 1,500 years. It's reassuring to find so many similarities in the 'menus' we have been served across the centuries and discover that 'feasting' has always been a worthwhile challenge. Knowing that our Host is just as relevant, real and welcoming to me in the twenty-first century as He has been for them gives my heart and will the strength to keep pushing through distractions to secure my assigned place at His 'table'.

I've had the privilege of sitting at this table since I was a little girl of ten. Together with my husband, I've spent more than thirty years working in church leadership as well as coaching, mentoring and training leaders in both business and church contexts, across nations and denominations. We've seen a multifaceted spectrum of how God's kingdom is growing and multiplying across the earth. There have been days of hard graft, tears and frustration outweighed by more days of wonder, worship, laughter and delight. We've also raised three strong daughters and an outstanding son, who are now making their own decisions to enjoy their assigned places and 'feast' on the various 'menus' they are being served. Whether we've been in Somerset or South Africa, Andover or Arizona, we have chosen to press in to know our Host more intimately as the years have unfolded, through thick and thin.

So, if you too recognise that in surrendering your life to Jesus and submitting to His will and purposes, you were never offered a trouble-free life, but you are hungry for a little more reality and a lot more intimacy with Him, then come with me; pick up your metaphorical/spiritual knife and fork, and let's feast together with expectation and thanks.

Jenny Sanders, 2019
Cape Town, South Africa

Appetisers

1. Feasts

To be much for God, we must be much with God.[1]

My favourite feast

There's a world of difference between laying a table for a regular family dinner and serving the kind of meal which marks a significant or special occasion. I've eaten countless good meals in my lifetime, but it's the ones which celebrated particular moments which stand out: a birthday party, a graduation treat, an anniversary extravagance. Of all of these, Christmas is the one which never disappoints. Christmas dinner in our family has always happened on Christmas Eve, a cunning invention introduced by my grandmother in the 1940s. This clever ruse ensured that over-excited small children actively celebrated the birth of Jesus, but also had a massive meal and went to bed completely flaked out, thus reducing potential shenanigans and staying-up-to-see-Father-Christmas nonsense; it also pretty much ensured that no one was up and bouncing around with undesirable exuberance at stupid o'clock on the morning of the 25th. What a wise woman. It also meant that Christmas Day was a generally calmer, more enjoyable affair...

---

[1] Leonard Ravenhill, *Why Revival Tarries* (Bloomington, MN: Bethany House Publishing, 1959; 1987), p26.

Twenty years later and the tradition had moved to my childhood home, where aunts, uncles, cousins and grandparents joined us for the requisite turkey feast, much squealing, a general bending of the usual house rules and, for the children, energetic, ill-concealed festive anticipation usually culminating in a riotous game of hide-and-seek. The bonus was that I could be upstairs in my pyjamas, teeth cleaned and hanging up my Christmas stocking almost before the extended family had driven to the bottom of the road.

Another twenty years and four children later, those magical Christmas Eve memories became the measuring post for celebrating Jesus' birth in December for a new generation. Marking the season with our wider family around food had imprinted the wonder of the festival on my young mind – the sight of the fairy lights, the feel of the old tinsel tree, the smells of a roast meal and flavours specific to the moment, all undergirded with the merry sound of infectious laughter: Christmas in glorious 3D and technicolour. It may sound like a corny greetings card, but in my family I had the good fortune of enjoying all of that in wonderful reality. I can barely think of the events that unfolded in a Bethlehem stable more than 2,000 years ago without such vivid memories also flooding my thoughts. The two are forever, inevitably and inextricably linked.

God's seven feasts

Long before David wrote his Shepherd Psalm, before Ruth met Boaz, before Samson started lifting weights, before Gideon pummelled the Midianites or Joshua had completed seven days of circuits around Jericho, God had His own plan for a cycle of feasts. We're familiar with the Ten Commandments of Exodus 20, which God gave Moses after he'd had led the Israelite people out of Egypt, but probably less so with the instructions and pattern of annual feasts He gave in Leviticus 23. Each one is rich in meaning and symbolism, much of which not only points towards the coming of the Messiah, but has also been fulfilled in the life, death and resurrection of Jesus Christ. The feasts were ordained as ongoing commemorative events to be celebrated by families across the nation as an opportunity to consolidate their sense of community and remember God's faithfulness, as well as to celebrate His goodness and provision as Deliverer. They speak loudly and clearly of more significant things than the various dishes simply laid on the table and thus, like my Christmas Eve feast, would be forever linked in the thoughts and memories of those who kept them.

In a society where literacy and accessibility to the written word was reserved for scholars and preserved on scrolls kept under lock and key by the priests, this seasonal rotation was an effective reinforcement of precious history. Jewish culture relied on oral tradition; a strong family cohesiveness was universally established in which tales of the faithfulness of God revealed in His dealings with the people could be told and retold around meals and firesides, on journeys and on street corners, all reinforcing and reminding young and old of His centrality in their corporate story. A regular pattern of remembrance, embodied and played out in visual symbols, enactments and traditions by ordinary people kept that story alive as one generation taught the next, long after the original participants were dead and gone. Children grew up saturated with the stories of their ancestral past; part of the warp and weft of daily culture. Commemorative feasts and historic events would become firmly, inseparably linked, so that even for generations to come who would have had no experience of the arduous Exodus journey and its accompanying miracles, the history and stories of the liberation of the Israelites would be kept alive and valued.

Why seven feasts?

The Bible repeatedly records times when God works in units of seven – seven days in the full week; seven years that Jacob worked for each of his brides, Leah and Rachel; seven circuits around Jericho, etc; seven feasts. It's the biblical number of completeness.

With such a full timetable of specific feasts to enjoy, you can be sure that this practice was far more familiar to God's people in Moses' day than it is for us in the present. Communities which still follow the Church calendar of festivals and saints' days may appreciate the rhythm of seasons more fully. They certainly have built-in opportunities to focus on specific values or emphasise particular biblical stories. The metaphorical Psalm 23 feast to which God invites us is one to enjoy all 365 days of the year, every year. You can easily research each of them for a detailed, in-depth study of their symbolism should you wish; I'm just going to outline them here.

Feast 1: Passover (*Pesach*)
Passover marks the crucial departure of God's people from slavery in Egypt; a hinge of epoch-making change in the chronicles of Israel. Since Joseph had first ended up serving Pharaoh there, and after a convoluted series of events that wouldn't be out of place in a modern soap opera, his entire extended family had also come to live there. Conditions must have agreed with them, because they flourished and multiplied with such success that some years later a new Pharaoh who, somewhat strangely, knew nothing of the history of their dynasty, was so alarmed by their escalating numbers that he imposed forced labour on the entire people group to keep them under his control. Approximately another 400 years later, God raised up a reluctant and stammering Moses to lead the Hebrew slaves out of this unbearable servitude, and across the wilderness to the Promised Land – an area promised to the patriarch Abraham, father and founder of the Jewish nation, three generations before Joseph. Abraham's multiple descendants had cherished this covenant promise in their hearts throughout their years of suffering, drawing comfort from the prospect of a land of their own and the freedom to enjoy it.

The Exodus took place after Pharaoh's obstinate resistance to Moses' demands to allow the people to leave, and his refusal to acknowledge the God of the Hebrews. This stubborn rebuttal of Moses' request initiated a series of ten spectacular plagues from heaven: a sequence of terrifying events culminating in the death of every firstborn in the country, including Pharaoh's own son, at which point the ruler capitulated.

On the night of the final plague, the Israelites were instructed to choose one unblemished lamb per family and smear its blood around the doorway of their house, marking the home as purified and protected, sparing them from the coming tragedy. The people were required to roast their lamb and eat it with bitter herbs along with unleavened bread, while dressed and ready to leave at a moment's notice, in preparation for the hurried departure and the long journey on which they were about to embark.

This is the commemorative feast/meal that Jesus shared with His disciples on the night before He died. On that significant occasion, the bread and wine they consumed together became symbols of His soon-to-be broken body, and His blood that would be shed at His imminent crucifixion. Jesus Himself was, and is, the pure and perfect unblemished Lamb of God. The symbolism is powerful.

The early Church used the sharing, or breaking, of bread and drinking of wine together as a time of reflection to remember the sacrifice of Jesus which had purchased their spiritual deliverance and forgiveness, and to focus on His impact on their lives. The New Testament Passover became both a reminder of liberation from Egypt, but also of salvation from the tyranny of sin and its consequences: death, hell, and permanent separation from God.

Feast 2: Unleavened Bread (*Chag HaMotzi*)
I like the idea of a celebration which uses bread as a focus; there's nothing like a warm, fresh loaf to tuck into. However,

this week-long event uses a very specific type of bread, more like pitta than a farmhouse bloomer, because it has to be made without any yeast. It's a feast of holiness which overlaps with Passover.

At the time of the Exodus, the time-strapped Israelites made unleavened bread for Passover night. With no time to allow the bread to rise, they simply took it with them, before the raising agent was added, to eat on the way. People commemorated this in later years by removing yeast from their households altogether during Passover. Yeast, or leaven, was regarded as a symbol of sin, so to remove it and sweep the house clean was illustrative of ridding the house of impurity.

Yeast may be small but its impact is relatively huge as a raising agent. Unleavened bread – bread without yeast – is therefore, biblically, a picture of something without sin and a reminder that even the smallest sin has a big effect. We delude ourselves when we start to categorise sins into large and small; there is no such thing. Sin is sin; a falling short of God's standard of perfection, and in every case, the consequences are disconnection and separation from God. Thank God for redemption!

Feast 3: Firstfruits (*Yom habikkurim*)

For Israel, this third feast in the cycle celebrated the first harvest reaping rather than the last. European harvest festivals usually happen at the end of the season when all the crops are gathered prior to the autumn plantings and the harsh winter conditions set in.

The Jewish celebration of firstfruits included waving a still-green sheaf of barley to the four points of the compass, in front of the altar, thus dedicating the coming harvest to God. It was both an expression of trust in God for His provision, and of faith for a bountiful harvest to come. It's a feast which focuses on fertility and life which are, of course, other traditions still celebrated around Easter time when believers celebrate Christ's resurrection.

Feast 4: Feast of Weeks/Pentecost (*Shavuot*)

This was originally the feast of summer harvest, to take place fifty (*Pente*) days after the Feast of Firstfruits; it would fall around our months of May or June. The grain harvest was now completed and the first fruits of olives and grapes were beginning to be gathered. Contemporary celebrants traditionally decorate their houses with greenery and flowers, and in many Jewish homes the book of Ruth is read, whose narrative takes place around the themes of harvest and community. Jewish tradition claims that King David – from Ruth's ancestral line – was born at this time. It also believes that God gave the Law, or Torah, to Moses during this period, and so part of the holiday is often spent studying and reading the Torah as well as praying.[2]

In the New Testament we find that this was the exact day when the lives of Jesus' followers turned upside down with the coming of the Holy Spirit. Fifty days on from Jesus' resurrection they were still together in Jerusalem when a supernatural wind and 'tongues of fire' (Acts 2:3) rushed through the room as the Holy Spirit arrived in power enabling them to speak in other languages.

The disciples were so empowered by the Holy Spirit that they were emboldened to leave their Upper Room hiding place and go out onto the streets of the bustling city where Peter boldly preached his first sermon. Some of the Passover pilgrimage crowds thought he was drunk, but others had a revelation of truth which radically changed their lives. The coming of the Holy Spirit meant that God could dwell powerfully with, and in, every one of His disciples in a way Jesus the Son could not do, bound as He was by the geographical and physical constraints inherent in His incarnation.

God's desire to take up residence in people, rather than simply in a building or on a mountain, was fulfilled that first post-ascension Pentecost; the feast became a celebration of a

---

[2] jewsforjesus.org/publications/newsletter/newsletter-jun-2005/shavuot-the-feast-of-weeks/ (accessed 29th January 2018).

different type of harvest – a gathering in of about 3,000 people who were added into the family of believers. Today we celebrate this event at Whitsun, but we can enjoy the reality of its fulfilment every day.

Feast 5: Feast of Trumpets (*Yom Teru'ah*)

One of three autumn feasts, this one takes place in modern September and is the only feast for which God gives no specific reason, apart from resting and making a sacrifice. However, it heralds a ten-day period of consecration and prayer in preparation for the Feast of Atonement. So, no regular work was to be done on this day, but the people were to gather together, summoned by the blasting of trumpets, and the priests had to prepare various offerings including a sin offering on behalf of the community. The sounding of a trumpet effectively called the workers in from the fields, indicating the time had come to stop harvesting at the end of the year and begin their grateful worship.

When God gave Moses details for the meeting place, or tabernacle, to be set up in the wilderness, He also commissioned two different types of trumpet to be made. Silver trumpets were to be used only by Aaron's priestly sons. Different blasts from them would indicate whether the entire multitude, or just the leaders should gather. They also had to be blown over the sacrifices which were made in the sanctuary as part of worship, when going into battle against enemies in their own land, and also in times of rejoicing. The silver trumpets became a visual representation of prayer illustrating a loud, clear, confident call from earth to heaven.

The other type of trumpet, the shofar, was made of ram's horn, reminding God's people of the original God-given ram which substituted for Isaac as Abraham's sacrifice on Mount Moriah.[3] There are multitudinous references to the use of this type of horn or trumpet throughout Scripture. It is used to

---

[3] Genesis 22:1-18.

sound a warning or alarm,[4] as an appeal for aid, in battle, in worship,[5] as well as in dedication or rededication events, for example: the completion of Nehemiah's wall and David bringing the Ark of the Covenant back to Jerusalem.

This feast isn't a time for lazing around though. The trumpets are seen as a spiritual wake-up call, summoning people to take seriously the prospect of meeting with God. The feast provides a period of spiritual self-reflection and an opportunity to ensure that personal holiness hasn't been relegated to the back burner of life. We could all regularly benefit from this kind of timely trumpet blast…

Feast 6: The Day of Atonement (*Yom Kippur*)

Technically, this is a national fast, not a feast, and is still considered to be the holiest festival of the entire Jewish year. Even Jews who are less strict in their observance of Judaic customs usually mark this particular day by subduing their physical appetite in a sign of humbling themselves before God. It is a day of confession and repentance of sins, the forgiveness of which requires, according to Old Testament Law, the spilling of a blood sacrifice.

This was the only day on which the high priest could enter the Holy of Holies where the Ark of the Covenant was kept, and where it was believed that the actual Presence of God dwelt. Separated off from the other parts of the temple by a huge, beautifully embroidered thick curtain or veil, this was a clear separation of a Holy God from sinful people. It would be absolutely impossible for anyone to wander in here accidentally. The high priest was required to wash scrupulously before and after the ceremony, wear special clothes and carry fragranced incense in order to blur his view; he could not be allowed to look on God directly.[6] Most importantly, he was required to

---

[4] Ezekiel 33:3-4.

[5] Nehemiah 4:18,20; Joshua 6:4-8,13-20; Judges 7:22; Psalm 47:5; Psalm 150:3.

[6] See Leviticus 16:3-5,12-13,17,23-24; Exodus 28; Exodus 33:20.

carry the animal blood which would be offered as atonement for the sins the people had inadvertently committed, as well as for himself and his household.

People were to treat Yom Kippur as a Sabbath, regardless of the actual day of the week upon which it fell. Regarded as a sombre day in some respects, it was, and is, also a day of rejoicing because of the cathartic element of cleansing – an opportunity to have a clean sheet before God.

The fulfilment of this day is clear in Jesus, the ultimate sacrifice, 'he entered the Most Holy Place once for all by his own blood' (Hebrews 9:12). No longer do we require an annual or animal sacrifice to pay for our sins; Jesus has paid the price once and for all, and taken the just punishment that we deserved, in order to make us clean. Symbolic lambs are obsolete. 'How much more, then, will the blood of Christ, who through the eternal Spirit offered himself unblemished to God, cleanse our consciences from acts that lead to death' (Hebrews 9:14). The barrier and separation between God and humanity has been permanently destroyed. This was dramatically emphasised when, at the point of Jesus' death, the thick curtain in the temple barring access to God's presence was torn in half, from top to bottom, opening access to all (Mark 15:38). It's significant that the curtain didn't rip from bottom to top. No human hands could have performed such a feat; this was truly an act of God. Imagine being in the temple when that actually happened – the noise; the fear; the furore; the questions; the awe; the dust!

There could be no clearer announcement that God had completely changed the way His relationship with us would function from now on. Two thousand or so years later, we may not grasp what a monumental spiritual shift this was. No more regular temple trips were required; no more animal sacrifices were necessary; no more intermediary priesthood was needed. An absolute spiritual revolution had just taken place in Jerusalem.

Not many years later, the beautiful temple was destroyed by the Roman army, in AD70; the culmination of a siege of the city which brought death to thousands. Animal sacrifice was permanently abandoned from this point in history. The temple remains in ruins, apart from part of the Western or Wailing Wall, where Jews still gather every Sabbath to pour out their hearts before God, and to 'post' prayers in the mortar gaps between the ancient stones. Messianic Jews and Jesus-following Gentiles know that such a temple is no longer necessary. Jesus is our living Atonement and we are the living temple in which He dwells.

Feast 7: The Feast of Tabernacles (*Sukkot*)
This feast falls just after Yom Kippur, and is otherwise known as the Feast of Booths. It's an eight-day festival giving the opportunity to remember the forty long years of pilgrimage and journeying the Hebrew people undertook as Moses led them through the rugged Sinai wilderness region during the Exodus, en route from Egypt and into the Promised Land. Without a permanent home, this multitude lived in temporary structures throughout that time and God provided supernatural food for them in the form of manna and quail. The Feast of Booths was, and is, the perfect opportunity to both remember and give thanks for God's provision, providence and protection throughout that important time in Israel's history. It is also a powerful reminder that all of us are temporary residents here on earth. Our permanent home is heaven; we are just passing through this world. This feast provides time for the Jewish people to specifically recall God's faithfulness in the past, the present and, by faith, into the future.

The week of celebration includes singing, dancing and rejoicing both at home and in the streets. We would recognise this as more similar to our own harvest festival celebrations in the early autumn when rural communities breathe a collective sigh of relief that everything has been safely harvested and stored in barns to keep them well fed in the leaner days ahead.

Some still celebrate with a triumphant supper and a service of thanksgiving in the local church, among displays of fresh produce.

Other symbols of this Jewish feast are water and light; it's no coincidence that Jesus offered the 'living water' (John 7:38) of the Holy Spirit to the Sukkot crowds and referred to Himself as, 'the light of the world' (John 8:12) during, and just after, His own visit to Jerusalem for this week. He was, and is, the fulfilment of every emblematic characteristic of God used in the feasts.

You will have your own stories about what Jesus has done in your life and how the images of light and water may have sustained you. Some of you will have proved His faithfulness over many years of walking with Him, through dry deserts and along dark roads. What a treasure house of stories you must enjoy.

Day by day, He still longs to fill and refill us with His Spirit; to shed His light along our individual and collective paths and satisfy our thirsty souls with His living water.

David's feasting psalm

This annual rota of seven feasts and holidays, unfolding in perpetual cycles, ensured that the Israelites were consistently reminded about their history and their God. Like my Christmas dinner associations, the food and accompanying traditions became inextricably entwined, cementing values and important events in the memories of the participants. Each one was designed so that God's chosen people would maintain eye contact, as it were, with their Creator, Deliverer and Lord.

The feast which David imagines in Psalm 23 probably has its source in one or any of the feasts which he would have enjoyed since his childhood. When you are the youngest in the family, assigned the unheralded, unglamorous task of looking after the sheep, there are probably days when even your packed lunch feels like a feast in the bleak and rugged Judean desert. While searching for pasture and water for his charges, watching for predators and alert to dangerous places, David had no idea that this was the preparation and training God had chosen for shaping him into the man he would need to be when he became king of the Jewish nation, living in a grand palace, presiding over a completely different scale of feast.

What he did discover was that solitude does not have to equal aloneness. Communing with God in uninterrupted thought, prayer and song while reflecting on memorised scriptures through those long working days, nurtured his relationship with the One he trusted so absolutely throughout his life. Whether he wrote the outline of this psalm song as a youngster in the company of the family flock, or much later as a seasoned warrior and beloved monarch, David knew that a banquet prepared by God would be a feast to gladden the heart and refresh the soul.

Palate-cleanser questions

- The Hebrew people were a consolidated community with shared experience, memories and values. Who is your community and what is the metaphorical glue that holds you together? How can you contribute to improving the quality of that community?

- What might de-yeasting your life involve? How can a period of living less comfortably strengthen our spiritual connection with God?

- Why does God want 'firstfruits', and what might this look like in the twenty-first century?

2. Invitations: Part 1

I want those you have given me to be with me where I am ...
(John 17:24)

Memorable invitations

As a child, the only certain way to receive mail for myself was to write to my grandparents. Not just the compulsory 'thank you' letters which didn't merit a reply, but everyday letters with news of school, my friends, bike rides and the like. Because I had some pretty amazing grandparents, my grandad would solemnly unveil his Olivetti typewriter and, with laborious two-fingered technique, hammer out a reply to his small granddaughter. My granny would add a handwritten paragraph to fill the space, complete with kisses, and the whole missive, often extending to two glorious pages, was stamped and then posted in the trusty red pillar box at the end of their road.

I cannot explain the thrill of my seven- or eight-year-old self in finding a personally addressed letter either on the doormat or waiting for me on my return from school. No adult could whisk it away or take charge of it. There was my name in blotchy but quite legible type: Miss J Johnson; sometimes the complete, Miss J H Johnson. Just for me. Deliberate; individualised; specified. I was the only person residing at that address owning that particular name and exact combination of initials; there was no possibility of someone else opening it in error.

Nowadays most communications arrive electronically, with the exception of formal invitations to weddings. Receiving these is a privilege. Over the years my husband and I have taken many engaged couples through courses of preparation for the adventure and challenge of marriage, so witnessing them make their vows on their big day is very special. We've had invitations in all shapes and sizes, embossed, embellished and embroidered. I know that logistics and resources are often tight for such an occasion, so seeing our names written there tells me that for some reason, the hosts have decided we are sufficiently valued by them to be honoured in this way. We have been specially selected and included in their important day. I'm always grateful for this.

The specificity of the table prepared in Psalm 23 for David's feasting pleasure clearly implies that he has been deliberately and personally invited, too, to take an assigned seat there with his host: the Lord.

Jesus' seven invitations

Jesus is clearly a giver of invitations: to parties, to life, to a wedding; and you and I are included on the guest list. There is a sense in which each invitation is generic and inclusive – to all. But, by His Holy Spirit God speaks to us as individuals, by name, challenging us each to accept and partake of these various invitations, to enjoy them in His close company, and metaphorically 'feast' with Him, even when no physical food is involved.

We'll explore seven invitations that Jesus makes over the next two chapters, ensuring the portion size is more digestible. This will give an important insight into the nature of truly 'feasting' with Him in the circumstances of our everyday lives, at the metaphorical table He has set expressly for us.

1. Follow

> 'Come, follow me,' Jesus said, 'and I will make you
> fishers of men.'
> (Mark 1:17, NIV 1984)

This is the first invitation that Jesus gave, endowing it with an immediate importance. It was issued to a rather motley, apparently unimportant, selection of manual workers on the shores of a lake. In Jewish culture, educated boys who wanted to push on into further studies would seek out a rabbi and apply to join him. Young men would spend their lives in that rabbi's company, discussing his interpretation and application of the Law and the Scriptures to every aspect of daily life; they would then emulate his outworking of these persuasions in their own way of life. The interpretation of their particular rabbi might differ from another, but this was considered to be a method of illustrating the many rich facets of God. Questions were raised, not necessarily to be answered categorically, but to be debated and discussed, exploring the nuances of the subject as one turns a diamond to catch different lights and so appreciate the jewel. Few followers were selected, and the fact that these young fishermen were working at home indicates that for some reason or another they had not been considered suitable candidates for rabbinic instruction in any local *Yeshiva*, or discipleship group.

Jesus was a different sort of rabbi in every sense; He actively went looking for disciples and it's no wonder that the Pharisees, scribes and other teachers of the Law were somewhat aghast at His choices. Among the dozen who made the final cut were a couple of hotheads who once wanted to call fire down on a village where they weren't made welcome, and a traitorous tax collector who worked for the occupying power of Rome in a position notorious for its cheating, corruption and sell-out ethics. Jesus found two sets of brothers who were either fishermen or owned fishing businesses, plus a selection of other blue-collar workers and a revolutionary zealot who identified with a group of low-life terrorists/freedom fighters who would cut your throat as soon as look at you if they thought it would help their cause: to encourage a Jewish uprising, bring about revolution and overthrow Roman rule. I imagine the disciples initially spent a lot of time looking sideways and suspiciously at one another, watching their backs rather than relaxing in one another's company.

When Jesus invites us to follow Him in our twenty-first-century context, what does He mean? Follow Him where? Is He saying that we all need to be more serious about spirituality, faith or religion? I don't think that's the whole picture; after all, Jesus consistently drove a cart and horses through the whole business of religion as a 'thing'. Indeed, history shows us that religion has generally been more of a hindrance than a help in solving any of the world's problems.

We must, therefore, make a clear distinction between religion and faith. Jesus and His finished work on the cross smashed through the rigid requirements of a law that was impossible to keep, releasing us from the oppressive need to do religious things and welcoming us into the favour-filled space of God's family where forgiveness and grace flow; here our true relationship with God begins.

So, no, Jesus is not asking any of us to get religious – thank goodness! He is not looking for people driven by duty. His call is not to modern-day do-gooders looking to achieve their own salvation by ticking required boxes, nor to pseudo-devout masochists who crush their own spirits in misplaced self-sacrifice in order to live a miserable life for the appearance of piety. Absolutely not. That is not the way to relationship with God, and relationship rather than religion is what living faith is all about.

We can only truly follow someone if we have a connection with them. Keeping, or at least aspiring to, a set of rules, a philosophy or, yes, a religion, spiritual or otherwise is not the invitation Jesus gives us.

The apostle Paul wrote, 'if anyone is in Christ, the new creation has come: the old has gone, the new is here!' (2 Corinthians 5:17). When we submit our lives to Christ, our previous way of life is eradicated; destroyed; killed off permanently. This also means that we are no longer at the helm. It's our new Captain who now gives the orders and steers the ship of our life. Every facet of our existence becomes subject to His command; there is not an option for negotiation.

As a new believer, my choices, motivations, family, career, outlook, values, sexuality, work dynamic, culture, ethos and values have been laid before Jesus for His stamp of approval. I am under His rule now, completely surrendering my own preferences for His standards; His kingdom culture holds sway over my own from here on.

Sometimes I think we have been given a soft-sell on following Jesus: pray the prayer; fill in a response card; turn over a new leaf; start showing up at a church on a Sunday; control that temper; don't swear in front of the boss… These sort of instructions trivialise discipleship; Jesus isn't asking anyone to shape up a bit, tweak their lifestyle or consider a change in philosophical outlook. He isn't suggesting that you just sign up to His teachings or be inspired by His example. He is not interested in our ability to stick to a set of rules which, just like most diets ever invented, usually ends for us in disaster, self-recrimination and shame.

God's intention for us is far more ambitious than ephemeral happiness. His desire is that we become holy – like Jesus – 'conformed to the image of his Son' (Romans 8:29). Happiness that's dependent on mere circumstance seems insipid and small when placed alongside holiness. Following Jesus means stepping into that new trajectory which will almost certainly involve moments in which we are not very happy at all, simply because we cannot have our own way if we are submitting to His ways; honesty requires me to admit that I won't always enjoy that. The longer we've lived as we pleased, the harder it is to give that up for the demands of Jesus and His kingdom standards; we've got used to doing things our own way and being answerable only to ourselves.

So what does God want from us?
Lives and destinies hang on this question. Jesus invites us to follow Him, but what is He really asking from us? The answer is: nothing; and everything.

How intriguing.

We must understand firstly that there is *nothing* we can bring to the table which impresses God. There is *absolutely nothing* within us – our abilities, our talents, our heritage, our intellect, our connections, our bank balance, our DNA – which will make the slightest difference to the way He sees us. There is not a single thing in us which can impress God. He can't love us any more than He does and He refuses to love us any less. The dimensions of His love for us are beyond our understanding and cannot be measured. He does not have any expectations of us which we are required to strive for, accomplish or live up to. That's grace! Our personal credentials are a big fat nothing in His book.

It has been accurately said that we contribute nothing to our own salvation except our sin. The only thing that bridges the gap between the Creator and the created, caused by that terrible disease – sin – is the powerful blood of Jesus, which cleanses, or purifies, us 'from all unrighteousness' (I John 1:9). 'All'; e-v-e-r-y-t-h-i-n-g – regardless of magnitude. What a relief!

Jesus didn't come to condemn us, shame us or humiliate us. Those things come from elsewhere. However, He did come to convict us, to redeem us and to restore us to friendship with God through His own love and sacrifice. It is truly all about what He has done; not what we have done.

At the same time, God wants *everything* from us: our whole selves, every corner of heart, body, mind and soul, 100 per cent. It's full disclosure, complete surrender. There can be no no-go areas in our life. Nothing is off-limits to His divine audit: job, relationships, past hurts, broken heart, finances, hobbies, TV choices, leisure time, any time, food, exercise, child-rearing, sex, politics, house hunting, etc. Everything, but everything, comes under His supreme lordship.

Does that sound intense? Remember then that this is not for the judgemental scrutiny of a harsh, overbearing taskmaster; it's so that God's life can flow through every single part of our lives with His power, authenticity, integrity and grace, which will bring the abundant life He promised to us, and to those around us, as well as reflecting His character wherever we go.

A word of warning before you reply prematurely to this invitation: following Jesus is not for cowards or those looking for an easy ride. Jesus said to His disciples, 'Whoever wants to be my disciple must deny themselves and take up their cross and follow me' (Matthew 16:24). He says the same thing to us today, and He doesn't pull any punches.

Following Jesus is not an easy option. Discipleship is costly. Laying down our lives is a requirement, metaphorically if not physically/literally. We give over control of our lives to Him; we are no longer calling the shots, no longer have the final say, are no longer at liberty to be masters of our own destinies. It's a huge decision; the ramifications are enormous.

His invitation extends to both princes and paupers, vagabonds and villains, the wealthy and the weary, the helpless and the hopeless, the young and the old, the broken and the bound. This invitation doesn't leave any room for compromise, and that's why it's such a serious challenge which demands sober consideration before you respond. However, if you really want the fullness of life Jesus promises (John 10:10) then your surrender will be absolutely worth it because, whether we understand it or not, this is what you and I were made for. We take the adventures He sends; walk the path He has planned for us with all its twists, turns, highs, lows and obstacles; and while it will not be the easiest life, it will be the best and richest life possible. Yes, Jesus is love, but He is Lord first.

2. Rest

> Come to me, all you who are weary and burdened, and I
> will give you rest. Take my yoke upon you ...
> (Matthew 11:28-29)

Here's an appealing invitation. From Old Testament times, even
slaves were included in the rules for Sabbath rest. Today,
preachers love to tell us how people are 'sick and tired of being
sick and tired'. It seems as though everyone, everywhere, is tired
for some reason or another.

The likely response when you greet someone with your
friendly, 'Hi, how are you?' is usually, 'Fine thanks; bit busy,
though.' You and I have been around the block a few times, and
we recognise their generic 'Fine' as a likely smokescreen for
detail – perhaps they really are expressing the in vogue tongue-
in-cheek acronym: Freaked out, Insecure, Neurotic and
Emotional! 'Fine' could mean anything, and honestly, when was
the last time you met someone who *isn't* busy? I don't usually
own up to having loads of time on my hands myself; perhaps I
am concerned that if I did, it would make me appear lazy,
directionless or insignificant? That's uncomfortable. If I probe
a little, I might discover that I am trying to justify, or big-up, my
activities and so seem worthy or important.

In a world where many are grappling with their identity, it's
all too easy to align what we do with who we are; but the truth
is that I am so much more than the activities of each day, my
job, my career or my bank balance. This sort of confusion
diminishes our value. When society equates worth with
employment status, it imposes a pyramidal structure on
populations that flies in the face of God's Word and how He
sees us.

We cram more activities into our days than our grandparents
would ever have contemplated. Most of us are driven by the
tyranny of the urgent and a relentless diary of events, deadlines
and responsibilities. There's no denying, too, that in a world

where global communication takes place 24/7 at the touch of a button, we are literally bombarded with stimulation from morning until night, from birth to the grave. Our personal and local boundaries of responsibility have mushroomed into perceived national and global responsibilities for situations in which we have no authority and very little direct influence. We've become more anxious, more stressed, more fearful and on more medication than any previous generation; we'd be foolish to believe there isn't some correlation between these things.

Jesus packed a lot into His three years of ministry, yet He was never *too* busy. He made space for children; He took time to heal a suffering woman even while He was on the way to help the dying daughter of a distraught synagogue leader; He paused to restore a devastated widow's son to life when she was already on the way to the funeral; He sat on the grass; He enjoyed a picnic or two; He sailed on boats; He loitered by a well so He could talk with an outcast Samaritan woman; He wrote in the sand; He walked pretty much everywhere. It's not that there wasn't a great deal to do: lepers to heal, blind men needing sight, the demon-possessed requiring deliverance, lame and deaf people to heal, disciples to disciple (obviously), crowds to teach and feed… But Jesus only did what He saw His Father doing; He only said what His Father said and in the way He was told to say it.[7] Jesus didn't heal everybody He saw; sometimes people weren't prepared to pay the price of following Him and walked away (Mark 10:17-23; Luke 9:57-62). He was never a victim of His schedule. That certainly gives me pause for thought as I contemplate my own diary.

In this particular invitation, to rest, Jesus offers us not just a one day in seven break, but daily mental, physical and spiritual rest and refreshment which will nourish our soul, recalibrate our pace and ensure that we are joined, or tied, not to a burden but to Jesus Himself. That's why His metaphorical yoke is not heavy

---

[7] John 5:19; 12:49.

or burdensome like the wooden ox yokes of agricultural use He referred to; it doesn't weigh us down but if we, as it were, strap it on properly, it will cause us to walk steadily, purposefully, rhythmically, in step with Him.

Here's the same invitation, eloquently worded in *The Message* version:

> Are you tired? Worn out? Burned out on religion? Come to me. Get away with me and you'll recover your life. I'll show you how to take a real rest. Walk with me and work with me – watch how I do it. Learn the unforced rhythms of grace. I won't lay anything heavy or ill-fitting on you. Keep company with me and you'll learn to live freely and lightly.
> (Matthew 11:28-30)

What an attractive, appealing prospect. Much of our weariness comes from wearing a yoke that isn't Jesus', in which case we shouldn't be surprised if it chafes and crushes us. Let's remove the rough, self-carved one we've made for ourselves and start wearing the bespoke one He has for us.

The kind of rest Jesus invites us to doesn't mean collapsing mindlessly in a heap on the couch doing nothing; Jesus is offering us the key to living fully, at a measured pace which will keep us flourishing as we walk through every day, regardless of our job title, salary, geography or responsibilities. To enjoy this kind of life, you and I are going to have to swim against the social and cultural tide, and, 'make every effort [strive, labour] to enter that rest' (Hebrews 4:11 NIV, ESVUK and KJV respectively). That sounds like an oxymoron – working towards rest – but we're going to have to be focused and diligent if we're to lay hold of this. It's an invitation I am still eager to answer in the affirmative, while increasingly realising that staying strapped in to Jesus' yoke is something I must attend to daily.

3. Drink

> Let anyone who is thirsty come to me and drink.
> (John 7:37)

I'm no athlete, but I have experienced the consequences of dehydration and they are extremely unpleasant. Hiking part of the Great Wall of China a number of years ago, I was aware of a complete dearth of public toilets or indeed, any toilets at all. The obvious solution to my potential quandary was therefore to reduce my liquid intake. Consequently, I not only had a mouth drier than the Sahara, but I struggled to speak, to breathe, will my legs to keep moving, and persevere; I suffered from thumping headaches and nausea. Not surprisingly, I was experiencing acute thirst unlike any I had ever known. Not such a smart idea after all.

Jesus' invitation to drink was given on the last day of the Feast of Tabernacles in Jerusalem when He had the attention of the biggest crowds of the holiday, as people gathered themselves and their belongings before beginning their various journeys home. His listeners were amazed that this man was so learned and spoke with such great authority, yet hadn't studied under any of the scholars or rabbis of the time.

Jesus repeatedly pointed the people to His Father in heaven as the origin and authenticator of His preaching and practice, sharply dividing His audience and increasing the jealousy of the Pharisees who continued their plotting to remove Him – permanently.

This invitation was offered to everyone who wanted to partake not of the physical H_2O I gasped for in China, but of something just as vital: life-giving spiritual water. This was a call to all who were, and are, parched and weary in their inner beings; those who long for the reality of God; who yearn for the lasting joy, peace, love and reconciliation with God, which deep down we are all made for.

Jesus throws a spiritual rope to those who are drowning in their circumstances, disillusioned with the world's solutions and conscious that no amount of their own good deeds, self-effort and law-keeping will ever be enough to bridge the gap that divides them from their original identity and intent.

The kind of water Jesus describes will not just refresh, but transform a life; here is satisfaction which brings eternal hope by the Holy Spirit bubbling up inside us like a fresh mountain spring. 'Whoever believes in me,' says Jesus, 'as Scripture has said, rivers of living water will flow from within them' (John 7:38). He is not simply talking about cognitive belief or intellectual assent, but a far fuller embracing of Himself as God's Son.

This is the same living water Jesus spoke about to the Samaritan woman He met at a well. To her He said, 'whoever drinks the water I give them will never thirst. Indeed, the water I give them will become in them a spring of water welling up to eternal life' (John 4:14). This living water is constantly flowing, and leaps up in our heart and soul – our inner person – causing godly fruit, or character, to grow.

In other words, we become more like Jesus in character as we keep on surrendering to Him – not with the reluctant gritted teeth of an obedient servant, but with the delighted abandonment of loved sons and daughters – and allow Him to mould us and shape us, in and through the circumstances and journeys of our lives, by the grace and presence of His Holy Spirit.

Palate-cleanser questions

- 'Every facet of our existence becomes subject to His command; there is not an option for negotiation ... I am ... completely surrendering my preferences for His standards; His kingdom culture holds sway over my own from here on.' Consider whether there might be areas of your life which you have not yet surrendered to God and explore these, asking the Holy Spirit to help you.

- How do you ensure that Jesus' living water is flowing in and through your life each day? Pause, and ask yourself whether anything might be blocking that flow.

3. Invitations: Part 2

Blessed are those who are invited to the wedding supper of the Lamb!
(Revelation 19:9)

We've seen how Jesus invites us to follow Him, to find real burden-free rest with Him and to drink living water. There are four more invitations which Jesus makes, all of which require a response from us.

4. Come apart

He said to them, 'You come apart into a deserted place, and rest awhile.' For there were many coming and going, and they had no leisure so much as to eat.
(Mark 6:31, WEB)

Here's another example of Jesus paying attention to the 'whole' person as He invites His close circle of friends to take some time out of the busy round of activities, and rest. This is more than the rest we experience when wearing His metaphorical yoke on our spiritual shoulders; this invitation requires a withdrawal from our usual activity. All of our lives need to be marked by those 'unforced rhythms of grace'[8] which Jesus offered when He invited us to rest. There is work we have been assigned to do in a variety of fields requiring different levels of expertise and skill. To be done well, it needs to be done from a place of inner rest and peace. Inevitably, each of us needs time to 'come apart' from the usual demands of the day and make sure we take physical, emotional and mental rest as well.

God so configured the universe that we have a seven-day cycle per week, within which He mandated that we take one day for a break from daily labours, however satisfying and/or fruitful they might be.

Daily life takes a lot out of us and whatever 'that' is, it needs to be replenished. This kind of refreshment needs both quantity and quality time. If you have given out physically, then you need to be revitalised physically; if your work requires intense emotional engagement, you will recognise how much that needs to be revived within you or, all too soon, you will feel the oppressive clouds of depression creeping up on you, and/or hit burnout.

It has been said that if we don't *come* apart then we will probably *fall* apart. Burnout is a very real problem in our frenetic world. If we try to keep going, soldiering on, even when our physical, mental, spiritual and emotional tanks are running perilously low, then all too soon we lose the resilience or clarity to make good decisions. You won't need to look very far to see that when one person crashes, frequently whole families begin to crumble; relationships are broken, trust is lost, joy vanishes… You know what I'm talking about, because it's more than likely that you know people who have found themselves on this tragic road; perhaps it's so familiar because you either have, or are, walking it yourself.

We were not designed to be machines that keep operating on a task *ad infinitum*. We were made for relationship with our Creator, and we need to prioritise the nurturing and deepening

---

8 Matthew 11:28-30, *The Message*.

of that relationship above every task and duty we claim to do for Him. We were made to enjoy Him and to embrace the journey He designed – this extraordinary adventure called 'life', which we are all navigating with varying degrees of success – and to relish the many blessings He has showered on us in all the spheres of our lives.

Every military battle or skirmish is followed by a time of regrouping and rest. Since we live in constant spiritual conflict with the secular world around us, wisdom tells us that our core, spiritual 'tanks' will also need to be regularly refilled and reinvigorated. Jesus knew all this first-hand. His tension-filled encounters with the Pharisees and teachers of the Law must have been spiritually punishing. Likewise, times of healing and deliverance required Jesus' full attention and the assurance from His Father of who to engage with, and what to say. He frequently chose to withdraw from crowds of people so that He could take time alone with God to refocus and regroup in the presence of His Father.

Before Jesus appointed the apostles, He spent all night by Himself, praying on a mountain. Rather than make a few snap decisions or rely on His 'gut feeling', He wanted to be fully assured that He was in tune with God's plans and purposes for both Himself and His friends. Even the Son of God didn't just take a punt on a list of names and hope for the best. It was strategically important for Him to take time away from the demands of people and realign Himself with God in prayer and quietness.

If the Messiah Himself did not look purely to His inner self in order to find the resources He needed to be and do all He was called to, then neither should we.

It probably doesn't matter much where you choose to go for this important activity, but it must be somewhere which lends itself to tuning in to God's voice. For me that usually means being outside enjoying fresh air and nature, preferably somewhere lush and green. For most it requires a physical removal from the business and busyness of every day, and the substitution of a different activity: maybe hiking, running or sport. For others it may need the stillness and solitude of fishing or painting. The emphasis is on a ring-fenced period of time which provides you with fertile space for specific reflection and communion with God. Jesus sometimes went to a lake for this. Perhaps your 'lake' is a bench with a view, a trip in the car or a quiet corner in your house. I believe Susannah Wesley used to throw her apron over her head and withdraw from the demands of her clamorous family for a few moments of restorative reflection and prayer.

It's not easy to retreat from the plethora of insistent demands around us, but the invitation remains. 'Arise, come, my darling; my beautiful one, come with me' (Song of Solomon 2:13); Solomon's love song echoes Jesus' invitation. It's a call to intimacy and delight; to warm exchanges of confidence and the exhilarating reconditioning of heart, mind, body and soul.

5. Eat

> Come and have breakfast.
> (John 21:12)

I love how immensely down-to-earth and practical this invitation is. What a great way for anyone to start their day: breakfast with Jesus!

Historically there is a pervasive temptation to separate the practical and spiritual life as if they were completely different entities. They aren't. We are whole people, and genuine, living faith not only undergirds but soaks into every aspect and fissure of our life. Artificial separation inevitably leads to a fracturing of holistic personhood opening us up to the accusation of hypocrisy, and ushering in nothing but the clammy hands of cold, dead religion...

In an Old Testament example, you may remember that some years after the Exodus, the prophet Elijah had an epic competition on the top of Mount Carmel with 850 pagan prophets to demonstrate to Israel, and particularly to wicked King Ahab, that the Israelite God of the patriarchs was still the supreme God above all other idols and contenders, and could answer by fire.

This spiritual warfare showdown was only the first part of Elijah's day. It continued with the routing and slaughter of the false prophets of Baal and Asherah, followed by an intense prayer time petitioning God to break a three-and-a-half-year drought. God then enabled the weary seer to run a personal best time from Carmel to Jezreel before a massive downpour. In his state of fatigue, poor Elijah received a life-threatening message from sadistic Queen Jezebel, who was out for bloody revenge and who scared the living daylights out of him. From hero to zero in the time it took to read the note; from God-focused to miserably self-absorbed pity in a heartbeat. Elijah ran again, another 100 miles to Beersheba where he sat down and, literally, prayed to die. But God knew that what Elijah needed was some deep sleep and some good food. Heaven didn't deliver inspirational verses, leather-bound words of comfort, or sweet-smelling flowers; God neither indulged nor rebuked Elijah. Instead, He sent an angel to provide practical sustenance: both nourishing food and refreshing drink between bouts of welcome slumber, the combination of which strengthened the exhausted prophet sufficiently to make a further forty-day trip to Mount Horeb. Marvellously practical.

While the Bible sparkles with supernatural occurrences, angelic visitations, provisions, miracles, signs and wonders, King David reminds us that God 'knows how we are formed, he remembers that we are dust' (Psalm 103:14). Our Creator is all too aware of our physical requirements; we need to sleep, to eat, to work and not be alone. He designed us that way. It's not glamorous and it may not be remotely surprising, but it is important.

Jesus' invitation to breakfast on the beach begins another post-resurrection encounter with His disciples, this time back in Galilee; the old stomping ground of at least five of them. Like

Elijah, this unhappy band had been through a tough season of unprecedented spiritual battering during the annual Passover feast; they had witnessed Jesus' betrayal and gruesome crucifixion, followed by two glorious resurrection visitations in the Upper Room. Their physical, emotional and spiritual tanks were now running on empty. In their fatigued state of puzzlement, they knew something good had happened (as did Elijah), but they didn't understand it, and certainly hadn't processed it. Their grief at the horror of the cross had turned to unsurpassed joy, and yet their life together with Jesus over the past three years had clearly run its course, leaving a gaping hole of painful uncertainty as they faced the future.

The default reaction when they had no clue what to do next seems to have been to go home to Galilee. Going back is often easier to manage than going on.

So it was that seven out of eleven had spent a futile night of fishing on the lake. I get the feeling they just wanted to be doing something familiar and undemanding, away from other people with all their chatter, invasive questions and insatiable curiosity. Out on the water these men could relax into their default pre-Jesus roles, share their hurts, memories and disappointments, or just enjoy the diversion of temporarily losing themselves in total concentration on the practical task in hand. Processing grief is often a lonely road.

The actual catch of fish seems to be fairly irrelevant for them. None of the men appears too disheartened when the stranger on the shore enquires after the catch, and on this occasion, they don't moan and groan about taking advice to throw the net on the other side. Perhaps the fishermen recognised this instruction from one of their first encounters with Jesus when He had borrowed Peter's boat to avoid the press of a crowd. The same outcome brought realisation to John who, suddenly, knew without a doubt that it was Jesus on the sand. Before you could say, 'Drop the anchor!', Peter had leapt into the sea and waded to the shore.

Like them, we see the thoughtful practicality of Jesus who had already lit a fire and was cooking a tasty breakfast of fish and bread. Jesus had gone ahead of them and provided what they needed; isn't that always the way? Everyone was catered for before their feet even touched dry land. The Saviour became the host of a welcome picnic after a wearisome night of activity. Jesus didn't weigh in with advice, explanations, or rhetoric; He just asked them to bring some of their fresh catch and join Him on the sand. This was a warm, inclusive, natural, uncomplicated invitation from a friend to other friends. It may have been a simple meal but it must have felt like a feast; I wish I had been there too.

6. Be blessed

> Then the King will say to those on his right, 'Come, you who are blessed by my Father; take your inheritance …'
> (Matthew 25:34)

'Blessing' implies the favour and protection of God; a transference of good things from one to another. In God's case, that's not just wishing good things for someone or sending them happy thoughts; there's a power in the blessings that God speaks that is backed up by the provision and resources of heaven. From the very beginning God did this, speaking approval, goodwill and security over His creation. For Adam, Eve and their descendants, 'God blessed them and said to them, "Be fruitful and increase in number; fill the earth and subdue it"' (Genesis 1:28).

God made a binding covenant with Abraham promising that his name would become great and that his offspring would turn into a significant nation. In essence, this was repeated after Abraham was asked to sacrifice Isaac when God said, 'I will surely bless you and make your descendants as numerous as the stars in the sky and as the sand on the seashore … through your offspring all nations on earth will be blessed, because you have obeyed me' (Genesis 22:17-18). Blessing runs through the narrative of Abraham and his family line; it's clearly important to God.

Most people want to have their family around them when they sense their lives are drawing to a close. I know my own dad was grateful for the special time we three daughters and Mum were able to spend with him, reminiscing, laughing, crying, reading out loud and praying with him before he was welcomed into heaven. He frequently expressed his thankfulness for the family and the joy we had apparently brought him throughout his eighty-seven years; he blessed us too, regularly pointing us back to our heavenly Father. I'm so glad.

The Bible records how men who realised their days were almost at an end, also gathered their families around them to speak blessing over them before they died – Isaac, Jacob and Joseph all did this. What a beautiful way to leave.

God ordained another delight-filled blessing which He commissioned the priests to pray over the Jewish people: 'The LORD bless you and keep you; the LORD make his face shine on you and be gracious to you; the LORD turn his face towards you and give you peace' (Numbers 6:24-26). Those warm words are still used in churches as a benediction prayer to close a service, and often on the occasion of dedicating or welcoming a baby into a church family. I like the way this same blessing sounds in *The Message*: 'GOD bless you and keep you, GOD smile on you and gift you, GOD look you full in the face and make you prosper.' It speaks so clearly of favour and goodness; I wonder whether Jesus thought of these words when he took the children in His arms, welcoming and blessing them in Mark 10.

Jesus invites us into His kingdom of blessing where God, as we see in Matthew 25, will also invite us into our 'inheritance'. Far wiser scholars than I have explored what this means, but inheritance is surely about more than a ticket to heaven. Our daily blessing includes being loved, accepted, forgiven and engaging in an ongoing process of transformation to become more like Jesus. We're blessed to live in the good of His victory over sin, death and hell throughout all our days on earth; no longer crippled by guilt, paralysed by shame, overwhelmed by fear, ambushed by popular opinion, blindsided by anxiety, fixated by our failures or obsessed by self-doubt. This is why Jesus came, so that we can enjoy life to the full; life so that every part is brimming with His prolific gloriousness. That's a life of blessing now, and clearly there is more to be enjoyed on the other side of death.

God has promised Jesus the nations as His inheritance, and since we are 'heirs ... and co-heirs with Christ' (Romans 8:17), they will be ours as well somehow. I don't fully understand what this will look like, but God has it all in His very capable hands.

John saw, in his revelatory vision, a new heaven and a new earth where distress, pain and tears are banished (Revelation 21:4). Living there in union with our Saviour is also our inheritance. What a compelling invitation, then, to come and be blessed!

7. *The Wedding Feast of the Lamb*

> Let us rejoice and be glad
> and give him glory!
> For the wedding of the Lamb has come,
> and his bride has made herself ready ...
> Blessed are those who are invited to the wedding supper
> of the Lamb!
> (Revelation 19:7,9)

Sooner or later, one of our tomorrows will take us right through the curtain of death and into that inheritance for ever. Jesus describes heaven as a wedding party. The apostle Paul was looking forward to this, not in a gloomy, morbid way, but with the certain hope of faith: 'We are confident, I say, and would prefer to be away from the body and at home with the Lord' (2 Corinthians 5:8). He told the churches at both Corinth and

Philippi[9] that he would far rather be away from this temporal world and was genuinely looking forward to throwing off his mortal coil, a body that was beginning to flag (not surprising after all the imprisonments, beatings, stonings, shipwrecks, etc he had experienced, 2 Corinthians 11:22-28), and a spirit that yearned for intimacy with Christ without the trials, hassles and heartache of first-century life in the Roman-ruled world. He could barely wait to take up the invitation, and who can blame him? It will be a unique privilege for the children of God.

Heaven will be a place of God's perfection. It definitely won't see us floating, bored and aimless on a cloud. Our certain hope will be far more real than anything we have known or experienced here among the shadows of earth and, as in the original blueprint, we will enjoy eternal and abundant life in His presence where our joy will be complete. Life now is just the preface to the real thing, a training ground for the reigning ahead, and apparently we have a wedding to attend – our own!

To understand the symbolic parallels of this marriage feast-yet-to-come, it's helpful to reference Jewish wedding culture, a four-step process: Choice, Contract, Consummation and Celebration.[10]

Step 1: Choice. Arranged marriages were the cultural norm, but before any contract could be negotiated and drawn up, a choice of bride had to be made, usually undertaken by the groom's father who would make decisions about strategic alignments and, perhaps, prior or existing affections. Abraham appointed his servant as marriage broker or representative to go to find the appropriate girl for Isaac (Genesis 24:2-4).

God the Father tells us that we too have been chosen 'before the creation of the world to be holy and blameless in his sight' (Ephesians 1:4). The apostle Paul refers several times

---

[9] Philippians 1:23.

[10] www.bible.ca/marriage/ancient-jewish-three-stage-weddings-and-marriage-customs-ceremony-in-the-bible.htm (accessed 18th March 2020). I have expanded the three stages to four for clarity.

illustratively to the combined body of believers – the Church – as the bride of Christ.

The picture of the Church as bride is perhaps best summed up by John the Baptist, who gave this apt reply to some men who were concerned that Jesus was beginning to eclipse his own ministry: 'The bride belongs to the bridegroom. The friend who attends the bridegroom waits and listens for him, and is full of joy when he hears the bridegroom's voice' (John 3:29). John knew that it was time for Jesus to take centre stage and proclaim His kingdom as He came to seek out the focus of His love – His bride.

Step 2: Contract: A betrothal took place between a man and a woman after the bride-to-be's parents drew up a legal document between the two parties including details of the financial responsibilities of the groom, the required dowry and the bride price. This was an effective deterrent to avoid frivolous suitors and the possibility of a broken relationship prior to the marriage, which would leave the woman destitute and sullied with a reputation she probably didn't deserve. It was a binding contract; at this point the protagonists were seen as absolutely married in every sense, even though the dowry was not yet paid and there was no physical consummation of the union.

Jesus paid for His bride, the Church, with His life-blood; the high price demanded as a spiritual dowry for His betrothal. This was the contract God had in mind when He sent Jesus to purchase our redemption. As part of His worldwide Church (the living, breathing organic family; not the institution, denomination, building, traditions or services), we are 'legally' betrothed to Jesus. We are a bride who has been fully paid for. Jesus is thrilled, and He will not break this contract. 'As a young man marries a young woman … as a bridegroom rejoices over his bride, so will your God rejoice over you' (Isaiah 62:5).

Step 3: Consummation: It could take a bridegroom as long as seven years to pay the dowry price in full before this step could be taken (there's that appropriate number of completion again). Then, the groom and up to ten of his friends would make their way to the bride's house in the evening, where she would be ready and waiting with up to ten of her own maiden friends. The groom would go into the room with his bride while the friends all waited outside (how awfully unnerving) for the shout of joy confirming that the bride was indeed a virgin.

I have found that understanding all this makes much more sense of both the parable of the ten virgins in Matthew 25, and John the Baptist's reference to himself as the friend of the Bridegroom.

Paul uses the marriage metaphor again when he refers to the purity of the believing Church. 'I am jealous for you with a godly jealousy. I promised you to one husband, to Christ, so that I might present you as a pure virgin to him' (2 Corinthians 11:2). He is urging the Church to stay spiritually clean before God and not be distracted or deceived.

When the things of this earth are completed, Jesus will finally be united with His bride and there will be the sound of rejoicing in heaven; this is what all of history has been about! Until then, like the bride and her friends, we are watching and waiting for His return; we don't know the exact timing, but we do want to have accepted the invitation and be ready for it.

Step 4: Celebration: Jewish wedding celebrations are still celebrated over seven days. In New Testament times, having consummated the marriage, the bride and groom, together with all the friends, would form a noisy, torch-lit procession through the streets all the way back to his family home where they would be met by more friends and family, and the feasting, dancing, merry-making and fun could begin in earnest, to continue through the night and the subsequent days.[11]

One day, Jesus will return to take us back, as a celebrated bride, to His Father's house in heaven where the wedding feast of the Lamb depicted in Revelation will be celebrated in eternity. We can be sure that will be a party like no other; a banquet of sumptuous lavishness beyond our comprehension, including a

---

[11] Ibid.

form of rejoicing which will be far, far beyond anything we could possibly imagine from our current vantage point, in this temporal, fallen world. Every nation, language, culture and tribe will be represented among the innumerable multitude of worshippers there, all enjoying a praise-filled celebration which will run and run…

RSVP

One Saviour; seven invitations; and our name is on all of them. What now?

You will know, as I do, that these are the four capital letters which appear at the bottom of any formal invitation: 'RSVP'. '*Répondez s'il vous plaît*' is a polite, if rather archaic, reminder to reply – an opportunity to either accept or decline the invitation. To simply turn up is rude and inconsiderate. It also runs the risk of arriving to find that you are not expected and that there is no place catered for you, which would be humiliating and embarrassing for both you and your host.

Having outlined the invitations that Jesus gives and described the biblical context for each one, it would be a massive oversight on my part to expect you to consider them simply as some kind of abstract idea, or a collection of teaching points for reflection and/or discussion. All of us have a responsibility to RSVP. If we have replied in the affirmative to the very first one, to follow Him – and not everybody does or will – then the other invitations are a given; but they still require responses… sometimes daily.

It would be tragic for any of us to miss out on such expansive, lavish and joy-filled invitations; but it's that first one which will determine all our other choices and draw us permanently into the company of Jesus, our host.

Palate-cleanser questions

- Elijah went back to Mount Horeb to pour out his heart and meet with God. This was the same place where Moses had powerfully encountered God years previously at the burning bush (Exodus 3). Where is your Mount Horeb?

- Jesus came to give us abundant life in which we need 'no longer [be] crippled by guilt, paralysed by shame, overwhelmed by fear, ambushed by popular opinion, blindsided by anxiety, fixated by our failures or obsessed by self-doubt.' How have any of these things conspired to steal your joy lately? Before you go on to the next chapter, spend some time putting this right with God and receiving His forgiveness and grace.

4. Preparation

You prepare a table before me
(Psalm 23:5)

Royal banquets and special tables

Buckingham Palace has, historically, been the venue for multiple state visits, investitures, ambassadorial visits and the like. These almost always include a banquet; no president or foreign dignitary will make do with simple cheese on toast and a cup of tea when meeting with Her Majesty the Queen. While the sovereign has, in recent years, flung open the doors of the palace to visitors in a refreshingly inclusive way and carried on the custom of Queen Victoria with her garden parties, tradition requires a more formal approach for international and governmental events, during which royal wealth and opulence are evident. The red carpets, shimmering chandeliers, valuable art collection and historic family treasures will all speak for themselves and contribute to the superlative and memorable affair.

It takes a year to plan for a state banquet; several weeks to compose the seating plan; ten days to prepare everything for each event, including three days devoted to laying the table correctly with 1,700 pieces of meticulously aligned cutlery – ten per person – and 1,104 glasses, each bearing the royal cipher – six per person – designated for water, champagne, white wine, red wine, a sweet dessert wine and port. The china is the valuable 1787 Tournai Grand Service which has to be handled with extreme care; it's composed of 4,000 pieces and was purchased by George IV in the nineteenth century. Each diner is allotted a dining area exactly 46cm wide; measuring sticks ensure this is adhered to precisely throughout the dining room.[12] Tables are swathed in pristine, steamed, white linen cloths, decorated with twenty-three centre pieces, and the seventeenth-century candelabras – made up of 122 constituent parts – are deconstructed, polished and then reassembled to dazzle the guests. Even the individual butter pats are stamped with an image of the royal crown. Pages serve guests in synchronised choreographed manoeuvres, signalled by a system of lights hidden in the ceiling. Finally, when the five-course meal is finished – usually eighty minutes later – pipers serenade the diners, and guests adjourn to the State Rooms for coffee and petits fours. The room is swiftly dismantled and then everything must be washed up by hand…[13]

Such an event requires sharp minds, excellent memories, meticulous planning, impeccable logistics, absolute concentration, tight teamwork, hours of hard graft, expert creativity, enormous patience and thorough commitment to the task. It's a massive and nerve-shattering undertaking. When every last detail has been given attention, the Queen herself comes and checks it all. Doubtless there is much holding of breath lest the monarch's eye spot anything out of place, overlooked or substandard. Giving her approval to the

---

[12] www.express.co.uk/news/royal/593359/Queen-Royal-Household-prepare-State-visit-Buckingham-Palace-summer-exhibition (accessed 30th March 2018).
[13] www.telegraph.co.uk/news/uknews/queen-elizabeth-II/11757987/The-secrets-of-Buckingham-Palaces-Royal-receptions.html (accessed 30th March 2018).

preparations is almost certainly followed by a collective sigh of relief from her staff. The stage is set.

Our own dining table has been the focus of less intense organisation, but witness to many years of conversation, debate, laughter, tears, blue-sky thinking, jokes, stories, birthdays, broken hearts, plans, guests, extended family and many meals – both good and not-so-good. Made from soft pine, bleached and aged with time and scrubbing, it was one I found in an antique store just before we got married more than thirty years ago. I loved its texture and patina, cherishing the idea that it might already have been handed down through generations and that we would now be guardians of all its untold stories until the next generation take it into their home somewhere. Unlike the Queen's banqueting table, it is a plain, simple farmhouse table of pleasing but utilitarian design, as appealing to me now as the day I discovered it. My children used it for study and homework; they leaned on it while they coloured countless pictures, learned to wield tricky scissors, sticky glue, gloopy paint and glorious glitter. We wrote letters and Christmas cards there, paid bills, filled in permission slips and wrestled over student finance forms. We have mixed cakes, served countless cups of comforting tea, read books, mentored newlyweds and taught three years of home school, as well as hosted hundreds of people around its friendly borders. My husband claims that should there ever be a house fire it is the only piece of furniture he would want to save (after family and photographs, of course), because of the memories it evokes.

Biblical dining

In Bible times, the dining table was a rather different piece of furniture. For most people, like Abraham, who was a nomadic herder, cushions and stools were the ubiquitous seating places. The 'table' was a mat or rug upon which dishes were placed.

David had a seat assigned for him at King Saul's table; Jonathan's orphaned son, Mephibosheth, ate at David's table throughout the monarch's reign. At the Last Supper, we find that Jesus and His disciples were reclining around a table as they shared the Passover meal together.

Unlike the usual daily meal, a banquet was one of those occasions when people attending went both to 'see and be seen'. The seating arrangements were particular, and places around the table were allotted by rank. I can only imagine the sinister disquiet felt by Joseph's brothers when they discovered that they had been seated in exact age order around his meal table in Egypt.[14] Still unaware that the stern ruler who hosted them was actually their long-lost brother, who had instructed his steward to arrange the table so precisely, its arrangement must have felt very unsettling. I imagine they all probably turned several dozen shades paler and instantly lost their appetites; wouldn't you?

A similar seating theme is illustrated by Jesus in one of His stories:

> When he noticed how the guests picked the places of honour at the table, he told them this parable: 'When someone invites you to a wedding feast, do not take the place of honour, for a person more distinguished than you may have been invited. If so, the host who invited both of you will come and say to you, "Give this person your seat." Then, humiliated, you will have to take the least important place. But when you are invited, take the lowest place, so that when your host comes, he will say to you, "Friend, move up to a better place." Then you will be honoured in the presence of all the other guests. For all those who exalt themselves will be humbled, and those who humble themselves will be exalted.'
> (Luke 14:7-11)

In this case, witnesses to the banquet would note how the seating of guests indicated their standing or rank, rather than age, in the eyes of both society and the host, sending an

---

[14] Genesis 43:33.

unequivocal message to the whole community. Favoured ones would be higher up the table, closer to the feast-giver and everyone would also be able to see who was not there. Notable omissions would, doubtless, provide fertile material for local gossip...

A place for you

Since God has prepared a table for us, we can be sure that He has also prepared a specific place for us at that table. We will not be asked to change places with someone more worthy, or to move down the table in consequence of having taken the place of a more important guest. No; God assigns us an exact place.

Many wedding planners arrange the tables with place name cards set out in the appropriate places. At Buckingham Palace, the Master of the Household goes to great lengths to seat the guests appropriately. More pedestrian hosts make strenuous effort, on a smaller scale, to avoid randomly seating their guests, but rather place them with friends they already know, or with people they envisage might have similar interests or personalities that they hope will connect well. Just as any wedding invitation I receive carries my name, so there is a 'divine place card' with my name across it at God's table.

When David was forced to escape the environs of Saul's palace where his life was actively threatened by the incumbent king, his absence at the king's table was noted (1 Samuel 20:24-27). In fact, that's how Saul realised his enemy was absent. No one else could use his place; diners could not come and go as they pleased. Similarly, God has created a particular place for us and allotted it to each one specifically – not a physical table, but a metaphorical one with a seat set aside and made-to-measure, as it were, for us. He is grieved if we choose to remove ourselves and spend our time elsewhere.

My head often knows this better than my heart. In other words, my cognitive understanding of God's personal care for me agrees that this level of His interest and love is true; but it doesn't always feel true.

My friend Ian has a pertinent story on this topic from a time when he was wondering where he fitted into a particular forum and was questioning whether God really was as interested in it all as he had hoped. He was on a retreat which had been organised by a local church for people involved in social activism within the area. The final meditative session was focused on considering the future. During this time Ian felt God say very clearly, 'Ian, you have a place at the table.' A reassuring word for sure, but somehow it lacked the specific clarity he was hoping for. After the event, he went outside into the garden area where he found a beautifully carved seat. Making use of it, he continued to think about the words he felt God had said, but persisted, 'What does that actually mean?' Still pondering this, Ian noticed a large, hand-crafted wooden table on a paved area, surrounded by magnificent, throne-like chairs. In his spirit, Ian felt God tell him to go and investigate and to sit at a particular corner of the table. Feeling rather foolish, he slumped into the chair, put his head in his hands, hoped no one was watching through the window and wondered what was going on. As he looked down, there, quite clearly carved into the wood, was his name: 'IAN'.

Despite subsequently examining the rest of the table with great care, there was not a single other piece of graffiti on it anywhere. Not only that, but this lone 'blemish' had green moss growing within its grooves; it was not a fresh cut. With a disquieting jolt, Ian realised this was more than a coincidence; God was kindly confirming His words of affirmation with this strange visual reinforcement.

This story reminds me of the wonderful words also penned by David, as he paints a poetic picture of the detail in which God knows each of us:

> For you created my inmost being;
> you knit me together in my mother's womb.

I praise you because I am fearfully and wonderfully
made;
your works are wonderful,
I know that full well.
My frame was not hidden from you
when I was made in the secret place,
when I was woven together in the depths of the earth.
Your eyes saw my unformed body;
all the days ordained for me were written in your book
before one of them came to be.
(Psalm 139:13-16)

The prophet Jeremiah heard God saying, 'Before I formed you
in the womb I knew you, before you were born I set you apart
…' (Jeremiah 1:5); the apostle Paul tells us that God chose us
'before the foundation of the world' (Ephesians 1:4, ESVUK).
Likewise, long before I was so much as a glint in the eye of my
parents, God saw me, knew me, loved me and chose me, and
then was somehow present in the cramped darkness of my
mother's womb, where the miraculous formation of my highly
complex human body was steadily taking place. How
thoroughly amazing! I don't think it is possible to engage with
these mind-bending truths without responding in grateful
worship.

Not only is there a wonderful specificity in where I am
positioned at this table of life but, more amazing, is that at the
ultimate Wedding Feast of the Lamb, we will all be seated with
Jesus as the central focus. Logistically I suppose we cannot *all*
sit next to Him, but somehow, unconfined by the limits of
temporal existence, I think it will probably feel both as if we are
celebrating en masse, yet sitting at an intimate table for two.
That aside, I'm sure that all of us will be so caught up in the
presence of the One we have worshipped and followed that we
will not be remotely concerned with the seating plan.

Which table?

Our Psalm 23 table is representative of our life circumstances – a place where we can know God's tangible, palpable presence and closeness as we sit down to 'feast' on the things that are served to us each day. This is not just vivid imagining; this is the divine nature of God's engagement with us each and every day. There are other 'tables' where we could go for sustenance, of course: career success (however you interpret that), financial buoyancy, popular acclaim, trend-setting, recreational drugs, thought-leading, coveted-image projector, celebrity, front-row guest, musical genius, social butterfly, scientific pioneer, non-stop partygoer, etc. The world has endless enticing 'tables' on offer which may give you a temporary buzz, but they will never compare with the one God has specifically prepared for you.

Personal preparation

So, the royal table at which we are invited to feast daily is prepared but, as guests, we also need to do some preparation of our own. If you've ever seen photographs from any of the garden parties held by the Queen at Buckingham Palace, you will see how the guests have gone to great lengths to dress appropriately: the women in beautiful dresses, often with elaborate hats and jewellery, and the men in crisp suits and perfect ties. Likewise, for a wedding or an official engagement, one would not expect the participants to arrive in casual jeans, T-shirts or old trainers.

Clothing

Jesus told another parable about a king who threw a wedding banquet for his son; you can read it in Matthew 22:1-14. It's an illustration of the kingdom of God in which God is the King and Jesus is the Son. The original guests refused the royal invitation, just as the Jews – God's chosen people – rejected Jesus as Messiah; and so, the request was resent to a wider circle of people, representative of the Gentiles or non-Jews. From our twenty-first-century perspective, we probably don't realise what a huge mental and cultural shift this was for the early Church; that God should generously expand the portals of His kingdom and the offer of salvation to everyone who named Him Lord would have shattered all their comfortable paradigms into baffling pieces.

Back in Jesus' parable, there is a guest who has arrived at the feast without the appropriate wedding garment. In Eastern culture, the royal wardrobe would carry exquisite, often highly decorated and embroidered garments, which were brought out for special occasions and distributed so that every guest could wear one. Thus a ruler could exhibit his wealth in a public forum which would be appreciated by impressionable visitors; a tasteful flaunting, if you will; a demonstration of status and riches. No one would bring their own fancy garments or come into the venue while wearing their ordinary clothes; that would be insulting to the host. It's no surprise, then, that when the king in the story arrived and found a guest without the necessary apparel, he wondered how the man could have even got into the banqueting hall without a change of clothing. This reckless guest was represented as thumbing his nose at the provision made by the master of the feast, and showing contempt for the lavish hospitality of the king. Refusal to put on the robe which was offered meant that this man was ejected from the proceedings.

Yes, God wants us at the feast of His Son but, as my dad used to say, while we can come *just as we are*, we cannot come *just as we like*. There are terms and conditions which apply. To be part of God's kingdom, a major clean-up act is required from the inside out. We cannot provide that cleanliness on our own or by our self-effort. Scripture tells us that the appropriate dress code for 'feasting' with God, whether in this life or the next, requires white robes signifying the purity and holiness of a righteous life which we cannot self-generate, but receive only as a free gift from the righteousness of Jesus, purchased for us by His sacrificial death, resurrection and ascension. Our heavenly Father has exchanged our dirty old clothes for new royal robes: 'He has clothed me with garments of salvation and arrayed me in a robe of his righteousness' (Isaiah 61:10). We can enjoy these right now.

The blessing and relief of walking spiritually clean allows us to face each day with confidence and our eyes fixed, not on our previous unworthiness, but on His absolute, undisputed worthiness which covers our own inadequacy completely.

Foot-washing

Another custom of Bible times was to provide water for washing a guest's feet. Way back in Genesis 18, Abraham was practising classic Eastern hospitality towards his three mysterious guests by giving shelter, food and water to clean their tired feet. The hot, sandy conditions of daily life in the Judean desert area meant that feet were inevitably dirty, and probably quite smelly, for much of the time. Offering water in this way demonstrated acceptance of a stranger, as well as welcome for a friend.

Perfume

In the same way, perfumed oil might well be provided by a host. This had the useful property of refreshing the visitor as well as reducing sweat and relieving the inevitable irritation of sand on the feet. The fragrance would disguise unpleasant smells of the personal hygiene variety, and possibly serve as a type of insect repellent as well – all of which would be most welcome to a hot, weary traveller.

Ruth's preparations to visit Boaz included washing herself and making use of perfumed oil before putting on her best clothes and heading to the threshing floor (Ruth 3:3). God told Moses to create a unique anointing oil which was only to be used on sacred items in the tabernacle and by the priests. They would enter God's presence as a fragrant offering themselves (Exodus 30:22-33).

Greeting

It was not unusual for a kiss on the cheek to be given as a welcome, particularly between relatives, but also as formal recognition of an individual. When Aaron was sent to meet his brother Moses in the desert, he gave him a fraternal kiss (Exodus 4:27). One of the greatest friendships portrayed in the Bible is the one between David and Jonathan. When David left the palace to avoid assassination by King Saul, they parted reluctantly with a brotherly kiss (1 Samuel 20:41).

Kissing is a universal gesture of intimacy practised in many cultures. What an irony then that Jesus Himself was betrayed by Judas with the kiss of a friend, in the Garden of Gethsemane.

A poor welcome

Jesus was provided with none of these welcoming things the day He went to supper at the home of Simon the Pharisee. Once inside and reclining at the table, He was approached by a woman of dubious character who used expensive perfume on His feet while He was eating (we'll meet her again in Chapter 15). The ill-disguised disapproval of Simon earned him a stinging rebuke from his guest as he was forced, against all cultural norms, to acknowledge her presence in the room. Jesus continued to ram His point home: 'I came into your house. You did not give me any water for my feet, but she wet my feet with her tears and wiped them with her hair. You did not give me a kiss, but this woman, from the time I entered, has not stopped kissing my feet. You did not put oil on my head, but she has poured perfume on my feet' (Luke 7:44-46).

Simon may have been a bigwig in religious circles, but he was not a good host, failing to offer any of the customary welcomes to Jesus, his guest. Was this just bad manners, I wonder, or an attempt to embarrass and discredit the young rabbi who was causing so much turmoil among the religious elite?

Gift-giving

This is another custom associated with visiting someone else's house as a guest; a small present expresses thanks and brings honour to the host, even though accepting the invitation does not require it. If you attend a birthday or wedding, you will probably take a gift. If going to a meal at a friend's house you may also arrive on the doorstep with flowers, a bottle of wine or box of chocolates. It's a thoughtful expression of gratitude rather than a trade, but the gesture indicates that you have anticipated the occasion with a degree of eagerness rather than just ticked off the next thing in your diary.

The desire to bring a gift of thanks is not new. Even the mysterious Magi brought gifts from the East for the new King when the indications of their astronomy charts led them to Bethlehem (see Matthew 2). Their exotic presents welcomed Jesus with a lavishness that would not have been out of place in a palace, and which must have made his parents' eyes boggle. Costly gold for a king; aromatic frankincense used in temple worship; and myrrh, an ingredient used in both the priestly anointing oil, indicating service, and in burial, prefiguring His death. These prophetically symbolic gifts spoke of the nature of the life Jesus would live as a man, yet still mysteriously embodied the whispers and stamp of heaven evidenced in His divine nature, position and calling. I wonder what Mary and Joseph did with those presents?

What should we bring to the banqueting table of God? In some senses God wants us to bring nothing, yet everything[15] – just ourselves. It may not sound like much, but perhaps Christina Rossetti's old Christmas carol sums up your thoughts as it does my own:

> What can I give Him, poor as I am?
> If I were a shepherd, I would bring a lamb;
> If I were a Wise Man, I would do my part;
> Yet what I can I give Him: give my heart.[16]

When we come to 'feast' with Jesus we can be sure that He has overseen both the preparation of the table and the food served on it. We must prepare ourselves. We need to have put on the garments of salvation He has provided for us, immersed ourselves in the water of the Word, and be slathered in the oil of the Holy Spirit. If the correct preparations have not been made, then we should not be surprised that we cannot enjoy the 'feast'.

Our psalmist also wrote, 'Who may ascend the mountain of the LORD? Who may stand in his holy place? The one who has clean hands and a pure heart' (Psalm 24:3-4). To be accepted by God we need to be saturated in Jesus so that we can come to Him confidently, with our heads held high, free from shame, guilt and fear. We are transformed, regenerated. Paul tells us that our 'life is now hidden with Christ in God' (Colossians 3:3). In other words, when God looks at us, He no longer just sees us, but the righteousness of Jesus because, spiritually, we are wearing those fine, linen wedding garments of salvation. Here on earth these metaphorical clothes need to look like the character of Jesus:

---

[15] See Chapter 2: Invitations – Follow.
[16] Christina Georgina Rossetti (1830-94), 1872; appeared posthumously in *The Poetical Works of Christina Georgina Rossetti* – Poem #426 (first published London: Macmillan and Co, 1904). Hymn *In the Bleak Midwinter* in public domain.

> Therefore, as God's chosen people, holy and dearly loved, clothe yourselves with compassion, kindness, humility, gentleness and patience. Bear with each other and forgive one another if any of you has a grievance against someone. Forgive as the Lord forgave you. And over all these virtues put on love, which binds them all together in perfect unity.
>
> (Colossians 3:12-14)

This is no easy task. Unlike slipping into your favourite sweater, this type of dressing is a process that's going to require time to change. If you expect it to happen all at once then you'll be sorely disappointed. 'Progress, not perfection' is the helpful mantra of one of my friends. Allow yourself time to change, and grace to smooth the transition.

The Holy Spirit helps us; He is the spiritual oil who provides the necessary lubrication for such a major gear change. Like the cogs in an engine, old patterns need to disengage before new ones engage; without oil there will be grinding, jarring, damage and pain. I've noticed that God is far more patient with us in seasons of change than we usually are with ourselves. Self-flagellation and recrimination is a sure-fire route to discouragement and even despair. God will never be the One leading us there. Instead, let's resolve to only keep in step with Him as we dress ourselves in these spiritual clothes.

Family resemblance

The glory of God is the character of God; therefore, of course, the glory of Jesus is also the character of Jesus. He told His disciples, 'Anyone who has seen me has seen the Father' (John 14:9). If we are God's children then we really should bear some resemblance to Him! Our very nature has been changed, our spiritual DNA irrevocably altered. We have moved from death to life; from darkness to light; from selfish self-government to joyful, submitted obedience to the new Ruler of our lives. We are literally under new management. The characteristics that Paul encourages us to put on, or clothe ourselves with, are not something to be taken off again at the end of the day. The nature of God will develop and grow in us by the power of the Holy Spirit, just as fruit grows on a tree. Fruit is a natural by-product of a healthy tree; the tree does not need to somehow squeeze them out by its own effort.

The New Testament identifies nine of these fruits: 'love, joy, peace, patience, kindness, goodness, faithfulness, gentleness and self-control'.[17] These characteristics will increasingly manifest in us as the inevitable consequence of remaining rooted in Jesus.

The Message version is helpful here:

> But what happens when we live God's way? He brings gifts into our lives, much the same way that fruit appears in an orchard – things like affection for others, exuberance about life, serenity. We develop a willingness to stick with things, a sense of compassion in the heart, and a conviction that a basic holiness permeates things and people. We find ourselves involved in loyal commitments, not needing to force our way in life, able to marshal and direct our energies wisely … Since this is the kind of life we have chosen, the life of the Spirit, let us make sure that we do not just hold it as an idea in our heads or a sentiment in our hearts, but work out its implications in every detail of our lives. That means we will not compare ourselves with each other as if one of us were better and another worse. We have far more interesting things to do with our lives. Each of us is an original.
> (Galatians 5:22-23,25-26)

To grow more and better fruit, we simply need to ensure that our hearts provide quality grade soil in which the seeds of God's

---

[17] Galatians 5:22-23, NIV 1984.

Word can flourish. The water of the Holy Spirit stops our hearts becoming hard, and the sunshine and warmth of His presence cause germination and healthy growth. This is not a collection of clichés, but profound biblical truth.

These characteristics are the fruit that grow in our lives; but God has also given His children a multiplicity of good gifts. Paul takes a great deal of time speaking to the first-century Church about the spiritual gifts which God has generously lavished on His Church in order that believers become mature, and so that His kingdom life will be replicated and multiplied throughout people groups across the world. You can do a study on these yourself from the ministries identified in Ephesians 4 – apostles, prophets, evangelists, pastors and teachers – to the long list in 1 Corinthians 12, which includes wisdom, faith, healing, discernment and administration; and don't forget the explanation of tongues and prophecy in chapter 14. Also note that the famous chapter on love, so frequently called upon in wedding services, is tucked in between them, emphasising how vital that attribute is above all others, and especially so in the context of using these important gifts.

It turns out that all the gifts we might bring to God's feasting table are actually gifts God has given us first. He gave us life and breath. He loved us while we were still far away and separated from Him (Romans 5:8). He chose us and called us. He appointed and anointed us for a life walked out with Him, and which is to be lived from the same mandate Jesus had:

> to proclaim good news to the poor… to bind up the broken-hearted, to proclaim freedom for the captives and release from darkness for the prisoners, to proclaim the year of the LORD's favour and the day of vengeance of our God, to comfort all who mourn, and provide for those who grieve in Zion – to bestow on them a crown of beauty instead of ashes, the oil of joy instead of mourning, and a garment of praise instead of a spirit of despair.
>
> (Isaiah 61:1-3)

This mission statement is the foundation and launch pad for the whole of our lives; it will manifest itself in myriad ways, but this is their essence. If you're ever feeling useless or aimless, it's a helpful piece of biblical signage to remind us in which direction we need to turn ourselves.

Chewing on truth

These truths are well worth digesting until they are naturally, truly a part of ourselves. Making them a part of our preparation for whatever the day may bring will help us tune in to God's voice. As we embark on each day, let's also follow the example of ancient worshippers as we 'enter his gates with thanksgiving and his courts with praise; give thanks to him and praise his name. For the LORD is good and his love endures for ever; his faithfulness continues through all generations' (Psalm 100:4-5).

Praise often activates faith. When we declare truths about God, lift up His name and worship Him in music, song and spoken words, we are also speaking to our souls and prodding them into life. Where we are spiritually flabby, worship sparks us into action and communication with God. It reminds us of things we forgot we knew, and serves as a form of prayer which lifts our eyes from the immediate back to the King of kings on His unshakeable throne. Thus we move from passivity to deliberate engagement with Him as we face our 'dish of the day', which ensures our focus is on God rather than on our circumstances. By lifting our eyes and hearts in active faith, towards our Father in heaven, we can prepare ourselves to embrace the day, even on a Monday!

We cannot truly worship if we are carrying offence around in our hearts, nurturing a grudge, sulking or withholding forgiveness from someone. This last one is worth particular attention since it lies at the root of so much bitterness, stress and so many fractured relationships; it can frequently show itself in physical symptoms too, robbing both us and those around us. The transformative power of Word and worship focuses our minds and compels our emotions to align themselves correctly in their light. The certainties of God displace the uncertainties of circumstance and our general human propensity to allow our feelings to dethrone those immovables. This serves as a spiritually healthy springboard into the many good things prepared for us by God, which are served up for us each day.

So, when we prepare ourselves to come and 'feast' with Jesus, we bear all of these things in mind and our hearts are free to be filled with a sense of expectant anticipation. The prospect of 'feasting' with Him each day – whether we perceive ourselves to be stuck in the trivial, mundane or routine, or whirling excitedly among the thrill of adrenaline-pumping adventures, or even in the heartbreak and pain of unwanted crises – stirs an expectation of deep connection in our thirsty souls.

Knowing we can walk the entire day not just in the company of our Creator, Brother, Lover, Friend, Saviour and King, but with our eyes fixed on Him as His are fixed on ours, beats everything else.

Palate-cleanser questions

- How do you prepare yourself for meeting with Jesus? In what way, if any, does your preparation for a personal quiet time differ from the way you prepare for a church family gathering?

- Colossians 3:12-14 lists characteristics with which we are encouraged to clothe ourselves. Which do you find the easiest, and/or the most challenging to wear?

- How can we have a consistently thankful heart and nurture 'good soil' (Luke 8:15) in our hearts? What action can you take when you are at a loss to find anything for which to thank God?

Main Course

5. What's on the Menu?

LORD, you have assigned me my portion and my cup ...
(Psalm 16:5, NIV 1984)

One person's feast is another person's famine

At the tender age of six or seven, I remember that we visited some old family friends who lived some considerable distance away. Once the boring adult conversation finally gave way to the welcome advent of lunch, I found myself perched on a low chair which just about gave me an eye-level view of the edge of the table. It was probably this unfortunate angle which gave the food on my plate artificially epic proportions when it arrived in front of me. What culinary monstrosity was this? A mountain of ominous brown slabs confronted me; with wide-eyed dismay, a noxious smell threatened impending disaster as my guts performed a series of alarming somersaults. Liver. Eugh; why was it that adults seemed to feel obliged to top up the iron intake of unsuspecting children by trying to disguise the vile taste of offal by slow cooking it in casseroles?

The merest whiff of liver today, and I involuntarily conjure the awful immediacy of that excruciating, visceral dilemma which my embarrassed but frightened self faced. I was overwhelmed; what to do? The rising panic as I helplessly surveyed the loaded plate is still with me. My head said, 'Run!' My experience said, 'The punishment will be swift and sure if you behave rudely to these people.' My tongue was paralysed, my vision blurred by the rising tide of inevitable tears as I faced this conundrum of manners versus stomach reflux.

This was no feast as far as I was concerned.

Can you relate to my story? You probably have one or two of your own. Time and history veil the eventual outcome of my semi-traumatic mealtime. Perhaps your tale spotlights some other 'delicacy'. Remember Spam? This horror featured in the 1970s school dinners of my primary school; I seldom found anyone who liked it. Perhaps your nemesis was prunes or semolina.

One person's feast is another person's famine…

Memory, curiously, can often retain the unpleasant experiences of life more poignantly and enduringly than the good ones. I have found it easier to remember the worst meals I've come across so much more readily than the best ones.

A couple of years ago, I visited a slightly macabre exhibition commemorating the sinking of the *RMS Titanic*. Among the salvaged articles were some pieces of china from the dining room which, chipped and cracked as they were, still held a haunting beauty. Cards, detailing menus of ascending quality reflected the spectrum of choices on offer for passengers from steerage to First Class, from the stodgy and bland to the rich and exotic.

What would constitute a feast for you? If you were called upon to produce one, and if money and calories were no object, would you hark back to some specialty your granny or your mum used to make, perhaps a reprise of a significant birthday banquet? Or would you throw caution to the wind, reach for an aspirational cook book and painstakingly create a new eye-popping, glorious, guilt-free dietary extravaganza?

The topic of food is, of course, completely subjective. Coming up with a menu can be as easy or as challenging as the guests or friends we are entertaining or hosting – and there's a world of difference between the formality or familiarity of those two events, of course.

How about God's 'menu'? What is being served up in front of you in this season of your life? Do you feel as though you are fine-dining in First Class, or languishing with the unpalatable fare of a steerage passenger? Perhaps you are surprised by the 'dishes' that have been allowed across your 'place setting', or maybe the 'menu' feels tired and old. Are you baffled by how to engage with what is in front of you, like a rookie diner fumbling with Asian chopsticks for the first time, or as horrified as I was by my liver encounter? You may be revelling in what is spread before you, but perhaps you find yourself more inclined to push it away.

Personalised menus

We know that every day has been planned and designed by God. Each has been prepared as a 'feast' to be enjoyed in His company and around the 'table' of daily experience, and that's inevitably going to look very different for each of us. The backdrop and circumstances of our lives cover a wide spectrum of geography, employment, social interaction, responsibilities, time management and so much more. Our waking hours are punctuated by highs and lows; delight and despair; excitement and dry routine; challenge, choice and change. Our myriad reactions to these things remain one of the many reasons why the study of people can be so endlessly fascinating. We are all truly unique. An energising, fruitful, satisfying, productive day for one can cause nothing but draining frustration for another. One person's feast…

If you are working in a corporate company, your 'feast' will look very different from the one faced by the person employed in a factory, a school, a retail outlet, the military or in an artist's studio. Obviously, it will be a world away from those who are sheltering in refugee camps, subsistence farmers battling drought, widows caring for their orphaned grandchildren, or those struggling as part of a child-led household in sub-Saharan Africa. Comparison is sobering.

There are always extremes of experience; then there are all the experiences in between. What some might find mind-numbing tedium, others might regard as a welcome consistency. Mundane, repetitive tasks at home or in an office may offer welcome relief for another who is craving the space to think, and the security of a regular rhythm to each day. One person's feast is another person's famine…

The same contrast exists every day of our lives: one person's adventure is another individual's nightmare.

Sooner or later – and you don't need to wait for a mid-life crisis for this – whether chosen or forced upon us, there will come a time (or times) when we manage to pause for reflection amid the busyness of life, and find ourselves asking some serious questions about the 'menu' God has devised for us. 'How did I get here?'; 'Why is this happening to me?'; 'How long will it be like this?'; 'Can I get off this roller coaster?' Like the Spanish nun, Teresa of Ávila, who lived 500 years ago, we may find ourselves saying to God, 'If this is how you treat your friends, no wonder you have so few'![18]

You may be finding your daily fare tedious – even wondering what the point of it all can possibly be – whether you are tussling with recalcitrant teenagers, exhausting toddlers or more days in the month than salary left in the bank, it's natural to feel that the prospect of another week is just too demanding. Perhaps you are a carer for a special needs child or an Alzheimer's octogenarian; you will almost certainly have persistently asked God to change your situation, or at least revise the 'menu'. Some of you will be struggling with other challenges: mental illness or depression, an unfaithful spouse, redundancy, loneliness, abusive partners, noisy neighbours, anxiety or bereavement.

---

[18] www.catholicstand.com/lord-if-this-how-you-treat-your-friends (accessed 20th March 2020).

Others wrestle with the consequences of unresolved trauma, addiction, family tensions, chronic pain, unexpected pregnancy, tormenting dreams and weariness. How many of these, I wonder, have ever appeared on your 'menu'? There is no exhaustive 'menu' of the kind of unwelcome 'dishes' some of us have been served up over many years. Most of us will recognise among them one or two which currently confront us, and quite a number will identify several of them being 'served' simultaneously, and maybe more besides.

Considering the 'menu' of others can certainly give us a healthier perspective on our own. Most of us who are breathing oxygen will, at some point, come to the end of ourselves and our own resources. The will to keep going in the face of trials almost inevitably reaches a breaking point. What do we do then? Panic? Retreat? Collapse? Left to our own devices, all kinds of fears and dark possibilities can pile in to offer apparent solutions, helpful or otherwise. There's no doubt that we often look for a quick fix long before we look for God's face or press in to hear His voice, in trying times.

Sometimes God takes us right to the edge of an apparent precipice in order to wake us up to His presence, to remind us that He is alongside us through the darkest of circumstances: 'Even though I walk through the darkest valley'[19] (Psalm 23:4). That sounds like a bleak place to be. It may look cruel, but be assured, we are *never* abandoned; His loving kindness and grace will pursue us, overtake us and embrace us again. Even if we tumble right over that precipice, He is just a whisper away.

Imperfect menus

If we were allowed to arrange a self-devised 'menu' for each day, I imagine it would reveal figurative 'food cravings' which feature more comforting and carefree items such as sunshine, laughter, debt-free days, invigorating jobs, healthy bodies, trouble-free

---

[19] Or 'the valley of the shadow of death', NIV 1984.

sleep, joy-filled family times and worry-free living. But Jesus categorically tells us, 'In this world you will have trouble' (John 16:33). Honestly, this doesn't sound like good news to me. But, apparently, part of the human condition is to find ourselves facing 'dishes' we don't enjoy so much, 'meals' which taste bitter. Why is this?

One of the consequences of living in a fallen world[20] is that life is not the perpetual paradise it was planned to be. That doesn't mean an eternal holiday; even the original global blueprint featured meaningful work in the form of ruling over creation in all its forms.[21] Our newspapers, Twitter-feed and regular internet updates keep us bombarded with the latest global unfoldings of tragedy, natural disasters and political mayhem, ensuring we are informed 24/7. Frequently, however, it's the stuff that happens on our own side of the front door, intruding into the immediacy of our everyday lives, which can make even the strongest faith-filled child of God quail and question what is on our plate.

Perhaps our expectations are at fault, or at least misplaced. The life we see portrayed in glossy magazines, TV series and advertisements spins the lie that there is a perfect existence out there, with our name on it, as long as we drink the right coffee, drive the right car, choose the correct insurance company or wear the latest carefully formulated perfume or aftershave. While part of our brain recognises that this is nothing more significant than image – a carefully crafted illusion to persuade us to purchase the featured merchandise – another part of us really does long for a life of contentment and peace. And that's where it can get so confusing, because that is actually the life God wants and intends for us. It's just that it is unlikely to look like the sanitised, materialistic, shiny fiction so continually thrust in our faces.

---

[20] See Genesis 3.
[21] See Genesis 1:26.

Jesus wasn't kidding. Imperfection, conflict, illness, stress and the results of our own poor choices and genuine mistakes, are all very much a part of our days, as are the consequences of whichever national culture and history pertains to you – the results of successive governmental choices over all the years until today. This is not to send us spinning into despair, though; it's not the whole picture. Crucially, Jesus also said, 'But take heart! I have overcome the world' (John 16:33).

Lessons from a stormy lake

To illustrate this, three of the four Gospels tell the story of the storm on the lake. After a day filled with teaching, storytelling and the demands of noisy crowds, Jesus got into a boat with His disciples on Lake Galilee with the intention of going to the other side.[22]

As they sailed, a violent storm blew in. Jesus soon fell asleep, but His friends – even the seasoned sailors – panicked. The wooden boat lurched alarmingly, the wind howled and waves crashed over the side. The men assumed their time had come and, fuelled by the fear that doubtless had grown in the way it so often does during the darkness of night, they woke Jesus. Here were a bunch of people thoroughly desperate for a change in circumstances. This 'menu' scared them to death; there was no peace here, no idea of 'feasting' whatsoever. Yelling into their Master's face, they accused Him of not caring for them. How could He be sleeping in such a time of crisis? Matthew remembers them shouting, 'Lord, save us! We're going to drown!' (Matthew 8:25).

Their combined perception was that this imminent, watery death would be the inevitable outcome of the events unfolding so dramatically around them. Their distress was exacerbated by the perception that their Rabbi and Master was unconcerned about both them and the drastic turn of events. What they failed

---

[22] See Matthew 8:18,23-27; Mark 4:35-41; Luke 8:22-25.

to take into account was that every circumstance, every natural force, every fear and anxiety was, and is, subject to Him. The Creator of seas and oceans simply reprimanded the waters back into order, and effectively told them to calm down. Immediately the wind dropped, the waves lessened, the boat regained its equilibrium and the disciples struggled to recapture their own.

If the fishing vessel tossed around in the tempest were a picture of our lives when trouble hits, I wonder with whom we would identify. All too often I behave like the disciples, deluged with anxious thoughts; my imagination goes into overdrive and, with the immediate circumstances eclipsing all else, I am sorry to say that I have found myself all too often crying out in a similarly urgent way, 'Where are you, God? Can't you see I'm drowning? Get me out of here!'

Because God is loving and kind and merciful, there are times when He does just that. Clearly, He did that night on the lake. Miraculously, He still steps into time and space and alters the things around me. He can restore order, effect change and generate manageable moments that don't seem quite so impossible, in which I find I can walk with a degree of competency and calm. But there are other times when rather than change the circumstances, I perceive that He wants to change me *in* the circumstances. In these instances, my prayers for a swift resolution are answered with a gentle 'No' or 'Not yet'. It's not that my prayers are unanswered or unheeded, it's just that God has an alternative outcome in mind. At these times, experience has taught me that my prayers need to take a different direction.

The challenge is to find the same peace Jesus had which allowed Him to sleep rather than fall prey to panic and fear. Rather than a simple SOS plea for a quick exit out of my trouble, in whatever form that takes, I need to find true connection with God as the place of peace within the raging storm. This is altogether more challenging.

My contentment and joy cannot be founded purely in my circumstances. These change arbitrarily, so if they are my plumb line, my trajectory will flail badly; I will find myself lurching across the scale of emotions, desperately trying to find a firm place to stand, and something substantial to which I can cling. There absolutely must be a firmer foundation, a stronger anchor, a steadier, more level place to plant my feet. If I can only find that place of tranquillity in God during times of ease, then one might justifiably question the depth and strength of my relationship with Him. Is my peace only dependent on the good things that happen to me, or does it rest solidly on the One with whom I walk through all things?

Nehemiah used these words to encourage the exiles who returned to Jerusalem for a fresh start, 'the joy of the LORD is your strength' (Nehemiah 8:10). It's a verse I learned as a child and it made me wonder, is the prophet talking about my joy in God, or His joy in me? Sometimes it's both, but the latter is sure to be a more consistent joy; it takes the pressure off my own fluctuating emotions if I focus first on His loving nature. He is the only consistent source of our strength in good times and bad.

Challenging biblical menus

The writer of Ecclesiastes tells us that 'there is nothing new under the sun' (Ecclesiastes 1:9). On one hand that sounds rather dismal, but on the other, it tells me that generations have navigated their own storms, their own unpalatable 'menus', and found a way either through, or in, their very real challenges. Some express it better than others. Let's unpack one of David's evocative compositions with which we can probably all identify:

> Listen to my prayer, O God, do not ignore my plea; hear me and answer me.
> My thoughts trouble me and I am distraught ...
> My heart is in anguish within me; the terrors of death have fallen on me.

Fear and trembling have beset me; horror has
overwhelmed me.
I said, 'Oh, that I had the wings of a dove! I would fly
away and be at rest.
I would flee far away and stay in the desert; I would hurry
to my place of shelter,
far from the tempest and storm.'
(Psalm 55:1-2,4-8)

David isn't just saying a trite prayer or singing a jolly song here.
He is in mental, physical and emotional pain to the degree that
he is no longer functioning in an effective way. Most of us will
have been there. Apparently, David has no inclination to brave
it out or to confront the many things that have his head tied up
with stress and anxiety. He just wants to escape his
multitudinous problems. He wants to run far and he wants to
run now. He yearns for a sanctuary; a refuge where the weight
of his trials will ease, where peace and calm can soothe his soul.
Don't you empathise?

Suffering always tries to separate us from God. To say that
we mustn't let it sounds simplistic, but it's absolutely true. To
make such a stand requires both grit and determination. David
knew that, and in this psalm he chooses to push the negatives
aside as he responds. Summoning his ebbing courage, he makes
the choice to find his 'place of shelter' in God Himself. See what
he does next:

… I call to God,
and the LORD saves me.
Evening, morning and noon I cry out in distress, and he
hears my voice.
He rescues me unharmed from the battle waged against
me, even though many oppose me.
(Psalm 55:16-18)

David makes a passionate and earnest entreaty that God would
step in and remove him from the pain and trauma of his own

particular raging storm, circumstances which have left him in turmoil. He engages in consistent, persistent prayer, trusting that God will hear him and save him, whether in or from his troubles. That's a good learning point for us too. Prayer needs to be a first resort far more frequently than a last resort; our trust in God grows with our walk with Him. David declares that he will not be harmed even in adverse circumstances because he knows that God is on his side, has plans for him and will be with him through all his days. He knows he will see 'the goodness of the LORD in the land of the living' (Psalm 27:13). Experience breeds confidence and gives us solid reasons to trust; David has found God faithful before and chooses to believe that He will be so again. That reality can be ours too.

So, what is his conclusion?

> Cast your cares on the LORD and he will sustain you;
> he will never let the righteous be shaken.
> (Psalm 55:22)

The Message version of the same verse reads, 'Pile your troubles on GOD's shoulders – he'll carry your load, he'll help you out.' Ancient wisdom; tried and tested advice, as relevant today as it's ever been.

God does not bring disaster and tragedy in our lives, but He does promise to walk through those things with us. This is not just a nice thought, a theological sound bite or a pithy saying for a fridge magnet.

The French poet and dramatist Paul Claudel said, 'Jesus did not come to explain suffering but to fill it with His presence.'[23] That's a profound statement. It flies in the face of our perpetual desire for rationales and commentary to make sense of our lives and keep suffering in any form at arm's length. Without the reassuring knowledge of navigating our shadowy valleys with

---

[23] Paul Claudel, *Le Heurtoir* (publisher unknown), p33, cited in Pablo Martinez, *A Thorn in the Flesh* (Nottingham: IVP: reprint edition 2007), p19.

God as our companion, we are left with a burdensome future, an emasculated faith, devoid of joy and marked only by leaden responsibilities, dry duty and drudgery. I am so thankful that this is not the case!

As a potter shapes clay, a weaver creates a tapestry or an artist paints a picture, God is producing His own masterpiece. It's you; and it's me. 'Feasting' with Him through our trials and challenges can become part of our story – an encouragement to others, a living signpost and an authentic testimony of His grace and faithfulness. Whether that story is long or short, straightforward or complex, He is completing the work He has started in us: to mould us in such a way that we become more like Jesus. We are all therefore, a work in progress, and we all have an unfolding story that needs to be told.

Palate-cleanser questions

- 'Jesus categorically tells us, "In this world you will have trouble" (John 16:33).' Why do you think He said this?

- 'But there are … times when rather than change the circumstances, I perceive that He wants to change me *in* the circumstances.' What do you find to be the most comforting and discomforting things about this statement?

- What have you discovered about trusting God in difficult circumstances?

6. When the Cupboard is Bare

*... you would be fed with the finest of wheat; with honey from the
rock I would satisfy you.*
(Psalm 81:16)

David was not the only one to wonder whether the 'menu' he
was served was really formulated and sourced in God. There's
a whole ream of Bible characters who faced pretty appalling
circumstances which they did not necessarily choose for
themselves. A glance through the history of the Church shows
the same pattern and a quick check of your friends will reveal
that none of them is living in a circumstantial utopia.

In this chapter I'll outline the 'menu' served up to six Old
Testament protagonists and six of my personal friends. Each of
them was faced with the stark choice of somehow engaging with
what was on their 'plate' and 'feasting', or pushing it away in
anger, disappointment and despair. In Chapters 9 and 10 you'll
find out how they each responded. Regardless of the dates of
these events you may find that some experiences mirror or have
similarities to your own. That connection is a timely reminder
that none of us is alone in facing our particular 'serving'.

Old Testament menus 1

1. Abraham (Genesis 12-13, 15-18, 21) had a promise from God about having children but knew years of childlessness, a source of intense pain to both himself and his wife, Sarah. When they got tired of this particular 'dish', they took matters into their own hands using Sarah's maidservant Hagar as a surrogate. The family dynamic unravelled fast and led to the little boy, Ishmael, and his mother being sent away. Ishmael became the father of the Arab nations, and history continues to play out the disastrous consequences of this unhappy liaison. If only they had waited...

2. Joseph (Genesis 37, 39-41) was served a 'dish' of fraternal jealousies that led to a narrow escape from death and being carted off to distant Egypt, where his reversal of fortune thrust him into a new culture, a new language, and the life of a slave. A brief promotion in Potiphar's house was followed by an extended spell in prison on an unsubstantiated rape charge.

3. Gideon (Judges 6-7) took some persuading to dig into the 'meal' he was served. Despite being the youngest in his family, from the smallest tribe, and with a reduced force of a mere 300 men against a combined enemy he couldn't even count and feeling totally inadequate, he was directed to lead his tiny army against the perpetually marauding Midianites.

4. Naomi (Ruth 1) faced a 'menu' of such devastating loss that she wanted to change her name to 'Mara' or 'bitter'. Losing her husband and both her sons left her heartbroken, bereft, and far from home feeling abandoned by God. Without any financial support and with days of loneliness and despair stretching ahead, she grieved for what might have been, and lost sight of her purpose. How was she going to 'feast' on such a paltry serving which primarily featured salty tears?

5. Hannah (1 Samuel 1) carried the cultural stigma of barrenness in a fecund household in which her husband's second wife consistently taunted and provoked her to the point of weeping, over her inability to bear a child. Her daily 'diet' as a figure of fun and disdain must have been extremely hard to 'swallow' given that her failure to conceive was continually thrust in her face with every laugh, shout or cry of Penninah's multiple children.

6. The most detailed example of a 'menu' which I know for sure that I wouldn't want, is the one that was served up to **Job**. In the course of a single day he lost 11,500 healthy livestock: all his oxen, donkeys, sheep, and camels. Not only that, but most of his servants were slaughtered and his ten children all killed in a freak accident. Losing possessions is one thing; losing your children is quite another. It was a blow of shattering proportions.

A short while later, he also lost his health to a strange wasting disease which saw him covered from head to foot in boil-like sores and resorting to scraping himself with broken pottery shards (Job 2:7-8). He then had to endure a most unsympathetic tongue-lashing from his wife, who treated him with complete contempt. This was followed by the feeble advice of his so-called friends, who no longer even recognised him. They were so overwhelmed themselves by the scale of his losses that, after weeping in sympathy, they identified with his sorrow in the culturally appropriate way of tearing their clothes and sprinkling dust or ashes on their heads. They then sat with him for seven days in total silence – perhaps a welcome relief for poor Job.

There are some 'meals' that feel rather too much for me – and those you've just read are only a few examples; you might like to explore the 'menus' faced by Jacob, Joshua, Jeremiah, Daniel and Hosea.

Modern menus 1

Restaurants which serve an *à la carte* menu allow you the liberty of choosing from a selection of meals. There are some occasions, however – family meal times, for example – when you get what you are given. 'Like it or lump it' were the only terse alternatives while I was growing up. The meal had already been chosen for me regardless of what my palate may have craved in the moment. Trust me, that will never be liver in my lifetime!

Let me introduce you to some of my friends who have also been served 'dishes' they would not voluntarily have picked, and were all faced with unexpected 'menus'. They tell their own stories in their own words except for Uncle Robin's which I have retold with his permission.

1. Paul and Julia's story: a baby bereavement

My husband and I were at the twenty-week scan of our second child when I realised that the ultrasonographer was taking just a few seconds longer than usual and his face was serious. Calling on a colleague to confirm his diagnosis, my fears were given words: 'Your baby is anencephalic.' As a midwife I knew what this meant; a serious neural tube defect affecting the development of the brain and skull; incompatible with life.

The next few days passed in a blur of tears and phone calls. We were asked to come to the hospital to terminate the pregnancy, but we did not feel comfortable with this. I knew of others who had terminated for this condition but we felt we should wait for God's timing and for what He might do in that time.

Many people prayed with us for our baby to be healed, but she was not. I had been confident that I would be able to have a second child when I wanted; but suddenly my confidence and life plan were in pieces. My first child was healthy; it had never crossed my mind that there would be anything wrong with a second. My sense of entitlement was challenged.

I gave birth at our local hospital as arranged, and came face to face with my lovely daughter who I had carried through the long nine months. She was beautiful, but she could not survive. The back part of her skull had failed to form and God had not healed her. We held her, cried for her and thanked God for her. We called her 'Anastasia' which means 'Resurrection'.

2. Dave and Gill's story: a baby with cerebral palsy

Ruben was our first child, literally a 'miracle baby', but that tricky pregnancy had faded from our thoughts when, four years later, Samuel came along. We were excited. Again, it wasn't an easy pregnancy. Complications from twenty-four weeks required frequent stays in hospital for Gill and permanent admission from week thirty. Samuel was born four weeks later and went to the Neonatal Intensive Care Unit. When we eventually got home everything finally seemed perfect; we felt blessed and happy.

But, just a few days later Samuel stopped feeding. He had no fever, no rash, and wasn't crying; he was just sleepy and not waking for feeds. I wasn't too worried, but the next day we found ourselves in A&E with a nagging feeling that something was terribly wrong. The doctor finally came and I could see the faces of the medical staff change; they did a lumbar puncture and drew fluids from Samuel's spine to see if an infection had developed. The word 'meningitis' hung in the air between them...

Samuel started having small seizures, then his little body started to blow up with all the fluids and antibiotics the medical team were pumping through his premature body. An MRI confirmed that there was significant damage in his brain, but I just blurred it out of my mind. I wasn't going to hear it or believe it. He needed an emergency shunt inserted in his head to drain the continual build-up of fluid. We spent long days in hospital and short days at home.

It wasn't until three months after he was born that we finally made it home. Samuel still gets febrile seizures when he is poorly, which is scary and challenging. After two years we received confirmation of the official diagnosis: full body cerebral palsy. He can't sit or stand unaided and will probably never be able to talk or walk.

3. Uncle Robin's Story: a murdered son[24]

On the afternoon of Sunday 12th January 2003, Uncle Robin (former Chief Constable of the Isle of Man) had a regular catch-up phone call with his son, my cousin Steve, who worked in Special Branch Manchester Police and consequently often faced tricky situations. Police work provides those quite frequently, but apart from some royal protection duties, Steve had also recently concluded a case of international drug dealing, having been alerted by a forged passport.

Two days later, he was part of a team for 'Operation Salt': Special Branch officers who visited a residence in Crumpsall Lane, as requested by MI5. They were in plain clothes, without special body armour and took no specialist arrest kits; it also later turned out that their police phones didn't work – the correct frequency had not been agreed. The objective was to detain an individual recognised by the Home Office as an international terrorist. Unbeknown to the officers, the two men they expected to find had been joined by a third. His name was Kamel Bourgass, aka Nadir Habra, a trained assassin and follower of Osama bin Laden, who was on the run from London.

The detainment should have been routine, but it took a different turn when the police recognised Bourgass as one of the men involved in a recent ricin (a potent toxin) raid in London. The danger of the situation had just escalated massively. Another officer was sent in and Bourgass was formally arrested but not handcuffed. Conventional non-sterile

---

[24] I have told this story from Uncle Robin's account, augmented by other sources. He tells the whole story in: Robin Oake, *Father Forgive: The Forgotten 'F' Word* (Milton Keynes: Authentic, 2008).

handcuffs can tamper with forensic evidence (traces of explosives, etc), and the necessary plastic bags and ties hadn't been brought. Despite being told to remain silent, the prisoner persisted in speaking loudly to the man in the next room, and finally launched himself at the new officer, laying a punch to the groin which felled him. Steve threw himself at Bourgass, wrapping his arms round him to restrain him. Other officers rushed to help, at which point the light went out. Bourgass broke free, dragging Steve behind him towards the kitchen where he grabbed a five-inch kitchen knife off the draining board and lashed out at the officers in front of him and Steve behind him. In an effort to protect his unarmed colleagues, Steve held on. His colleagues finally overpowered Bourgass, but it was too late for Steve. One sergeant tried to resuscitate him to no avail; Steve had received eight stab wounds, three of which would have undoubtedly been fatal on their own.

It was evening when Uncle Robin's phone rang. Lesley, Steve's wife, relayed the news she had been given, that Steve had been involved in an accident and she was just going to the hospital. They both wondered whether Steve had fallen asleep at the wheel of his car, overcome with exhaustion from his long hours and habitual early start with time spent reading his Bible and praying. The reality was very different and Uncle Robin was home alone when the next inevitable phone calls came from Lesley, and a colleague in the Greater Manchester Police. The shock was enormous and Uncle Robin realised he would have to prepare for a mandatory press conference the next day. Through the shock, pain and sleeplessness, he found that all he could do was pray.

4. Charlotte's story: a child fallen into depression
I was a school nurse for a number of years and during that time became aware of the increasing number of children, and particularly teenagers, who struggle with complex mental health issues. As a mother-of-three myself, I felt huge compassion for

them and their parents, but had no inkling that it would ever come calling at my door.

I remember the feelings of total helplessness when I was called into school because my own precious daughter had caused physical damage to herself through extreme self-harm. I felt that, somehow, I'd failed as a parent. How could I, as a trained nurse, have missed this? We had known that she was struggling with some issues, but we had put it down to hormonal teenage mood swings. I hadn't experienced any mental health issues myself and now I struggled to really understand how she was feeling. To my shame, I often resorted to angry outbursts and very unhelpful comments and suggestions.

Our heartache and sadness at the spiralling destructive behaviour and poor life choices she was making was very, very painful. I can't remember how many doctor's appointments and counselling sessions we attended with very little change to show for it.

I had prided myself on having a good relationship with all our children and on being a family who could talk openly and share our problems, yet during this time I felt totally unable to reach her. She was completely trapped in a sunless prison of despair and isolation, and I was powerless to help her. My frustration was overwhelming as I grappled with my desire to 'fix' her. In a well-intentioned effort to protect her from others, we told very few people about our situation and so found ourselves carrying a huge, lonely burden. The pressure was immense for the whole family; it was like walking through a minefield, testing our emotions to their limits.

5. Sally's story: an unfaithful husband

I was a youth worker in a church when I met Mike there, who was also a youth leader and on the leadership team. I had never known a man who carried such peace before, and found myself falling in love with him. We spent a lot of time together and became close very quickly. Although we were both very young and, in retrospect, somewhat broken, he also fell in love with me and we soon got married. Two years later we started our family and before long we had three amazing children; life was full and busy.

As the years went by, something changed. I felt that Mike's heart was not as soft as it had been in the beginning towards God or towards me and the children; it was strange. We had been married for ten years at this time and our youngest was three years old. Then I found out that Mike had been having an affair which had gone on for a couple of years. To be honest, I had suspected something like this might have been happening and I realised I had been living in fear of it. But the reality was a real shock; I had always trusted that surely he wouldn't go there.

The pain was massive, but not just for me. Mike left us: me, the children, our family home. I was sure this wasn't how God meant things to be for us; Mike had a call on his life, surely? As I reviewed the previous years together, I realised that our love was tainted through anger and unforgiveness, but I never foresaw this outcome. For two years I lived in the hope that he would come home. These were such difficult days; I had to manage my hurt and find emotional reserves to meet the children in their feelings of confusion and rejection.

Mike told me that he wasn't seeing anyone else, but wouldn't come home either. It looked like I would have to start thinking about divorce even though it wasn't what I wanted. A while later I found that he was still with the woman he'd had the affair with; he had lied to me and this second blow was massive too.

6. Julie's story: a husband's health crisis

James and I have always worked closely together throughout our adult lives. Some years ago, we felt God calling us to leave England and move to the French Alps, where we planned to use our gathering and evangelistic gifts to plant authentic communities of believers among the villages on the French/Italian border. We started a skiing business to integrate with the local community, learned the language, and became familiar with local habits and culture, all of which was demanding, but fun. We had our share of successes and heartbreaks, but the company grew so successfully that we soon realised we needed to recruit some more help. Our daughter, Asha, and her husband, committed to help us through the coming winter season. We helped them decorate and move into a rental property in the village and on the completion day, James and Davey went wood-cutting together to provide fuel for the new burner that had been installed.

That afternoon we went on to a village party to celebrate a friend's fortieth birthday. Before long James said he did not feel very well; perhaps he had overdone it chopping wood in the sun earlier. I didn't think much of it, and we sat down to enjoy the party. But when James stood up he suddenly felt very ill. He started to vomit; his legs would not move and he lost his balance – it was frightening. I had worked with stroke victims in the past, and recognised the classic symptoms.

Our predicament was immediate. We were in a remote village up in the mountains and the local doctor and *'pompiers'* – who double up as volunteer paramedics – were all at the party, drinking and making merry. To get anyone to take James' condition seriously was very difficult. They said he had had too much sun and drink, and then made him lie down on a bed to sleep it off. I tried to phone Asha and Davey and some other friends to please come and help, then I tried to explain to the doctor again that something was really wrong. It was so frustrating that I didn't know the French word for 'stroke'.

At last the doctor realised things were more serious than she had first thought. By this time, I had got hold of Asha and another Christian friend had arrived. The air ambulance had been phoned, and after an hour of horrible anxiety there was the sense that something was finally happening. Meanwhile, James seemed to be deteriorating and all we could do was give him a kiss as he was lifted into the helicopter and disappeared over the horizon.

A twenty-five-minute airlift took 160 minutes for us in a vehicle. All the time we were not sure whether James would be alive or not when we arrived. We simply hung on to hope and prayed that he would be alright. The diagnosis of a serious stroke was devastating. The next few days would be touch and go. My imagination ran away with me at times. How would I ever pay all the bills – hotels, travel, rehabilitation as well as run the business? How would I cope if James didn't get better? What if he died? We just prayed and prayed.

These stories are all true and their consequences are still playing out. We will find out what happened next with the biblical characters in Chapter 9 and how my friends chose to respond to their unpalatable 'menus' in Chapter 10.

I have other friends who could have also told their stories of being presented with 'menus' of childlessness, abuse, poverty and long-term unemployment. None of those 'dishes' is easy to face. When the walls press in on us, the unexpected ambushes us, the lights seem to be extinguished, and the 'menu' takes a turn for the worse, remembering that God – our divine chef, if you will – is aware of all the ingredients on our 'plate', is a great comfort. Being conscious that we are part of a narrative much bigger than ourselves can give us some helpful perspective as we gather our strength, our wits and our faith, and face the important choice of 'feasting' or pushing the dish away.

What's on your menu?

I wonder what you find on your 'menu' today. Are the courses of your own choosing, or has your heavenly Father entrusted you with less appealing 'dishes'? Perhaps you have had more than enough of 'dishes' that are hard to swallow and crave some basic staples or exotic treats. Perhaps you are facing things of such magnitude that you barely have the vocabulary to convey them.

Perhaps you share elements of your 'menu' with my friends, in which case, I pray that you will find 'the peace of God, which transcends all understanding, [and which] will guard your hearts and minds in Christ Jesus' (Philippians 4:7), even as you prepare to pick up your spiritual knife and fork. Whatever else is going on, I can assure you that God sees, He hears, He knows and He cares.

May you find refuge and a song today 'in the shadow of [His] wings' (Psalm 63:7). May you take strength and courage from remembering that this is not the end of any of those stories and neither is it the end of yours.

Palate-cleanser questions

- With which of the biblical characters and their stories do you most identify, and why?

- Which of my six friends has a story which resonates with you? What factors struck you most forcibly as you read them?

- What is the most challenging 'dish' on your 'menu' today?

7. Feast or Famine: Part 1

Go, eat your food with gladness, and drink your wine with a joyful heart, for it is now that God favours what you do.
(Ecclesiastes 9:7, NIV 1984)

Pull up a chair and tuck in...

Other people's 'menus' can be luridly fascinating. Hearing their painful stories and discovering their calamities can help put our own lives into perspective; but they can also have the same macabre effect on us as on the motorists who slow down to view the results of a car crash. We're intrigued by the troubles of others – how would soap operas ever sustain their ratings if we weren't? We are curious about how the protagonists react; how they process tragedy; who they blame and whether their unresolved anger will fester until recrimination, regret, self-pity, or simmering bitterness boil over into all-out revenge. There's something in such plot twists that satisfies our sometimes voyeuristic curiosity.

I wonder if we are equally aware or engaged with our own stories, our own 'menu'? Whatever life has served us, God unequivocally invites us to come and 'feast'. We are not asked to view our 'meal' from a distance or give our opinion on its merit or otherwise. Instead we are required to metaphorically sit at our assigned and prepared place, tuck in our chair, arrange our napkin, pick up our knife and fork and get seriously involved with everything which is put before us.

My husband tells the story of how his dad used to call him and his two brothers in from the garden where they were, doubtless, whiling away the school holidays playing yet another game of football. 'Would you like to come in for dinner now?' he would call. Not a difficult question. But – and this he remembers all too well – although it sounded as though his dad were giving an invitation, in reality there was not space to say 'No'. The request was, in fact, a summons; a command; an imperative. He chose to speak politely, but what he was really saying was, 'Boys, come in and eat now!'

This is the true nature of the invitation God gives us: '... he commands all people everywhere to repent' (Acts 17:30). That's not a suggestion. Declining God's invitations is a choice that will lead to a whole new set of dilemmas.

I was talking to one of my daughters about the subject matter of feasting while I was putting this material together. A little message came through from her, 6,000 miles away. 'It's not an option to just not eat, is it?' she queried hopefully. Nope; not really, honey. Telling God we're really not that hungry; not quite in the mood for what we've been served in the past, or are being served right now, is neither a helpful nor satisfying way to receive anything from Him, or to enjoy His company while we're getting to grips with the portion before us. In fact, there's a whole world of actions which might qualify as 'eating' but probably don't meet 'feasting' status.

What feasting isn't

For ease of emphasis and to identify some things which feasting most certainly isn't, I'm going to summarise with bullet points.

- *Fasting* is not feasting. In fact, it's the opposite. A feast suggests generous portions and the opportunity to eat one's fill and more. Fasting is about restraint, denial and personal sacrifice for a season, usually – biblically, that is – for the purpose of focusing on God, denying the sense of appetite for the sake of sharper spiritual hearing.

- Feasting is not a *packed lunch*, thrown together with last night's leftovers, or with dubious-looking out-of-date items lurking at the back of the fridge. Much more thought has been given to this 'meal'. It is not supposed to be eaten on the run, alone, at your desk, or while your attention is focused elsewhere.

- Unfortunately, what lies before us is not a *picnic* either – a casual meal eaten over the course of a lazy afternoon where the emphasis is on restful dining beneath shady trees and a friendly summer sun. This meal will be eaten, 'in the presence of [our] enemies' (Psalm 23:5); it's an act of war (more on this in Chapter 13).

- *Being picky* is not feasting. I used to loathe the kind of birthday parties where overexcited, energy-hyped children would lunge for every treat in sight, and then proceed to pick at them, leaving a trail of waste and debris. Some wouldn't eat the crusts off the sandwiches; some ate only the icing part of the cake; some only ate the middle of the sausage rolls… Perhaps God feels the same about those who try to dine like this on His 'dishes'.

- *Replacement options are not available.* In other words, the menu is the menu. No swapping one item for another. There will not be an option for any special dietary requirements. You and I do *not* know better than this particular Master Chef which, to be honest, is annoying at times. Many a time I have wanted to substitute a period of lack for one of plenty, or a difficult training time when circumstances felt like

115

another hefty helping of liver, for a season of comfort – another reason that feasting can so often be a challenge.

- *Armchair experts* on how you should 'eat' are not given airtime. Each of us has our own dining assignment with Jesus, just as we each run our life race in the figurative, specific track lane which we have been allocated. Not only do we tend towards voyeuristic interest in the circumstances of others, but it is amazing how, from a more comfortable vantage point, a handful of people can choose to dispense their personal wisdom regarding the decisions they think we should make, the root causes of our pain, etc. Wisdom and empathy expressed through trusted relationships, couched in kindness, experience and encouragement, may be welcome balm to our wounds; but they need to be delivered in an environment of trust, and with sensitive timing.

- Feasting is not a *spectator sport*. We have not been invited to this table to watch others eating. One of my grandfather's favourite mealtime maxims was, 'Eyes on your own plate.' Flitting our gaze to what others have been served, comparing and assessing how fair the portion sizes seem or the more or less appetising nature of what is being presented, will ensure that we miss out on the deliberate care that has been given to our own carefully devised 'dish'. Why has someone else been given such an apparently easy ride when we are plagued by perpetual disappointment and are let down by people who, we think, should know better? I don't know. Why does the fun-to-be-with individual get 'served' aggressive cancer while the miserable, sour-faced gossip gets a free holiday? Again, I don't know. Differentiating trials will tempt us into a disgruntled discontent which is incompatible with genuine 'feasting'. Take the advice of Paul, who says, 'We do not dare to classify or compare ourselves with some ... When they measure themselves by themselves and compare themselves with themselves, they are not wise' (2 Corinthians 10:12). Far better to take some of his other words to heart and keep our eyes fixed on Jesus so we can truly 'rejoice with those who rejoice; mourn with those who mourn' (Romans 12:15). The world needs more authentic Christians of this calibre.

- Feasting is not a *competitive activity* either. Whatever faces you today, somebody, somewhere will let you know that they, or someone close to them, has had it much worse. Instead of coming alongside and empathising with you in your trial, they stand at a distance and send detached sympathy without identifying with you at all. It's heartless, disappointing and does nothing to build a relational bridge. Insisting on reviving their own pain at the expense of yours lets you know that they probably still need some healing of their own.

- *Fakers* will be found out. Celebrities and public figures who attend numerous functions, which often include rich and calorific food, develop the knack of looking like they are eating even though they probably aren't. Their lifestyle demands a strategy to avoid appearing rude, but if they really ate all the wonderful goodies prepared by expert chefs and served over multiple courses, they would all be as round as beach balls and facing serious health problems. Their forks need to look busy as they push the food around the plate, but often very little will actually go into their mouths. When God prepares a feast for us, however, He desires that we tuck in, not just 'play' with it on the plate.

- There are no relevant *allergies* here. God knows how we will react to our 'menu' and everything can be digested without damaging consequences when we 'eat' with Him. He knows us better than we know ourselves and has set boundaries on what can be served (see Job 1:12; 2:6). God oversees the portion size (time and length of the trial), calorie count (excess or lack) and the combination of food groups (perhaps we could interpret these as: loss, pain, joy, disappointments, satisfaction, frustrations, etc). While the enemy may intend them for harm, God intends to draw good out of them all as we access His grace and discover that even the worst 'dish' can drive us into His loving arms.

- *Hiding* the unpalatable bits will be found out. My granny used to hide the chewiest bits of her meat – of which presumably there were many back in the 1920s – on a little shelf she discovered, conveniently positioned underneath the family dining table. History fails to tell us if she was ever found out… Similarly, as a child, I listened open-mouthed to a missionary account of a trip during which the protagonist and his friend donned wellington boots to navigate the thick mud of a far-flung, rural village where they were preaching. Sharing food out of their poverty was a gesture of great honour from the villagers, but dishes of fish soup, complete with heads and eyes still in situ, caused the same kind of reaction as my childhood liver experience. There was no helpful dog to foist it on, no convenient house plant, and nowhere else to hide it so, inventively, but surreptitiously, bit by bit, the soup went into the wellies! They just couldn't face eating it and simply didn't have time on their trip to be ill. Walking home must have been a nightmare…

  God's invitation is to feast on the entire meal. We can't hide from Him and we can't pretend. If it feels as though there are bones in our serving, or unidentifiable components, it's not a mistake, even though it may not be pleasant.

- *Gorging* is not appropriate. This kind of eating implies appetites out of control, a self-indulgent stuffing of oneself. Proverbs says that, 'if you are given to gluttony', you should 'put a knife to your throat … Do not crave [those] delicacies, for that food is deceptive' (Proverbs

23:2-3). Self-control is listed among the fruit of the Spirit for a reason. One mouthful at a time is the sensible and steady eating etiquette and will get you through even the largest and most intimidating serving of any meal. Perhaps this tip would have helped me when faced with that childhood mountain of liver…

- *Portion control* is entirely at the discretion of the host. You and I may think we've had quite enough of this 'dish'; a favourite dessert or alternative course would be welcome very soon… He knows.

- Feasting is not the same as an *Instagram* post. It is not there to photograph like some still-life masterpiece: to appreciate the way the light falls on it, the creative plating, or sparkling crystal. The whole point of any feast is that it be eaten, not just observed. In fact, we may feel our 'menu' has been served on old chipped enamel or a cheap paper plate. We don't need to capture our serving as a memorial; it's part of our journey but it's not our destination. It may refine us, but it is *never* supposed to define us. God lovingly meets us at His table each day and transforms the 'meal' by His presence.

- Nominating a *stand-in* is not a possibility. The Bible talks about sharing our burdens but, in a military comparison, each of us carries our 'own load' (Galatians 6:2,5). In other words, we can't delegate our 'menu' to someone else when we don't like the look of it; there are no surrogate diners at this table, no body-doubles to take over when we'd rather be elsewhere.

- *Gritting your teeth* or holding your nose and swallowing – all great childhood fall-backs – will only make your face hurt. This is not feasting; neither is it honouring to your host.

- *Resigning yourself* to what lies in front of you is not feasting. That attitude of stoicism will rob you of the joy that is hidden (sometimes, admittedly, very well hidden) in the 'dish' before you. There will be no victory over your enemies with a self-induced martyr spirit.

- Similarly, *enduring* may get you through the meal but it will be a joyless affair; not really feasting. While there are elements of enduring which are admirable – pushing through, refusing to give up – it's all too easy to do this in your own strength. Very quickly it can be a mental battle of wills; a case of mind over matter. The task may get completed but at the expense of your peace of mind. It's just exhausting to live like this. God has other resources to help us through and discover true joy and lightness of spirit, even in the toughest places.

- *'Coming to terms'* with the menu is not feasting either. This comes close to that other great British trait: 'making the best of it'. Traditionally, good Brits roll up their sleeves and get on with it – whatever 'it' happens to be. There's an implication in the expression that we are probably rationalising what is before us; perhaps, through some warped theology, we may decide that this is exactly the unpalatable 'dish' that we somehow deserve. Even God's cherished children have sometimes been deceived into believing the lie that their circumstances are God's punishment for something they've said or done. This reflects and perpetuates a very wonky perception of God, grace and ourselves. True 'feasting' is not going through the motions only. This approach encourages that ugly martyr spirit, identified by the appearance of self-sacrifice but performed with an attitude of (usually) quiet resentment or seething, ill-disguised anger. It manages to keep ourselves at the centre of everything and relegates God to the sidelines; that's actually a subtle form of idolatry.

- In the same vein, don't waste your time by *scoring* the dishes. God's feast is not an episode of any popular TV cooking or baking show. We haven't been invited to assess the menu, but to tuck into it with thanksgiving even when we struggle to be grateful for the substance of the actual 'meal'. I know that this is more than we feel we can face some days, but nevertheless, the invitation remains.

By itemising all the things 'feasting' isn't, we have a much clearer idea of what it actually is: the diametric opposite! It's important that we consider this if we are taking God's invitation seriously. He is looking for people who are prepared to surrender to His will in all things, who allow their faith to be stretched, their ears to become more attuned to His voice, and whose yielded hearts are resolved to follow and enjoy His presence, power and provision through whatever life throws at them, to the end of their lives. I want to be one of them.

This is a good moment to reflect on your own current 'menu', regardless of how appetising it may or may not look. Can you see the hand of God in its preparation and presentation? Perhaps you can't. It's OK to be brutally honest; God won't be fazed and he's not in the same tearing hurry that we so often are. If you can't see Him, are you still prepared to trust that He will meet you in your place of need and carry you through it all? That is His burning desire.

Palate-cleanser questions

- What are the implications of considering Jesus' invitations as commands?

- Recall a circumstance during which you considered not 'feasting' with God. What happened?

- To which of the non-feasting approaches are you most prone?

8. Feast or Famine: Part 2

Taste and see that the LORD is good ...
(Psalm 34:8)

The royal champion

A number of years ago I was at a ladies' breakfast which I had organised. Since I didn't have the responsibility of speaking on this occasion, I found I was able to engage with the worship time more fully than usual. From my mind's eye a picture, or mini-movie, appeared, of such clarity that I was quickly aware that God was showing me something significant. I paid full attention although I didn't understand what I was seeing to begin with.

I was in a desolate, dry, desert-like landscape with nothing to be seen on the horizon ahead. Quite a distance behind me was the wooden palisade of a substantial fort from which flags were flying strongly in a stiff breeze. Suddenly a shout rang out followed by a blast on a trumpet. I turned to both see and hear the drawbridge lowered, with a crash. An accomplished rider emerged in full chainmail, including a helmet with the visor pulled down, a plume on the top, and seated on a huge white horse, which was also decked out in the vibrant colours of the king. They came towards me at full gallop which was extremely alarming, not least because I thought the mounted figure held a lance in combat position, which made me feel very vulnerable. As he came closer, I saw that this champion, who was without doubt the king's son, held not a weapon but a long pole, or stake, with a pennant, of the same colours as those on the fort, attached to one end. He pulled up beside me and, with great force, did what seemed impossible: he secured it by thrusting it deep into the rocky ground beside me, like a marker post, the flag flapping in the wind. Barely stopping for more than a moment, he spoke to me with a promise: 'I will come back to break up the hard ground.' With that, he galloped away leaving me awestruck and alone.

It was a powerful picture and I was sure that the rider was, or represented, Jesus. If so, this was an important impression; I was prompted to pray for wisdom and understanding as I wondered what it could mean. Gradually, and somewhat apprehensively, I realised that God was preparing me for some spiritual heart surgery. I had to face the uncomfortable truth that there were areas of my life which, for one reason or another, over the years, I had allowed to become as hard and impenetrable as the ground in my picture. Some of that was an attempt at self-protection; some was the inevitable result of various relational wounds which I hadn't allowed to heal properly. What God showed me was that He was well aware of the pain I was carrying, saw how I had so inadequately tried to cope with it and, from a place of Fatherly concern and wisdom, was committed to bringing His healing in due course. He had an incontestable claim on my heart. For some reason He let me know that although this was not going to happen immediately, He knew all the heartbreaking details, and was owning the spiritual ground of my heart by planting His colours securely into it, like a land claim.

Although in some ways this was an intimidating prospect, I actually found it a relief; after all, it's difficult to live fully when you're walking around with a debilitating injury, whether physical, emotional or spiritual. I found it reassuring that God knew and cared for me enough to send me a compassionate but firm promise of intent. It was a mercy-filled preparation of tenderising my heart in advance. That Jesus Himself would fight for this end to become a reality for me, took away any disinclination or reluctance on my part to meet Him in the healing process, whatever that might look like in the days ahead.

Any medical practitioner will tell you that sometimes, healthy tissue has to be cut out in order to get to an infected area; that's going to hurt. Metaphorically, it has felt rather like that at times; but I am so thankful that I was able to 'feast' with Jesus even in this painful season of healing and that He knew exactly when, what and how much of each portion I should be served at any one time. I am also very well aware that God has not finished with me yet. He will continue to challenge and shape me in the days ahead, relentlessly, passionately pursuing my heart and is committed to completing what He has started: making me more like Jesus.

The challenge of change

Ever-present distractions and a natural unwillingness to engage with the demanding process of personal change can keep us far away from the 'feasting' table. Acknowledging areas of life which need change requires courageous vulnerability – something many of us have actively suppressed, often for years. The knowledge that God knows us through and through, even better than we know ourselves and down to the tiniest detail, can unnerve us to the point that we may prefer to keep our eyes firmly on the ground and not face Him at all lest we be exposed to humiliation, hurt and shame.

But God doesn't deal in these currencies. His gaze is all about hope, love, compassion, forgiveness, grace, healing, delight and longing to draw us closer to Himself. If we choose to look away from Him we will never be able to 'feast' and never become all that we were created to be. Instead, we must remain on the outskirts of His table where meagre crumbs will be unable to truly satisfy our souls.

With this in mind, let's take a collective deep breath, and remind ourselves that despite and whatever you and I face today, God is once again giving us an opportunity for 'feasting' with Him rather than scraping, or starving, through self-enforced famine or by employing any of the itemised non-feasting approaches of the last chapter. God has allowed it, plated it and given divine permission for it to be served specifically to us in the time and places where we are right now. God loves us fiercely, and our 'meal' is no accident; it's neither a punishment nor a rebuke. There may have been some poor choices that have brought your journey to this point, but take heart. Today is a new day with abundant opportunities for making fresh choices. My story isn't finished, and neither is yours.

Jesus is, and always has been, inviting you to come and sit at your assigned place around the table with Him. That will be the life-changing key to the entire experience: the One with whom you 'feast'.

Part of the joy of eating together is the relational bonding that goes on around the table. One of the ingredients that has marked the 'Alpha' evangelistic course as so successful around the world is that it takes place over the informality of a community meal. The atmosphere is relaxed and people find it easy to talk openly there.

How do you react to the lone diner in a café or restaurant? I know my heart goes out to them and I tend to jump to wild conclusions about why they're alone, to the point that I often wonder whether I should ask them to join us, even though they are more than likely there by choice and enjoying their moment of peace.

At Jesus' table, no one eats alone because He is right there with us. He has something special, something perfect, for you. There's no getting round it, some of it may be hard to swallow. Eat it up regardless. We may well experience some spiritual indigestion as we tuck in, but that's OK; we can trust this chef. Forget Michelin stars; this Master made the originals! His 'feast' will nourish us beyond our imagining if we seek uninterrupted connection with Him through the whole thing, whether it feels like an ordeal or an oasis. It's choosing to 'feast' with Him, which makes all the difference.

My friends in Chapter 6 all faced that choice. Each was confronted by a moment of crisis when normal routine was interrupted and temporarily displaced by a particular event which has consequently, unalterably, permanently coloured their lives. We left their stories rather on cliff-hangers, but there will be more to tell when we discover what their choices were and what happened next.

There may be some readers who have had no such monumental crisis; I'm so glad. Truly, I hope you never do; but one day you might, and enjoying your place at God's table now will be the best preparation for navigating such a moment or season. Even during easy, comfortable, mundane days, just be aware of His company in every moment of your day; enjoy Him!

Let's not forget that 'feasting' can be equally challenging among those ordinary routines and the relative comfort of Western life. Restlessness, discontent, lack of purpose and boredom can all leave us craving for almost anything except what actually lies in front of us, just as much as crisis and trial. Yet, even the most boring, staple or stodgy 'menu' can become a 'feast' when our host is the King of kings.

Grief and trauma

Basic psychology tells us that when a catastrophe or crisis happens – regardless of its proportions – we will probably face a journey of five distinct stages. Perhaps you can identify with some of them, or can trace seasons in your own history via their marker posts. Traditionally, they are:

1. denial
2. anger
3. bargaining
4. depression
5. acceptance[25]

Some feel this is too simplistic and have expanded the process to include seven stages:

1. shock and denial
2. pain and guilt
3. arguing and bargaining
4. depression, reflection and loneliness
5. the upward turn
6. reconstruction and working through
7. acceptance and hope[26]

These are useful handles, or markers, which normalise some of the emotions that ebb and flow with varying degrees of violence as we react to adversity and calamities. They will be familiar to any of us who have been confronted by trauma or grief in some shape or form – I think that must include just about everyone who draws breath. However, we won't necessarily have navigated them in a linear, chronological or predictable way. Our pains, shames, failures and losses may be vastly different in type and scale, but unless we travel through a process of 'good' grief, sooner or later we may find ourselves psychologically and emotionally stuck.

While these insights are enormously helpful, there's no doubt that navigating them would be a smoother journey if the traveller were walking in the company of Jesus. He doesn't

---

[25] Elisabeth Kübler-Ross MD and David Kessler, *On Grief & Grieving* (London: Simon & Schuster, 2014). Also: grief.com/the-five-stages-of-grief/ (accessed 12th November 2019).
[26] www.recover-from-grief.com/7-stages-of-grief.html (accessed 12th November 2019).

guarantee either that quick fix we'd all prefer, or that the timespan of healing would be speeded up, stations omitted, or the passage of healing become an anaesthetised, pain-free experience. Within that journey, however, the added ingredient of the Doxology blessing will be present in glorious abundance: 'the grace of the Lord Jesus Christ, and the love of God, and the fellowship of the Holy Spirit be with you all' (2 Corinthians 13:14).

We know that God's love is constant and consistent, underpinning our every breath and heartbeat – a great foundation for every step of life. The Holy Spirit who was sent from heaven at Pentecost is indeed spirit, which means that He can be with everyone, everywhere, at every minute of the day or night. What a wonderful provision for us. He was described by Jesus more than once as the 'Comforter' (John 14:16; 16:7 – both KJV); the word evokes a serene parental picture of gently quieting a child through their hurt and vulnerability. Breaking the word down, you'll see the word *fort* which itself means, 'strengthen'; the Latin word is *con fortis* – 'with strength'.

But the Holy Spirit doesn't just say, 'There, there,' or the equivalent, He also invigorates us with divine power.

The Bayeux Tapestry contains a scene entitled: 'Bishop Odo comforts the troops', which depicts the armoured cleric (half-brother of William the Conqueror) waving a club at his Norman soldiers, urging them forward to battle and victory with enthusiastic prodding. It doesn't sound very comforting in the usual sense! While he isn't beating or abusing them, he *is* actively furnishing them with the strength and motivation they need to keep going.

The Holy Spirit enfolds us while encouraging us onwards through trials and challenges. We are not supposed to stop and make camp. All of us are on a journey; none of us has reached our destination this side of heaven. The compassion of the Godhead manifests itself in lavish consolation so that not only will we be empowered, but 'we can comfort those in any trouble with the comfort we ourselves have received from God. For just as the sufferings of Christ flow over into our lives, so also through Christ our comfort overflows' (2 Corinthians 1:4-5, NIV 1984).

Heaven is not stingy with its resources. There's always more than enough for us; in fact, there's such a plentiful supply of the Holy Spirit and His comfort that He is to overflow from us, to spill out from us, to those around us with the same gentle, healing balm.

And then, of course, we have access to the amazing, unmerited, unfailing, unlimited grace of Jesus. His delight in us and His favour on us doesn't evaporate at the first hint of trouble. Paul was unequivocal in his declaration that it was this grace which was enough to uphold him as he wrestled with whatever his debilitating 'thorn' was (2 Corinthians 12:6-10). It is not unreasonable to conclude that grace is therefore proportional; His grace will *always* be sufficient for the circumstance. Whether you feel you need that in small drops, to soothe a bumpy relationship with a cranky neighbour, a stubborn teenager or an obstructive traffic warden, or in bucket loads, to face another round of chemotherapy, a red bill or a life-altering injury – there is enough. More than enough. Not because church says so, a preacher preached it, or you read it in a book, but because the Author of the universe has decreed it.

Don't pull away or recoil in dismay; lean into Him; access the grace which He always planned for you to enjoy. You'll need courage to engage with Him in this, but you will find so much more that you ever dared to dream when you sit with Him; and there you will undoubtedly find peace in the storm.

The reality of trials

How we stand in the face of trials reveals what is happening beneath the surface. I'm sure you're familiar with the picture of the swan who glides serenely across a lake but underneath may be paddling frantically, belying the surface impression of tranquillity. Storms and hardships tend to draw out what's really in our hearts, how we perceive the world, ourselves and God. Emotions and actions bubble up from deep within us, unleashed by the pressure brought to bear on us; it's not always pretty. Some are overcome with crippling self-pity, rage and bitterness. It's tragic that this can be true for individuals who not so long before had thrown themselves on God's mercy and verbally surrendered to His will.

When things don't go our way, some of us are prone to stick out our bottom lip and sulk. Lest you think I am being judgemental here, I can tell you I'm very aware that I've done this myself at times. Taking note of this ugly reality, I want to exhort us all to authentically engage in some self-reflection and count the cost of saying a genuine 'Yes' to God.

When we surrender our all to Him, we can't know what lies ahead, but He still calls us to trust Him anyway. My observation may be painful, my confession awkward, but difficult days draw these truths into the light. Can any of us truly bear the pain, the weariness and the crushing suffocation of the many things life throws at us, without falling prey to bitterness, gloom and defeat? Some days are so full of bad news that it's difficult to even breathe. How many more stories of violence, corruption, abuse and disaster can anybody take?

But, can we – however feebly – choose to look beyond these circumstances to the hope of Jesus? Can we, by faith, focus on the victory He can bring rather than the darkness that threatens to defeat us, drawing on those proportional resources of heavenly grace, strength and courage, convinced that even the smallest flickering light can dispel complete blackness?

This is not some clever mental gymnastics. It's the arena in which our faith has space to develop, grow and mature. We need to place that faith, not in some natty mantras, slick sayings, the latest podcast or flavour-of-the-month preacher, but in the steadfast, unshakeable God whom we worship.

Faith is not a fickle emotion; it cannot be whipped up out of nowhere. A charismatic leader can hold a crowd in the palm of their hand, directing them towards the heights and depths of excitement, hysteria or sorrow. It may be irresponsible, morally and ethically questionable, but it is possible. A good theatrical production can do the same. It may serve a purpose for a dramatic moment, but it's not faith. It has no substance; it won't hold you like an anchor holds a ship in a storm. In fact, that feeling will probably evaporate not too long after you've left the venue.

That's show business, and that's atmosphere; great in the right context, but it has no place in the family of God.

We know that 'faith comes by hearing, and hearing by the word of God' (Romans 10:17, WEB). There's no lack of voices we could listen to for advice and inspiration; but if we're looking to increase our faith, we need to be listening to the right one. Secular voices won't deliver; spiritual gurus who are not trusting in Christ alone for salvation are barking up the wrong tree. God's Word comes to life under the direction of the Holy Spirit, igniting mere believing – cognitive knowledge – into faith in Him, and consequent action. That's a relationship, not an intellectual stance. This is the massive, vital difference we've already explored and which, given a determined, faith-filled response, grows over time regardless of the joys and griefs we bear.

Jesus was identified by the prophet Isaiah as 'a man of sorrows, and acquainted with grief' (Isaiah 53:3, ESVUK). In His humanity, Jesus knew what it was like to feel the cold stab of bereavement, and to grieve. He cried when His friend Lazarus died, even though He was just about to raise him from the dead. You might think that His tears were unnecessary in this instance; they do seem strange. After all, if He knew what He was about to do, why waste tears? The point is, not so much that Jesus was sad or even that He was empathising with His friends Mary and Martha, but that Jesus knew what life was *supposed* to be like; He was part of the eternal Trinity that put the blueprints together for how the world was meant to function and flourish from the start. I believe that the terrible gap between the intended and the actual is what brought Him to tears. They were not wasted at all.

Hope deferred

People – including you and me – were and are the pinnacle of all creation; death was not an original element in the plan. And then, tragically, sin crept in and wrecked its havoc across the whole beautiful, perfect idyll, scourging and scarring everything with its toxic kiss of death, and subjecting the world to the terminal consequences it carried: sin and death and hell. No wonder 'Jesus wept' (John 11:35).

Some of us carry grief, not for things that have happened, but for things that haven't. Expectations of people, or events that fail to materialise as we anticipated, can trip us up. Perhaps you envisaged your life panning out a certain way: a career, a relationship, a business opportunity, an academic achievement, a chance to live abroad; but it hasn't happened. Or maybe it began well, floundered and ultimately crashed. If it's a source of pain and grief then it needs to be addressed. I know a number of people who expected things of God which haven't happened and their palpable disappointment has been allowed to fester into something darker and more debilitating.

You may feel that there are promises God has given you for the future but currently, there is no sign of them coming to pass. That's a legitimate grief too. Don't ignore it; process it and ask God about it. Some things wait for an 'appointed time';[27] other things have been misunderstood or spoken out of turn by people who wish us well and speak with big hearts, but not necessarily with wisdom. Sometimes there are more steps in a process that leads us to the desired destination than we had foreseen, but right now we feel stuck, or even lost, somewhere on that journey. Proverbs 13:12 says, 'Hope deferred makes the heart sick'; how true that is. It's worth pausing and unpacking

---

[27] Habakkuk 2:3.

these things before they ferment and understandable sorrow turns to resentment, anger and an opportunity for the enemy to exploit our grief.

Part of our anticipation for the glories of heaven lies in the description that Jesus' friend, John, gives us in the book of Revelation: "'He will wipe every tear from their eyes. There will be no more death" or mourning or crying or pain, for the old order of things has passed away' (Revelation 21:4). Here we will get back to those original blueprints of how life – abundant life – was supposed to be lived.

In the meantime, we need to learn to grieve about the things that don't feature in that blueprint: loneliness, broken relationships, poverty, disappointments, hunger, homelessness, broken hearts, slavery, abused bodies, exploited children… It's a list that could stretch around the world; you don't need me to spell it out for you because we're surrounded by these painful realities. The natural and godly response to any of these things is grief. When I talk about 'feasting', I am certainly not suggesting anyone should ignore the realities of their situation, or bury the height, depth or breadth of their particular personal pain and experience.

Walking in reality

You may have met people along your way who do just that, but insist on saying, in effect, 'Hallelujah anyway.' The problem is that if their declaration doesn't genuinely come from the heart, then this type of coping mechanism in a crisis is actually inauthentic and fake. It's a pseudo-spiritual attitude that only serves to squash down the whole process of untangling, or making sense of, what is on the 'menu', usually for the misguided reason that it is considered, somehow, unspiritual to be struggling, or challenged, or losing one's grip, or even heading for total meltdown.

These are things which some people erroneously believe that Christians are not *supposed* to feel; so they either deny such feelings or suppress them as thoroughly as they are able. I don't know where such a lie began, but it needs to be called out as the nonsense it is: a dangerous unreality. If there's a community around us who have taken on this kind of false spirituality, then it's no wonder we can often feel so lonely trying to navigate our emotions internally. Frankly, it's a disastrous way of dealing with them; an echo of the old 'stiff upper lip' personified in many a caricature during the era of the British Empire, when emotions were not given any space to play out lest anyone 'let the side down'.

In our more enlightened times when expressing emotions is positively encouraged, we recognise that good mental health requires voicing our feelings and can even extend our lifespan by reducing internal stress. Keeping everything bottled up tends to lead either to a damaging implosion or a devastating explosion, neither of which is healthy for us or for the family, friends and colleagues around us. That *supposed to* behaviour brings no glory to God; in fact, it diminishes His power and presence to actively carry people through their trials. It does not reflect anything of His true character and can ultimately do ourselves and those around us irreparable damage if it's left to fester.

Even a superficial reading of the Psalms will evidence how David frequently expressed anger, disappointment, frustration and astonishment at events which impinged on his experience. Venting and laying them out before God with passion and honesty is not only cathartic, but it allows God's peace to flow into the space they occupied. It also provides a context for processing and identifying *God's Truth* – His promises – from what *feels true* in the moment – our immediate experience.

When we come to 'feast' we aren't denying those feelings or pretending they are somehow more or less worthy than others. We recognise that God has us in His sight-lines and that He is doing a work in us which will require His love, patience, grace, mercy and the gentle infilling of the Holy Spirit. And that's fine, because He isn't going to run out of any of those resources, and we have the assurance of His promise that He will walk with us through the darkest parts of our lives where the clouds of despair and defeat threaten to overwhelm us.

Whatever huge thing it is which has cast such a giant shadow across the banqueting table of our lives, we can take heart too, because physics tells us that where there is a shadow there must, by definition, also be light. Remember the reassuring truth that Jesus is 'the light' (John 8:12) and that He has 'overcome the world' (John 16:33).

So, feast or famine? 'Feasting' implies a full-on engagement with the meal; it's lavish, energetic, enthusiastic, engrossing. It appeals to each of our five senses: sight, smell, taste, hearing and touch. Colourful presentation, fragrant spices, tantalising flavours, clinking cutlery, sizzling dishes; they all combine to make the experience a living, visceral, all-consuming focus of delight. 'Feasting' with Jesus is an activity to be enjoyed whatever is served, even on those days when it's an enervating challenge.

Palate-cleanser questions

- Think about the merit and value of 'good grief'. Reflect on any disappointments, unmet expectations or unfulfilled promises in your own life which still carry grief for you. Ask God to give you the courage and honesty to face them again. Perhaps you have a trusted friend who could help you walk through this worthwhile process.

- Jesus was 'a man of sorrows, and acquainted with grief' (Isaiah 53:3, ESVUK), but also anointed with 'the oil of joy' (Psalm 45:7). This seems like a contradiction; what might it tell us about the character and nature of Jesus?

- Paul states that 'godliness with contentment is great gain' (1 Timothy 6:6). What do you think that means?

9. Pressed Down, Shaken Together[28]

A feast is made for laughter, wine makes life merry ...
(Ecclesiastes 10:19)

A quick study will reveal that there is more recorded biblical narrative around meals and food than you might imagine, but what about the metaphorical 'feasts' which make up our daily diet of work, leisure and sleep? The items on our 'menu' may be troubling or delightful depending on how much sleep we've had the previous night. But *can* we feast when we don't like the 'menu' served to us and feel we can't face this so-called 'feast'? Is it even possible; and if so, how? These are crucial questions. Is this an instance in which I should primarily ask God to change my circumstances, or is it actually one of those times when He seeks to change me in the circumstances? How will I be able to tell the difference?

Truly following Jesus

There is no comfort or illumination in trite answers for any of these questions. The 'sound bite theology' so beloved of social

---

[28] Luke 6:38.

media will not give us the robust ground work or context that we need in order to engage with, let alone embrace, these things.

Jesus specifically said, 'Each day has enough trouble of its own' (Matthew 6:34). Some days you and I both know for sure how true that is! Successive cold-blooded decisions will often be the key to unlocking genuine contentment, regardless of the 'menu' in front of us. Sometimes I need to speak to my soul like David did[29] and not forget the eternal truth that God's intentions for me are always good.

Reminding myself of some of the names of God, which reveal the facets and depth of His nature and character, has proved to be a good way of stirring my faith and helping me to lift my eyes off my circumstances and back to Him and His throne. You can do this with a simple Bible study search or an online concordance. Every name underlines an aspect of who God is and allows me to move from generic truths – God loves me; God wants to bless me – to more particular specifics through which the Holy Spirit quickens a response in my heart. That simple practice helps me focus, stirs my faith, lifts my eyes and enables me to be rightly positioned and motivated to face the 'dish of the day'.

At some point we will all need to decide whether what we read and know about God is true or not. Do we dare to believe it, or will we choose to put our trust elsewhere?

'If Christianity is just one more bit of good advice, then Christianity is of no importance. There's been no lack of good advice for the last few thousand years. A bit more makes no difference.'[30] C S Lewis is right. Just because we say our faith is real and true doesn't mean that we live according to, or in the good of, its truth; that will be challenged umpteen times in our spiritual walk and we will be forced to make one of those cold-blooded decisions to either lean into His truth, or to discard it

---

[29] Psalm 42:5; Psalm 103:1-5.
[30] BEYOND PERSONALITY by CS Lewis © copyright CS Lewis Pte Ltd 1944.

altogether. Either He will be your point of reference, or something (or someone) else will have that role in your life. Even the most hardened atheist has a point of reference which serves as a bottom line for their moral, ethical and daily choices.

Living consistently in the outrageous goodness and grace of God, with Holy Spirit peace and joy, takes us way beyond anything the world can offer in terms of life hacks and philosophy. We can only live this way if we know Him, the eternal 'I AM'.

Jacob only knew God as 'the God of my father, the God of Abraham and the Fear of Isaac' (Genesis 31:42) for many years, until he truly met with Him for himself at Mahanaim, near the fording place of the Jabbok River (Genesis 32:22-32). His 'menu' that day was to meet with his estranged brother, Esau, from whom he had stolen both birthright and blessing. In the ensuing years he had made a small fortune in flocks, herds and camels; accrued a large number of workers; married two wives and fathered twelve children. He was, nevertheless, very frightened at the prospect of meeting his aggrieved brother; a fight was almost inevitable. In fact, before facing Esau, Jacob was involved in an all-night wrestling match – an 'appetiser', if you will – with a mysterious man who turned out to be God. As a result of engaging in this strange nocturnal bout, Jacob got a new name – Israel – and a dislocated hip. For the rest of his life he walked with a limp.

When we truly choose to 'feast' we will meet with God and, like Jacob, be irrevocably changed. When the natural meets the supernatural, that's fairly inevitable. Such an encounter will be an important milestone in our lives for good or ill, depending on our response. Meeting with God is worlds away from knowing about God. Our faith is not just a creed to be referred back to from time to time in order to check whether we're still in cognitive agreement with the tenets of Christianity. This was always supposed to be about genuine relationship with God.

Remember, way back in Genesis we see Adam and Eve walking in the garden with God, in open, honest, transparent relationship. That was the original intention. It hasn't changed; it's just that sin got in the way, introducing guilt and breaking the precious relationship.

Sin is an ugly thing entangling us in its inherent weight of condemnation, fear, lies and shame. The only way out of its grip is through Jesus. At the cross everything else falls away, our crooked past gets straightened out and, like John Bunyan's famous pilgrim, our burdens are rolled away forever.[31] It is, we will discover, less about us finding God and so much more about Him finding us. By His grace, there comes a time when, drawn by the Holy Spirit, our eyes are opened and finally, we see and recognise Him.

Conviction, repentance, forgiveness and restoration, all ignited by faith, mark the path of all God's children into His abundant life and give notice on the enemy's hold over us. By being adopted into God's family, a line has been drawn in the sand and all other claims on us are rendered obsolete. This is where we live from now on, under God's banner, as part of His family; we are clean and we are home.

Much of our struggle through life stems from an innate need to realign ourselves with our original purpose and identity. No other philosophy, ideology or religion in the world will provide the life-giving answers to these issues – always, only, Jesus. 'Never doth a soul know what solid joy and substantial pleasure is – till once being weary of itself, it renounces all property [and] gives itself up to the Author of its being.'[32] That is what we were made for; that is where we find 'home'.

A menu of trials

But, make no mistake, child of God or not, at some point our 'menu' will include a dish we do not relish. Countless biblical

---

[31] John Bunyan, *The Pilgrim's Progress* (London: Penguin Books, 2008).
[32] Henry Scougal and George Garden, *The Life of God in the Soul of Man* (first published 1677; Boston, MA: Pierce and Williams, 1831), p4.

examples show us that meeting with a holy God is not a warm, fuzzy experience; it's not about atmosphere and it's seldom comfortable. While God often encourages us, frequently reassures us and continually loves us, He is thoroughly and absolutely committed to shaping, changing and challenging us. How else will we move on from being spiritual babies? How else could His image stamped in us become more evident? How else can we grow to be more like Jesus? We certainly can't do it by our own efforts, however well intentioned they may be.

More often than not, when God breaks into the temporal world, or sends an angel as a heavenly ambassador, the first words are, 'Do not be afraid'; the usual reaction, we can conclude, is one of fear. The encounter will almost certainly be painful too and, like Jacob, we will truly experience the strong hand of God, bear the marks of God in our scars, and never be the same again. But, we have a valuable opportunity to grow more like Jesus if we respond with humility and faith; if we can find connection with Him in the trial, we will not veer off our course but elevate and dignify the experience. Strange as it seems, if we can do this – and remember He is always far more anxious to meet with us than we ever are to meet with Him – we may find something that looks like joy even in our pain; even 'treasures of darkness' (Isaiah 45:3, ESVUK).

Under pressure

It has always been an encouragement to me that the most precious things on earth – diamonds – are formed deep in the lonely, dark places of the earth and under immense pressure. God's value on us indicates that we will also be shaped and refined in similar conditions, so that His treasure can be revealed in us and through us.

One of the real problems with darkness, pressure, shaping and trial is that they frequently fracture our relationship with God. They tend to be times when fears of abandonment, hopelessness and despair rush in to block our view of His goodness and even His presence. Do we move away from Him, or does He withdraw from us? Anger finds ready fissures to exploit if they've been neglected, resentment bubbles up from deep within and trust can wobble and break. It's a dangerous time too because you can misinterpret what's happening and find yourself agreeing with your feelings if you don't realign them with the things you truly know about God. Those agreements serve to cement the chasm between yourself and God, whether you begin to blame Him or yourself. Such breaches need to be mended, discarded and space made for healing, reassurance and truth.

Have you felt this? I know I have. Like the involuntary reaction which makes us leap back from a burn, I remember recoiling in a situation when I felt that someone I respected and admired behaved in a treacherous way towards me. If that sounds emotive, then I can tell you that it really was. It's not an exaggeration to say that I could have had a fairly solid court case rule in my favour had I chosen that path. My emotions exploded and imploded simultaneously as I reeled in pain, baffled by the actions of another, but feeling powerless to protest (I really had no desire to embark down a legal route; see 1 Corinthians 6). I was flailing for a while, as my perception of what I thought was reality was turned on its head and the desire to have my voice heard almost drowned out everything else. In my situation I could easily have fallen down into such a pit if I had remained focused on my desire for justice which, unfortunately, had a lot more to do with my honour than with Jesus'. Without the support of godly praying friends and a loving husband, I could easily have concluded that God had hung me out to dry. The cold water of disappointment is very sobering. But don't be fooled or taken unawares; this type of reaction to events is exactly what the enemy desires and schemes for. We cannot afford to give him ground or surrender to his foul lies. There is a redemptive element in our blackest moments and deepest valleys if we can but discover it. I'm glad my friends helped me find that then; it gave me the courage and resolve to press on without allowing bitterness to take hold of me.

Redemptive possibilities in times of challenge

The modern world fails to find much of any value or usefulness in suffering, so it reaches for human solutions to banish it from the world altogether in the shape of abortion, suicide or euthanasia. But this binary outlook – make the suffering stop or stop me suffering – is too simplistic, too childish and too narrow. It leaves no room for God; it assumes that He is outdated, irrelevant or absent. This is certainly not the case.

In one of his letters to a young church, Paul writes that he wants 'to know Christ ... and the fellowship of sharing in his sufferings' (Philippians 3:10, NIV 1984). I don't believe Paul was a masochist, but he knew that Jesus' sufferings were not pointless. Quite apart from salvation, which was purchased by Jesus' death and resurrection, Paul recognised a link between the troubles we face and those which Jesus endured. In each case, there is a peace-filled complete submission to the will of the Father and a determined trust that He will rule in the situation and reign over the outcome. It's actually, therefore, an honour to share His sufferings. It doesn't mean we have a perverse desire for the same brutal crucifixion, but it does mean that we have the same opportunity to connect with the Son and the Father as we keep our eyes fixed on them throughout our days, prioritising God's will over our own, whatever comes our way.

Jesus knew what it was to be an outcast, lonely, abandoned, betrayed, unjustly accused, verbally and physically abused. You must have felt at least some of those things. It may take enormous strength to keep on seeking God's face when the evidence suggests He is absent; but He will be there.

The Old Testament worship leader, Asaph, writes, 'Your path led through the sea, your way through the mighty waters, though your footprints were not seen' (Psalm 77:19). From a time of personal disaster he is recalling how, years before, God had led the Israelites through all manner of calamities under the care of Moses and Aaron. His point is clear: when the waves are huge and life-threatening, when you can't see God (or any evidence of His presence whatsoever), or catch so much as a glimpse of where He is taking you, He is still there. His commitment to shaping us means that even when the circumstances remain unaltered, He continues to invite us to 'feast' with Him, trust Him, and endure with Him.

I remember a time when God spoke clearly to me about something similar. The picture in my mind as I prayed about the uncertain days ahead was of a steep descending path disappearing as it wound its way down a mountain and into a dense wood. The way looked dark and lonely; the destination was obscured by the trees. It felt intimidating in the extreme; where were all the people? I wasn't at all sure this was remotely encouraging; was I really supposed to take this track? A sense of reassurance came when His familiar voice seemed to say, 'Just because you can't see them doesn't mean they're not there.' Your way may be dark or unclear too; this is the season where, more than ever, you need to lean into God and feed on the sustenance of His sure Word. 'Your word is a lamp for my feet, a light on my path' (Psalm 119:105). In other words, the light of God's truth will illuminate the path ahead.

In my case, I can look back and see how God has brought all sorts of fantastic people – fellow labourers, pilgrims and friends – across my path since that encounter. This psalmist doesn't describe a spotlight or floodlight, but indicates the provision of enough brightness merely for the next step; and that's all we need. When I was a child, my dad used to turn my bedroom light off, but he was still very much standing in the room. The same applies with our heavenly Father.

We may struggle to find any purpose in the dark moments, but these are the times when we can push into God with a new desperation that will evoke a loving response, and where we will later understand that our true growth in the realities of our faith has occurred. Asaph bore witness to the testimony of the escaping Hebrew people, that the way through any raging storm is to keep following the One who led you there in the first place.

Paul had an unspecified trial in his life which felt like his own personal storm. He would much rather have had it removed but although he prayed three times for his 'menu' to change, he heard God say something else: '... he said to me, "My grace is sufficient for you, for my power is made perfect in weakness"' (2 Corinthians 12:8-9). Paul didn't see a change in his circumstances; but he did 'see' that God wanted to work a change in him in those circumstances. In so doing he plumbed the riches and depths of heaven's grace with such thoroughness that he is still able to communicate to us via his letters to the New Testament churches, many hundreds of years later, giving us hope, clarity and the tools to access that same grace. The way we approach a trial directly affects how we emerge from it and what we glean through it emotionally and spiritually; we can drown, or we can dominate if we 'feast' with Him.

Old Testament menus 2

The 'menus' of biblical characters you read in Chapter 6 only tell part of the story. The narrative unfolds to tell us what happened next and how they responded to their various 'dishes'.

1. Abraham and Sarah had the child of promise through whom, hundreds of years later, the promised Messiah would come. They had had to wait twenty-five years and were so old that by then, naming their son Isaac – 'Laughter' – was appropriate. They saw the faithfulness of God throughout those years as they leaned into His promise, despite having dropped the ball along the way with Hagar and Ishmael.

2. Joseph became the second most influential person in the known world, saving thousands of people from famine by his strategic, God-given plan and administrative skills; but that was only after he had submitted to the humbling experience of finding the reality of God while alone in prison. It was there that he must have learned to 'feast' on his particular 'menu'; there that his heart was changed and his character shaped sufficiently to be able to handle the next 'course' of leadership at such a dizzyingly high and public level, where the seduction of power could have gone to his head just as his youthful dreams had once done, and with potentially far more dangerous consequences.

3. Gideon led his rag-tag army to an emphatic victory which ended seven years of Midianite harassment and conflict, pulverising the Midianites, including their two kings, in a decisive battle after accepting God's dismissal of 31,700 potential soldiers (Judges 7:3-7). This was not just a victory; it was a landslide conquest which ushered in forty years of peace.

4. Naomi embraced a new season after calamitous losses and a long journey home, where the demonstrable grace and guidance of God brought her and her daughter-in-law, Ruth, from a pit of bitterness to a place of peace, belonging and contentment. By pushing through her sorrow and connecting with Boaz, a kinsman-redeemer (and so a forerunner of Jesus), she found a new lease of life. In time she became great-grandmother to the boy who would become mighty King David, Israel's greatest monarch, thus taking her place in the extended family line and genealogy of the Messiah Himself; what an honour.

5. Hannah, in spite of her pain – or maybe because of it – took her sorrow to God. Rather than giving way to self-pity and recrimination, she poured out her damaged heart with many tears, trying to find the voice and will of God in her lonely barrenness. God heard her sincere prayers and was moved to give her her heart's desire in the form of Samuel, who was dedicated to God before he was even conceived. Hannah's son grew up in the house of God where he was tutored in the things of God, and became the last of the judges, paving the way for the season of Israel's kings, and faithfully represented God throughout his long life of service. Hannah's beautiful prayer-filled worship is expressed in 1 Samuel 2 after her heart-wrenching sorrow; it is challenging, provocative and deeply moving and is mirrored by Mary in Luke 1. God also abundantly blessed her with three more sons and two daughters.

6. Job refused to fall into the trap of blaming God for the dramatic downturn in his circumstances. He dismissed the idea of being a fair-weather God-fearer as foolishness. 'Shall we accept good from God, and not trouble?' (Job 2:10). Despite his devastating losses, harridan wife and useless pseudo-philosophic companions, Job (mostly) silenced them with ironic comebacks and kept his focus on his long-term relationship with God.

Job longed for his past days of respect and prosperity, acknowledging the Almighty as righteous and wise, and appealed to no one but the all-seeing God to be his advocate. His story closes with a knee-wobbling encounter with God who roundly rebuked the empty words and false accusations of his companions and gave Job a fresh perspective on the majesty, scale, scope and dealings of the Upholder of the universe. At no point did Job receive an explanation for the terrible 'dishes' he had been served, but the season of trauma was followed by a season of unparalleled blessing: a restoration of health, wealth, another ten children and a long lifespan during which he enjoyed his great-great-grandchildren. While recognising that what had happened to him was not fair in terms of a recompense for his lifestyle, he still honoured the wisdom and character of God. He never questioned God's power, only His justice. His was primarily a crisis of faith, not of suffering.

Shape up, soldier!

I truly wish Job's question about what we accept from God was a truth more prevalently recognised and discussed among the people of God today. The general tendency is to blame God very quickly when things aren't going as smoothly as we hope. We would perhaps do well to take the time to ask better questions about suffering in any and all of its forms. Academic debate is of very little value on the topic; what is required is a true personal encounter with Jesus Christ.

Here is the crux of the matter, which connects with our very heart. Unless we truly embrace and understand this, we will remain immature, spineless, feeble and unfit soldiers who struggle to operate in any effective way in the battles and spiritual warfare to which we have been assigned in God's army. If we continually turn tail at the first sign of the enemy's threats, we are not going to make the inroads we should, or recapture ground which he has temporarily taken from the jurisdiction of the kingdom of God. Training in God's school for warriors includes lessons in perseverance, unwavering trust, seeking His face in the darkness and fog, and a healthy respect for the Architect, Sustainer and King of all universes. As one old fighter put it:

> Soldier of Christ, you will have to do hard battle. There is no bed of down for you, there is no riding to heaven in a chariot. The rough way must be trodden, mountains must be climbed; rivers must be forded; dragons must be fought; giants must be slain; difficulties must be overcome; and great trials must be borne. It is not a smooth road to heaven ... Yet it is pleasant; it is the most delightful journey in all the world ... because of the company ... the sweet promises on which we lean ...[33]

When we 'feast' in His presence, the troubles of the world take on a different perspective, and our challenges another hue. With Abraham, such seasoned warriors can say, 'Will not the Judge of all the earth do right?' (Genesis 18:25). This consistently challenges me to my core.

---

[33] Charles Haddon Spurgeon, Anthony Uyl (ed), *Spurgeon's Sermons Volume 01:1855* (Independently published 2017), p79.

Palate-cleanser questions

- Have you ever 'wrestled with God' in a metaphorical sense? What was the issue? Who won?

- Why is sin often so difficult to face?

- "'For I know the plans I have for you,' declares the LORD, 'plans to prosper you and not to harm you, plans to give you hope and a future'" (Jeremiah 29:11). Take a few moments to meditate on this promise, allowing its truth to soak deep into your heart.

10. Full and Running Over

My soul will be satisfied as with the richest of foods;
with singing lips my mouth will praise you.
(Psalm 63:5, NIV 1984)

Modern menus 2

My friends, whose stories you read in Chapter 6, all found that
their crises opened the door to a new opportunity to either
'feast' at the table that had been so abruptly and unexpectedly
set for them, or to refuse the invitation and walk away from the
One who longed to sit and eat the 'meal' with them. Like them,
we face daily choices to press in or walk away.

I am encouraged and inspired by them all. Each has proved
the unfailing reality of Solomon's wisdom: 'The name of the
LORD is a strong tower; the righteous run to it and are safe'
(Proverbs 18:10, NIV 1984). In Part 2 of their stories, they once
again explain how they came to a place of 'feasting' in their own
words.

1. Paul and Julia's story: Anastasia
I gave birth to our beautiful daughter, Anastasia, one October
night. She lived for only a few hours and I held her in my arms

for much of that short time. The medical staff gently put a bonnet on her so that the back of her head was not exposed.

This was not what we had hoped for, not what we expected. So many of our friends were still praying with us that God would step in and miraculously heal her. We had no doubt that He was able to do so, and we still believed He could override all the medical advice and prognoses we had been given. It was not to be.

The funeral took place with our church family not long afterwards. Grief was exhausting and ever-present. As I cried by our baby's grave, my husband, Paul, said, 'This is not the end.' I believe that's true; one day I will see my child again. This life is not all there is.

The truth of James 4:13-15 certainly became very real to me at that time:

> Now listen, you who say, 'Today or tomorrow we will go to this or that city, spend a year there, carry on business and make money.' Why, you do not even know what will happen tomorrow. What is your life? You are a mist that appears for a little while and then vanishes. Instead, you ought to say, 'If it is the Lord's will, we will live and do this or that.'

I had assumed some things about our future which were based on nothing but my own preferences.

I learned to thank God for the blessings I already had, rather than demand from Him what I thought was my right, and stop the comparison game. My empathy and my faith grew. Many people have far more difficult things to bear than us, but looking back, I do think it was a time which required our determined perseverance which, itself, changed me.

Romans 5:3-5 says: '... but we also rejoice in our sufferings, because we know that suffering produces perseverance; perseverance, character; and character, hope. And hope does not disappoint us, because God has poured out his love into our hearts by the Holy Spirit, whom he has given us' (NIV 1984). I recognise that God definitely grew those things – character and hope – in me. The difficulty of the path we trod wasn't an indication that the journey was pointless. I realise that we need to hold our goals and hopes for this life lightly, and make sure they are directed by God and not by the pressure of the world or the expectations of others which get put upon us.

In subsequent years, God gave us more children: a son and a set of twins. I felt that the twins especially were God's way of giving us a double portion after what we lost in Anastasia.

2. Dave and Gill's story: Samuel
Dave: Both of our kids have been God's great teachers of our hearts as we reflect the deep love, the joy, the pain, the hope that burns inside the Father for His children.

Samuel spreads joy wherever he goes. He is gentle, kind and our little sunbeam. Ruben is a ball of energy who knows what he does and doesn't like, including broccoli and spinach. In a way, Samuel is the broccoli and spinach in the meal that God has laid before Gill and I. We often find ourselves vehemently protesting at what is presented to us. It's hard to swallow the spinach of what we lost and the broccoli of what looks like unfairness that leaves the taste of pain and despair in our mouths.

But, the reality of God graciously bearing with us has gently led us into deeper relationship with Him and a more intimate understanding of His heart. Our trust in Him has become more tangible as our love for Him has been developed in a place of pain. We recognise that we are small parts of His story, rather than Him being a part of ours. We sit at His table and He chooses what is served; so, we choose to eat with thankful hearts, knowing for certain that He loves us more than we can ever hope to understand.

Sometimes we feel that we are separated from our family and friends by a fast-flowing river where the mud is thick and sticky. Their easier path continues; we can feel that we're shouting from a great distance as we slog through the mud on our side.

That's been very tough. We don't need pity, but we do need love as we persevere.

Gill: Yes, I asked how God would allow this to happen to *me*! I have been in denial; I've been mad, sad and disappointed. It's a deep, broken sorrow. But, even if I tried, I discovered that I could not run away from God because I need Him more now than ever before. Every day reminds me that I am not in control, and I can vividly see how precious and fragile life is; that there must be more…

I know that God is doing a work in me that can only happen if I surrender fully and not fight against it. Samuel is teaching me to be vulnerable, to reach out, ask for help.

Each day there are choices to be made: I *choose* to trust God, even if there is no healing; I *choose* to see the miracle that is my son; the everyday miracles – breathing, swallowing, smiling, laughing. I *choose* to be thankful, to find the good in each day. I am finding that true joy comes when I give out of my place of brokenness.

3. Uncle Robin's story: Steve

The inevitable press conference came after a sleepless night the day after Steve's murder. As both his dad and a policeman, I was asked what I thought about my son's killer. The silence seemed to go on for a long time because I was praying for the right words. There was quite a reaction from journalists when I said that I forgave the killer; but I meant it then and I mean it now. I still pray for the man every morning when I get up. Without Christ that kind of forgiveness would be impossible for me.

Steve's funeral took place in Manchester Cathedral a couple of weeks later. Far from being an intimate family occasion, the streets were closed and crowds of people lined the route of the cortege which was escorted by six mounted policemen. The coffin arrived to the sound of *Amazing Grace*, a hymn Steve had often played on his trumpet in the church worship group. Loud speakers outside relayed the service to which the then Prime

Minister Tony Blair and his wife, Cherie, came, along with supportive police officers from New York who had been involved in the aftermath of 9/11. Steve's minister gave a clear gospel message and some people met Jesus themselves for the first time that day. Amazing grace indeed! We were determined to try to celebrate Steve's jokey personality as well as his faith. Following the example of Jesus, Steve laid down his life to save others. I can say with confidence now, as I said then, people who believe in God never meet for the last time.

We miss Steve every day more than I can say. He died a very brave man of whom my wife, Chris, and I are very proud. I can honestly say that out of the tragedy has come triumph. Life has taken us in a completely new direction as we now have the privilege of helping other bereaved people, especially those who have lost children. Helping people navigate their experiences and walk through their own pain towards forgiveness has now become part of our counsel. Forgiveness has been key. It's taken from us the bitterness and the anger that we might have had and we might still have. I know we've been healed from that.

It doesn't diminish the loss, but I know that we will see Steve again. Until then I will continue to pray for the perpetrator of his killing and seek God's forgiveness for him. I pray that he will seek God himself and find true peace and forgiveness in Him.

4. Charlotte's story: a daughter

I initially responded to our daughter's mental crisis by becoming angry and frustrated with God. We had approached our parenting by reading the 'right' Christian books, and followed all their advice. What had gone wrong? It just wasn't fair. I ranted and railed against God: 'Why us? Why *my* family?' And ultimately, 'Why me?'

I am so grateful for my family and friends who stood with us during those dark days when mental illness tormented our daughter and dogged our every waking moment, in all its forms. The situation became a wake-up call for me in a way, as I realised that having been a Christian since my childhood, what I really wanted from God was more of a problem-free life, than a 'not my will, but yours be done'[34] life.

It was a reminder that following Jesus is not the promise of a fairy tale life. I knew that Jesus said we'd encounter storms and have trouble in our lives. I've read those words so many times over the years, but now I finally started to understand what they must mean. In the times when I felt that faith was slipping in my heart, I discovered a greater depth of God's love and He met me in my brokenness and pain. He was and is my Saviour. He healed my heart and He gave me new hope and strength to face another day.

Our daughter was given a place at a wonderful Christian residential centre which provided medical care, counselling, practical support and prayer ministry. Here, God broke His light into the land of darkness and shadows where our daughter was trapped. From being literally paralysed by fear and despair, she was released into a new freedom and began to walk towards that light of health and wholeness.

I don't know whether this journey has finished for us, but I do know now, with far greater certainty than ever before, that even when the road is unfamiliar and difficult to navigate, I am not alone. I have seen how Jesus, the 'light of the world',[35] can reach us even in the darkest darkness. Isaiah 9:2 in *The Message* says, 'The people who walked in darkness have seen a great light. For those who lived in a land of deep shadows – light! sunbursts of light!' This is the light that has shone so brightly into our family, and I love sharing that truth with others who also need His light to shine and dispel their own dark places.

5. Sally's story: Mike
It was the third year of our separation when I felt that I heard God say very clearly, 'Here and no further,' in my mind. Other

---

[34] Luke 22:42.
[35] John 8:12.

things confirmed this and so I was sure God was speaking to me even though divorce wasn't the path I had wanted to pursue.[36] I found a lawyer and the process began. I believed God was in it the whole way along, confirming that I was doing the right thing. It was so hard, but I am convinced that there is nothing that the blood of Jesus cannot cover and heal.

So, here I am as a single parent, raising my three children in a less-than-ideal situation and facing the future in faith, trusting that God will provide and guide me. By the mercy and grace of God I have been able to look Mike in the eye and say 'Sorry' for my part in the breakdown of the marriage. I take 100 per cent responsibility for my part, and have released him to God to deal with his part. I know that God hasn't stopped loving him. Soon he will tell the children about the woman he is living with. Amazingly, I have found that I am able to pray for her, that she will be a good stepmum and that our children will grow to love and respect her. I know that God loves her too.

Each day I am choosing to believe the truth that God does 'immeasurably more than ... we ask or imagine' (Ephesians 3:20). He goes above and beyond. He didn't say we wouldn't have any trouble in life, but I have found that in that He is still good and He never changes. He raises us up to a standard for living and following Him in purity and wholeness, in restoration and redemption, so that we can live life in all its beautiful fullness.

6. Julie's story: James

Julie: I was so grateful to God that I was not alone in the emergency of James' stroke. As we prayed together, I can honestly say we knew God's love and peace, and amid the sorrow there was the news that we were expecting a new grandchild. I wept and wept as I saw God's hand in hearing all my own cries through the crisis. The rest of the family joined us from the UK, and it was so precious to have their support.

---

[36] Matthew 5:32 – Jesus on the topic of divorce.

The journey that I had to walk brought me closer to God than I had ever been before. I learned that God does not depend on our strength or abilities in a crisis, but He is great in our weakness.

James started to improve. At first, he had trouble moving his arm and leg and would sound muddled, starting his sentences in the wrong place. Gradually, over weeks, he was able to start walking again and his strength began to return. I could see that although it was going to be impossible for him to continue his life at the pace he had been living before, he was still with us, and I was so grateful. However, I still had no idea how we were going to carry on. The family jumped in and together we got through that first season; we were all so aware that God's grace was there.

Whenever I feel overwhelmed, I have found myself saying, 'Satan, you will not take my joy.' James has had some setbacks, but we have known the reality of God's grace in it all. I think the truth is that we all have a choice to make in times of crisis; we either do it with our precious Lord Jesus or we choose to do it alone. As we face our future years the challenges seem huge. Without God's grace and presence, I am not prepared to go on this journey; but this is my confidence: that He will sustain us just as He has on the journey to date.

James: During those first few weeks in hospital I experienced two things I never had before. First was the sense of God being around me. I knew that many were praying for me across the world, and all I can say is that I have never been so aware of His presence. We talk of 'a thin place', and that hospital bed felt very much like a thin place between heaven and earth. I was, and am, renewed in a deep belief in the power of prayer. As the weeks went by and the praying moved on to other urgencies, I could sense the change. Our Father was still very much with us, but nothing was like that first phase – a small foretaste, perhaps, of our life that is to come. Secondly, for the first time in ages, I had a long, uninterrupted time to meditate and ponder. A dear friend of ours has termed it: 'Time to be impressed by God rather than to try and impress God.' As life has become busier and the diary refilled, I miss those days of chilling ('feasting') with God without any other agenda.

Choices

One of the things which stands out as I read the stories and 'menus' of my friends, is the choices of reaction which were made by the 'diners'; how they 'feasted' in places of devastation. They did not slide into a place of uneasy acceptance; there were stark moments when choices had to be made. Without those moments, they could have been swept along into maelstroms of unfettered sorrow or withdrawn numbness.

There is an apocryphal story of a Jewish man who once debated with a Gentile over where they believed God's Word came to rest. The latter claimed it is to be written in our hearts. The Jew disagreed, 'No my friend, His word is placed *on* our hearts, so that when they are broken His words can flow into them.'[37] That certainly seems to have been the experience of my friends. For some it was a decision in the moment; for others it continues to be a daily decision. Be assured, these were not taken lightly or automatically. Not one of my friends claims to be a super-saint. Like Jacob, some wrestled to get to a point of peace; undoubtedly, none of them will ever be the same again. That proportionally sufficient grace seems, of necessity, to be greater and somehow deeper and more wonderful in seasons of suffering than in the seasons of normality.

Emotions are good servants but make very bad masters. If we choose to live purely from our feelings, we will live a very yo-yo, roller-coaster kind of life, in which we react to every stimulus, and every twist and turn of fortune, like the ball-bearing in a pinball machine ricocheting around, damaging ourselves and others. To maintain an even keel, we need the steadiness which keeping our eyes fixed on Jesus gives us. Like

---

[37] Original source unknown.

a twirling ballerina, we need a fixed point of focus or we will become giddy, disorientated and crash to the floor. Emotions give us a heads-up call, like the lights on a car dashboard. We ignore them at our peril, but they do not determine where the vehicle will go. All these metaphors illustrate the same point. God has given us those emotions, but they operate best when steered by the things we know are true.

The decisions we make in a time of crisis are enthroned and established in our experience and psyche, becoming default avenues of thought for pretty much every decision from there on. If we choose to agree with the promised fact of God's goodness, in spite of what we may see circling around us, we will engage, or 'feast', in an entirely different way from those who choose to blame God and embark on a destructive 'feast' of hatred, blame, bitterness, unresolved anger, recrimination and self-pity. Just choosing to take the next step can be, relatively, a mammoth leap forward.

My dad often used to refer to the old adage, 'How do you eat an elephant?', to which the answer is, of course, 'One bite at a time.' In other words, when the obstacle in front of us seems overwhelming and we don't know where to begin, rather than try to solve or resolve the situation in its entirety, engage a slow and steady, methodical approach (see Chapter 7: *Gorging*). If the 'plate' of your circumstances is piled high with metaphorical liver (or its equivalent for you), maybe begin at one edge, taking small bites or nibbles. The portion may still seem formidable, but you will be making progressive inroads which will see you conquer the entire 'meal' given some time.

You may find yourself a victim of circumstance, in so far as you neither chose nor desired the things that happened to you. None of us received a pre-birth application form to state our preferences for the life ahead of us regarding nationality, social or economic demographic, year of birth, academic expectation, etc. That would be absurd; I understand that. My friends know that too. But, what they have proved by living out a life of 'feasting' is that this does not necessarily mean you have to be a victim of the things that come your way.

We stumble when we begin to lobby for our 'rights', forgetting that these were left at the foot of the cross when we relinquished control of our lives. In the seasons when everything is stripped away from us, our vulnerability can be a source of fear. Trusting ourselves into the hands of God for daily strength and a secure path is a choice; relying on ourselves, we will come up short. Perseverance will prove that His resources will see us through, and provide what we need for maturing in Him en route. That's really food for thought.

If we have an immovable foundation of certainty that God is good, God is faithful, God is trustworthy, God is King – then we will not easily go off course. Looking at our circumstances is like Peter being invited by Jesus to walk on water but focusing more on the choppy waters around the boat than on the One who invited him to be there (Matthew 14:22-32). That way lies discouragement and disaster. The eyes of faith see beyond the information provided by the immediate, and firmly fix themselves on God's unfailing promises and the certainties of His goodness. Our senses and emotions only tell us part of the story; they supply a small part of the whole picture. In the microcosm of our life they can shout very loudly, but in the macrocosm they will be acknowledged but eclipsed and, ideally, subsumed, by the pervading, solid fact of the goodness of God. We may yet discover the thrill of walking on that water.

If we embrace the truth of God's words that He plans good things for us, then we will find ourselves standing on solid ground. More than that, we are actually invited to go beyond standing, which in many ways is static, to do so much more than uphold the status quo. We can move into those things, wrestle to possess the promises God has given, declare His purposes to ourselves and our situation, stir our spirits and our souls to engage thoroughly with everything we know about God and His character – to debunk the lies of the enemy, see mountainous obstacles crumble and His life burst out everywhere we go. So, whether God changes our circumstances, or changes us in our circumstance, He is still very much in charge and worthy of our utmost devotion and worship.

The story is so much bigger than what is happening in our small corner. There's a whole world out there that has no idea about and, so far, no personal encounter with the lavish and extensive goodness of God. These truths are so radical, so countercultural that they can change individuals, cultures and nations. The invitation to 'eat' and 'feast' is open to all who respond to Jesus' invitation; there is an overflowing abundance of nutritious 'food' and excellent 'wine' to nourish and bring life to all, whether in palaces or in rubbish dumps. 'Enough' seems a stingy word; there is so much more for those who dine with Jesus.

True 'knowing'

There is a world of difference between knowing these things as abstract concepts and knowing them as reality. In the same way we can read the words of the Bible as *logos* words – general truths – or know the revelatory impact of a *rhema* word, when a truth hits us with the accuracy of a sniper's bullet, getting straight to the heart of our situation – very different. A crisis will still be painful, frightening, disappointing, confusing and a thousand other things, but we will not inevitably dissolve into a puddle and throw away our faith. I expect you know of people who have chosen that route when faced by a 'menu' they did not like. Tragically, the frequent comment is often, 'It didn't work for me,' as if God were a formula to apply, or an insurance plan to wave in the face of every barrier on our path. No; that's dry, legalistic religion which offers no hope, no comfort and no real life. It's a far cry from the abundant life that Jesus promises and which is evidenced by those who choose to 'feast' at His table.

Trying to be satisfied with mere religion is like expecting to be nourished by junk food. There's a frustrating emptiness to it; don't settle for it. There is no lack and no rubbish at this divine table. The blessings and favour of God have no limit and no sell-by date; as His children we can access them 24/7 and share them with those who so desperately need to know Him.

Every trial, storm or rancid 'dish' provides an opportunity to accept again the invitation to 'feast' with the Mighty One, who has set His immeasurable love upon you – even in the 'presence of [your] enemies' (Psalm 23:5) – and to prove that He is just as real today as He ever has been.

Palate-cleanser questions

- What did you find the most encouraging, and what the most provocative, element of my friends' stories?

- Forgiveness was the path to freedom from bitterness which Uncle Robin found through the tragedy of losing Steve. What part has forgiveness played in your own life?

- 'Consider it pure joy ... whenever you face trials of many kinds' (James 1:2). This is very countercultural for us. How might it be possible?

11. 'It's Not Fair!'

The kingdom of heaven is like a king who prepared a wedding banquet for his son.
(Matthew 22:2)

There was a time when my parents must have thought they would never hear the last of the 'It's not fair!' phrase; the last syllable mangled and extended to make it hang in the air for as long as possible. The whining anthem of my childhood became: 'It's not faaaaaaiiiiir!' Being the youngest of the three children, I frequently vented my frustration at the age-related perceived injustices that rankled so badly, whether in reference to bedtimes, the last piece of toast, curfews, dress codes, allotted space on the back seat of the car, the latest stalemate Monopoly® marathon or disagreements about whose turn it was to do... well, almost anything, actually; this was my default response. Poor old Mum and Dad. At least, that's what I eventually thought, with considerably more empathy, once I began to hear the phrase cranked out with monotonous regularity from my own four. I believe we banned it for a while.

One of the most sobering but informative lessons of growing up is just that: life is not fair. Whatever 'fair' is, and whoever is the arbitrator of this elusive thing, there's no doubt that much of what goes on in the world does not fit the bill. The disparity between social, economic, demographic and national groups is vast, and while taking into account the hundreds of years of history which has brought us all to this point is illuminating, it provides very little in the way of immediate solutions to the multiplicity of global problems we face.

Life is certainly not fair out there; but closer to home where comparison is second nature to us, fed as it is by our competitive school system and perpetuated primarily by the advertisement industry, we may find the complaint of yesteryear on our lips once more. When our 'menu' looks unpalatable, it's natural to wonder who on earth came up with it. Did they seriously want anyone to eat at this 'restaurant' of life? In fact, no one 'on earth' could probably come up with some of the twists, turns and complexities which our lives can take.

It's the sober reality that we all have to face: nobody suggested any of this was 'fair'. Theologians, writers and philosophers have grappled with the random, or otherwise, nature of suffering for centuries. Hundreds of books have been written on the subject, some of which may help you get to grips with the topic should you wish. Doubtless the stories you read in earlier chapters are just the tip of the iceberg in terms of all the scenarios with which you are acquainted, quite apart from your personal ones.

Learning to 'feast' clearly didn't happen overnight for my friends, and it won't for us either.

WWJD?[38]

If, in the face of difficulties we ask, 'Why me?' – which we probably will at some stage or another along life's road – we are unlikely to come up with a satisfactory answer. My own conclusion, therefore, is that a far more apropos question might be, 'Why *not* me?' After all, if we live in a fractured world full of brokenness, sorrow and pain, is it really likely that we will walk through it without any of these things touching us? That's as

---

[38] What Would Jesus Do?

ridiculous as walking through a muddy puddle and expecting to come out the other side looking as though we've been freshly laundered. I'm not talking about a fatalistic, 'what will be, will be' mentality, either; not at all.

Jesus Himself in His incarnated humanity was not wrapped in divine cotton wool, shielded from the sufferings of the world. In fact, He partook of all those things. He knew the reality of a tired, sweaty body; the rumble of a hungry stomach; the reality of a mouth parched by dust and heat – universal irritations rather than specific 'sufferings'. More poignantly though, Jesus knew the stigma of being conceived out of wedlock; the slicing pain that comes with the betrayal of a friend; the crippling sorrow that accompanies bereavement. He knew about living with a reputation He didn't deserve – the consequence of hanging out with 'low-lifes' and prostitutes. He experienced caustic judgementalism and green-eyed jealousy dressed up as religion, the sanctimonious dismissal of His teaching by those who thought they knew better, and the loneliness of being shunned by people who should have welcomed Him with open arms. He knew the disappointment caused by an easy lie of another friend, the injustice of false accusations, the searing cuts of a Roman whip, and the humiliation of public mockery, to say nothing of an illegal trial and the consequence of a weak man looking for an expedient political get-out. On top of all this, Jesus experienced the awful, intense reality of being separated from His heavenly Father not just physically, but spiritually.

Jesus could have avoided all of this if He had fallen for Satan's temptation in the desert just after His baptism in the River Jordan. There, at the start of His ministry, Jesus was offered 'all the kingdoms of the world' (Luke 4:5), which were, indeed, legally his to give at that point. Since Adam's Fall, the world and everything in it fell forfeit and the enemy took charge until the sacrifice of the only innocent man in history redeemed the entirety of what had been surrendered in Eden that dark day. All it would have taken for an anguish-free life, would be for Jesus to worship the fallen Lucifer rather than His heavenly Father, just for a fleeting moment.

Since Jesus was fully man as well as fully God, make no mistake, the temptation must have been real. Satan was sneakily offering Jesus a short cut to what God had already promised Him: the nations. If He had succumbed to that temptation and taken the offer, the human race would have been condemned forever. There would be no way back for us; no possibility of escape from the consequences of our sin. Thank God that Jesus refused the enticement and held fast to the path of righteousness, countering Satan's vicious attack with 'the sword of the Spirit ... the word of God' (Ephesians 6:17).

As His earthly ministry came to a close, Jesus was faced with the immediacy of His God-ordained 'menu' of crucifixion. Are you surprised that He asked in the Garden of Gethsemane whether He could please have an alternative? "'*Abba*, Father," he said, "everything is possible for you. Take this cup from me. Yet not what I will, but what you will'" (Mark 14:36). This was not a light request; Jesus was not ambivalent about how He felt when faced with such a 'meal'. This would be a trial like no other. Dr Luke records that in His state of anguish, and despite an angel being sent to give Jesus divine support and strength, He sweated blood which dripped onto the ground (Luke 22:44). Medical science is aware of this phenomenon, called hematidrosis, which has been linked in some cases to the extreme stress which tips the body into a recognised 'fight, flight or freeze' response.

So what got Jesus through the mental, physical, emotional, psychological and spiritual ordeal which lay ahead of Him? The Bible tells us that He endured it all 'for the joy that was set before him' (Hebrews 12:2). Jesus knew that there was more going on in His deepest suffering than could be seen with the human eye. There was a redemptive purpose unfolding, and my goodness we, collective humanity in our broken world full of broken people, needed it.

Our spiritual situation was more perilous and more desperate than our temporal minds can grasp. Only the blood of an innocent man could reverse the legal claim that Satan had over us. There has only ever been one such man: Jesus. That is why He alone held the key for our redemption. God's plan of salvation, to reconcile us to Himself, bringing us back into correct spiritual alignment and restoring the tragically broken relationship, required nothing less. Justice demanded that God's wrath against all the sin of humanity and its destructive effects on His creation be disgorged in its fullness on an innocent substitute: Jesus.

Crucifixion doesn't sound like joy; it certainly doesn't sound fair, but it was both divine justice and extravagant grace. It didn't look like much to celebrate at Golgotha that day, but by Sunday morning it was a different story…

The joy Jesus anticipated was that of completing the task for which He had been sent: redeeming the ruined human race. There was also the prospect of returning to His Father, of regaining the glories of heaven which He had gladly and obediently forfeited for thirty-three dusty, earth-bound years, and the ultimate consummation of all history when the nations would become His rightful inheritance with countless thousands, 'from every nation, tribe, people and language' (Revelation 7:9), taking part eternally in the largest worship celebration ever known.

Surrendering to shaping

Where has your 'menu' taken you through the years, I wonder? And where will it take you next? I don't know; but I do know that if you lean into it, if you seek God's face rather than just His hand in it – and there is a vital, critical difference – then you will find yourself changed and shaped according to His good pleasure, and become more like Jesus in the process, which is, after all, God's goal.

We have only the vaguest, shadowy idea of the kind of beings He has in mind for us to be, but it is His intention rather than our own which takes centre stage when He is King. We say we want this in a thousand worship songs and in seemingly sincere prayers, but stop and ask yourself, do you? Do I? Really? The passionate evangelist Leonard Ravenhill identified this foolish error as a reason why Christianity has known years of decline in the West: 'we sing His praise but shun His person.'[39] That's a provocative statement. To be honest, it immediately makes me feel defensive and challenges some of my assumptions, but actually, it deserves some brutally honest consideration if I am to be authentic in my faith.

Sometimes it's as though we haven't read the small print – the bit about the cost of such a choice. It's almost as if we've made following Jesus too easy.

We are foolish if we underestimate the effects of any life which has been completely surrendered to God. Such a person doesn't simply talk about faith but, welcoming the unhindered power of the Holy Spirit, faith rules their entire life. This is how we are supposed to live out our Christian faith.

When we willingly submit our lives to God, when we ask Him to take control and be pre-eminent in our thinking, our decisions and our plans, we are stating that we are proffering full surrender. Nothing less will do. C S Lewis once gave a pertinent illustration of this, comparing God with a dentist who is ready to give thorough treatment to a pain-riddled patient.[40] Like the dentist, God never planned to just give us a cursory clean up, but to extract the entire source of our agony. There can be no half-measures when we hand our lives over to God.

Submitting our lives to the rule of God means that He now has a behind-the-scenes, access-all-areas pass to our past, our present and our future. We have given Him the keys to every

[39] Ravenhill, *Why Revival Tarries*, p103.
[40] BEYOND PERSONALITY by CS Lewis © copyright CS Lewis Pte Ltd 1944.

dusty corner of our minds, hearts and lives. Let me repeat: nothing is off-limits. Simply filling in a response card or repeating a standardised prayer of commitment are not practices we see in the New Testament. Becoming part of God's family isn't like taking out membership at the gym where we can pick and choose which activities we'll engage with, or like joining the library and only ever selecting a certain genre of literature that particularly appeals to us.

Perhaps, in an effort to boost numbers, be seen as relevant or promote an attractive vibe, churches have made it too easy to join of late; some have undoubtedly sold people short on the truly radical, countercultural, uncomfortable and dangerous path to which Jesus calls us. Could that be why some people are surprised by what is served up along the journey of life? Were they expecting that all their problems would be solved, the consequences of their past choices eradicated and the road ahead furnished with nothing more demanding that the odd coffee rota responsibility? Please understand, I am being neither critical nor facetious here, but we must resolve to avoid childish naïvety. Let's not diminish the mighty work and person of Jesus by diluting either Him or His message.

Sometimes salvation and discipleship can be watered down into something quite unrecognisable from what Jesus spoke about. There are instances where that has subtly morphed into little more than an insipid collection of self-help mantras, do-it-yourself-psychology tips, fridge-magnet truisms, or sanitised middle-class values focusing primarily on self-fulfilment. This trivialises the profoundly revolutionary demands of our Saviour.

The unequivocal placing of every thought, feeling and action which doesn't bear the mark of holiness into God's refining furnace, doesn't make for popular sermon fodder. Perhaps it's time it had prominence again.

'We must alter the altar, for the altar is a place to die on', said Leonard Ravenhill.[41] This is not the kind of soft-soap,

---

[41] Ravenhill, *Why Revival Tarries*, Chapter 6.

comfortable message designed to ignite warm fuzzies in any congregation. He probably didn't win many friends either when he declared, 'We have many organisers but few agonisers; many players and payers, few pray-ers; many singers, few clingers; lots of pastors, few wrestlers; many fears, few tears, much fashion, little passion, many interferers, few intercessors; many writers but few fighters. Failing here, we fail everywhere'.[42] That's quite a rebuke and, whether it's your experience or not, I think it's as potentially relevant now as when it was written in the 1950s.

Wake up and grow up

One of my friends recently preached a Sunday sermon in the UK entitled 'Growing in Maturity'. Apparently it received 'a mixed review'. Despite having a reputation as a cutting-edge church, it turned out that some people didn't appreciate being encouraged to stop being spiritual infants and start to grow up in God. I know the point was expressed with grace, tact and compassion because I heard it myself, but I was still baffled to hear the reaction.

Preachers are not in the pulpit to tickle the ears of their congregations. Of course, they must not deliberately cause offence, but they are not entertainers either. Their sober responsibility is 'to equip his people for works of service, so that the body of Christ may be built up until we all reach unity in the faith and in the knowledge of the Son of God and become mature, attaining to the whole measure of the fullness of Christ' (Ephesians 4:12-13). That requires persistent, consistent encouragement and affirmation, but also challenge; it's not always going to be pleasant; we would be naïve to think otherwise.

Jesus spent most of His time making somebody in the crowd uncomfortable and frequently caused offence. His goal was to catalyse real change at root, heart level; sometimes that requires

---

[42] Ibid., p25.

an unconventional or even a slightly disagreeable approach that probes beyond our natural comfort zones to be effective.

It's wonderful to have a revelation of God's heart for us as His dearly beloved and chosen children, but because He is a good Father, God will also teach, train, rebuke and discipline us. That's an important part of the parenting process, but it doesn't mean that grace is replaced with condemnation.

God loves us too much to allow us to be indulged brats without any spiritual backbone. Good preachers, like good parents, know this and take to heart Paul's words to Timothy: 'All Scripture is God-breathed and is useful for teaching, rebuking, correcting and training in righteousness, so that the servant of God may be thoroughly equipped for every good work' (2 Timothy 3:16-17). Of course, we all enjoy hearing a good teaching session far more than a rebuke. I can be in the moment and/or shelve the former if I choose; the latter requires me to take responsibility for its application in a far more rigorous way. If it's uncomfortable, I can try to brush it off, assume it's for someone else's attention, or I can choose to carry my offence indefinitely.

At the first hint of difficulties, ill-equipped people shed their faith and opt for an easier route. I have heard too many stories of people walking away from God because their grandmother died. Once again, please understand, I am not being heartless. Of course it's sad when a loved one passes away, terribly sad. I was devastated when my own lovely, godly granny died and I still miss her enormously. But we need to wake up: health fails, bodies stop working; no one lives forever. It's foolish to think that because God did not step in to reverse the natural ageing process in a cherished relative, He cannot be real. Yes; we must wake up *and* grow up.

Facing our giants

I am told, by those who play cricket, that there is a right and wrong way to catch the ball. If I were going to partake in that particular sport, I think it would be advisable for me to master this skill. It might spare me the agony and inconvenience of broken fingers. When that sphere of stitched leather comes zipping towards you at speed, the correct procedure, apparently, is to curb your natural instincts to protect yourself from the ball and cup your hands in such a way that the ball is drawn inwards towards your body. In this way, the energy of its momentum is somewhat dissipated. You have, effectively, welcomed the ball and provided it with a pliable, accommodating reception rather than a rigid wall. I have a permanently wonky finger from a similar, but gentler, volleyball incident which is testimony to what happens when you don't do this. Perhaps your own experience in various ball-related sports also bears this out.

The same principle can be of enormous help when facing a crisis. When David faced Goliath, the entire army of Israel was falling back in fear, but the feisty shepherd boy *ran towards* him (1 Samuel 17). He not only faced his problem, he raced to meet it head-on; not because he was too young to know any better, but because he had years of practice slaying would-be predators out in the desert and his skill was enhanced by his confidence in God. We could learn a few things from that shepherd boy.

Our own 'desert years' may be a preparation for more challenging days. Curiously, facing – even absorbing – pain rather than resisting it with every fibre of our being, can actually bring a measure of relief to the whole affair. The Holy Spirit is the One who keeps our spirits soft, amenable and available to the things God wants to 'throw' our way; a spiritual antidote to defensive rigidity.

Pain that refines us

The seventeenth-century Scottish theologian and pastor Samuel Rutherford knew that God's 'menu' wasn't always very tasty. He spent seventeen months holed up in Aberdeen, and was banned from ministering in public after publishing a book which Charles II found so abhorrent that he burned it. Rutherford was persecuted for both his book and his theology but He encountered the Holy Spirit in such a powerful way that heavenly fire marked his ministry as preacher, writer of letters and as Rector of the University of St Andrews. His wise exhortation to one friend, 'I hope he [God] shall lose nothing of you in the furnace, but dross'[43] has resonated with me many times through the years.

Rutherford knew first-hand that trials and tribulations are inevitable and bring all manner of dirt and muck to the surface of our lives for removal in the process of refining and purifying our hearts. The unpleasant truth is that those pollutants were lurking within the whole time; it's the presence of increased heat which draws them to the surface. We would be wise to embrace the opportunities to have them permanently extracted and eliminated with thanksgiving rather than resistance, for with them come the openings to move deeper into holiness and Christ-likeness in a way that no smooth path, or 'menu' of insubstantial, undemanding, spiritual jelly-and-ice-cream equivalent, can bring.

We are never as aware of pleasure as we are of pain. Think of how excruciating the pain of the tiniest splinter can be: out of all proportion to the size of the imposter. C S Lewis rightly said: 'Pain insists upon being attended to. God whispers to us in our pleasures, speaks in our consciences, but shouts in our pains. It is His megaphone to rouse a deaf world.'[44]

Sometimes the items on our 'menu' grab our attention in a more focused way. Back in 1989, my friend's husband fell dangerously ill; there were several times when we thought he would certainly die. Every time I prayed for her during that

---

[43] A letter written to William Glendinning on 6th July 1637, Aberdeen. Rev James Anderson and Rev A A Bonar, *The Letters of Samuel Rutherford with Biographical Letters of His Correspondence* and *A Sketch of His Life* (Edinburgh: William Whyte & Co; London: William P Kennedy, 1848), p419.
[44] THE PROBLEM OF PAIN by CS Lewis © copyright CS Lewis Pte Ltd 1940.

period, I felt God was saying that it was as though she were in a crowded room and He wanted to get her attention. My initial thought was that this seemed unfair, even cruel; but I know that He succeeded. God wasn't toying with her; He loved her so much that He was determined that she know Him in a better, deeper, fuller way and with greater intimacy than any of the previous years had brought her. He is motivated by passionate, relentless love for us, and sometimes that means He will back us into a corner until we have little option other than to connect with Him authentically. It can be dramatic, or not; but if the result is that we banish distractions and give Him our full attention, then we have stationed ourselves perfectly to grow in relationship with Him and are positioned for a greater, more extensive, wholehearted and satisfying seeing, hearing and knowing of Him.

When life is plain sailing, we can end up relying on our own wits, education, capabilities, skills, qualifications and talents to see us through. God loves us too much to allow us to do this for long. His desire is for that close, intimate relationship with us, and sometimes it's pain, suffering or a crisis that drives us into His open arms. That is the only reason why we are ever able to say with trusting confidence and faith that, despite the immediate landscape around us, 'The circumstances of my life are perfect.'[45] This is completely and utterly different from saying they are *ideal*. Few of us live there! When the crises happen, we choose to either cling to Him and pursue Him more passionately, or resist Him, lashing out with words and metaphorical fists.

We know that God is the Supreme Power over the whole earth, which He created, and over which He rules. We often forget that, astonishingly, we are the pinnacle of His creation and His heart longs for us with the same longing the prodigal's

---

[45] John Sutton-Smith: English teacher (1969-88) and deputy headmaster (1979-88) of Scarisbrick Hall School, Lancashire; retired pastor (Southport Community Church); inspiring Jesus-follower and mentor to many, including my husband. Used with permission.

father had for his far-away foolish son in Jesus' parable in Luke 15. The Bible tells us that God is 'a jealous God' (Exodus 34:14). In other words, God will brook no competition; He will not and cannot share that place of pre-eminence with anyone or anything else in the entire universe. His greatest delight is when we are in close, clean, ongoing relationship with Him.

Thirsting for Him

But the truth is that it's all too easy for us to become 'professional' Christians who go through the motions of a 'Jesus life', but who gradually lose our passion, our fire, our focus, our conviction and, inevitably, our joy. Like any repetitious activity that creates muscle strain, our spiritual life can suffer the same way and prove injurious to our spiritual health. All of us have probably fallen prey to this malady at some point, when duty has squeezed the life out of our daily walk, when we're concerned again about what we deem fair, and the delight of 'feasting' in proximity to Jesus becomes little more than a fading memory.

So then, we should not be surprised if sometimes there seems to be a little too much salt on our spiritual food. 'Thou hast put salt on our lips, that we may thirst for Thee,' noted St Augustine, who lived in the fourth and fifth centuries. Sixteen centuries later, when we struggle to swallow what faces us on our 'menu', we can nod in agreement but still be absolutely sure that God's intended outcome is the same: for us to press further in, not to walk away.

The Old Testament sons of Korah express the same kind of longing for God as the desire for water which they would feel in the excoriating heat of the sun-scorched desert: 'As the deer pants for streams of water, so my soul pants for you, my God' (Psalm 42:1). It's worth reading the whole psalm to catch a glimpse of their desperation. In the midst of a dark and miserable time, the writers long to connect with God in a meaningful way. They dig deep into their collective memory to pull out the qualities of God they remember and have proved in past experience, as a motivation to continue to seek His face now. Their heart's desire is to be face to face with Him again. It makes me wonder if I have ever desired God with this sort of nothing-else-will-do passion.

Asaph, another psalmist, uses a similar pattern in Psalm 78, where he captures in vivid, poetic language, the journey and history of the Israelites in the great Exodus. In spite of seeing extraordinary miracles every day and enjoying God's protection, the Israelites doubted that God could provide for them in the barren desert and constantly felt that life was unfair. How wrong they were on both counts. For forty years God gave them a daily physical feast of heavenly manna, and neither their clothes nor their shoes wore out. Many people, including my friends in Chapters 6 and 10, have found that even in times that seem as spiritually dry, desolate and dusty as the Judean desert, God can indeed come to meet us and provide us with sustenance and refreshment.

I love the story of Corrie ten Boom, who knew the reality of this when she and her sister, Betsie, were sent to Ravensbrück concentration camp, near Berlin, in 1944.[46] Their family had been hiding Jews in a secret room in their old Dutch house from which the family watchmaking business operated. In circumstances that were far from fair and in spite of the 'salty' horrors of the camp, they refused to give in to hatred and bitterness, discovering that when they fixed their eyes on Jesus, they could even thank God for the infestation of fleas which kept the camp guards away, thus allowing them the freedom to pray and read the Bible, which Corrie had miraculously smuggled in with them.

Remarkably, Betsie, who suffered from weaker health, was still able to say with conviction that in her darkest experience God was deeper than any chasm into which they might have

---

[46] Corrie ten Boom, *The Hiding Place* (London: Hodder & Stoughton, 2004).

fallen. So, even with all the deprivations of a Nazi death camp she found a way to 'feast' at the meagre table that was set before her, because she did it with Him. For Corrie, the choice to press into Jesus in the midst of unspeakable suffering was made based both on the firm foundation of God's character and promises, and on her walk with Him over the previous fifty years or more. She too was able to say without a trace of resentment that God was faithful regardless of circumstance. Whether the sun shone or her sister died of starvation in Ravensbrück, He was still the same good God. In the light and in the darkness her trust remained, despite being tested to the limit.

The 'Why' question

When life feels unfair, it's not unusual to try to elicit answers from God about some of the 'dishes' He serves us from His 'menu'; but we can be inadvertently sucked into a trading mentality. If God can give us a satisfactory, or even just an adequate answer, to why some of these things happen to or around us, then we imagine that we will be content to carry on. If He explains 'a', then we offer to return with 'b'. But God never planned this relationship to be on any basis of trade. He is not a merchant looking for profit; He is a Father looking for His children. We are to be family, not retailers or business transactors.

My husband, Bernard, has had cause to consider this himself over the past forty years or so. His own father was tragically killed in a car accident when Bernard was just seventeen years old. As the eldest son, overnight he became the father-figure in his family. Crucially, when the terrible news was broken to him, he felt God clearly reassure him that He would be his Father from now on.

Over the years, fathering with grace has become one of the hallmarks of his character and calling; but there is no doubt that he still misses his dad. One day, when he was praying and wondering why such a drastic event, which has coloured his life as well as that of his mother and brothers for all these years, was allowed to happen, he felt God come close. 'If I told you My reasons son, would that make it alright?' In a moment of unhindered clarity, Bernard realised that the grief he continues to carry would not and could not be eradicated by any explanation, not even one which came directly from heaven. No words would be sufficient to make it 'OK'. The loss is the loss, the pain is the pain regardless; and it's real. The wound was deep, heartrendingly painful and excruciatingly real, because so was his love for his father; but it is clean because God came in with His healing love. The scar is ever-present, but the blow was not allowed to fester or become infected with bitterness; it is evidence of wrestling and engaging in the real-life battle that has been assigned to him.

With the realisation of God's close presence came a measure of peace; Bernard knew he could trust such things to his loving Heavenly Father, and deliberately choose to rejoice and 'feast' on all the riches he has discovered and enjoyed in His presence over the years. So today, he is none the wiser as to why this 'unfair' trauma was allowed into his life, but he can and does declare with confidence that 'God is good; all the time'.

Palate-cleanser questions

- How has God used your circumstances to catch your attention and compel you to look to Him?

- What unchanging truths have you discovered about the character of God through your experience in recent years?

- How can you guard against becoming a 'professional' Christian? What is the path back to an authentic, Spirit-filled life that reflects the character of Jesus?

12. Staying Hungry and Thirsty

Blessed are those who hunger and thirst for righteousness, for they will be filled.
(Matthew 5:6)

Authentic feasting

It is crucial that we live in a place of ongoing hunger and thirst for Jesus and His righteousness – not just for experiences, goose-bump moments, slick conferences or the latest Christian fad or show in town; only Him. If He is truly your heart's desire, then you can be fairly sure that He will somehow take away everything else so that you are compelled to connect with Him in the way you were designed to do. Nothing and no one else will satisfy that spiritual part of us which is searching for its true home.

Our hearts can long for the kind of testimony which sounds dramatic, even glamorous, but in reality, most of us shrink back from the roads which might take us to such dark places as my friends have experienced or which cause us personal pain that leaves us desperate for God's intervention; certainly, we would not choose them voluntarily. The cost is just too great. However, if we stay connected with God, we will find that, should we be required to walk such a road, or 'eat' such a 'meal', something else is going on beyond that which we can see, even in the midst of our trials. With Paul and Timothy, we will arrive at a place where we can also say, 'Praise be to the God and Father of our Lord Jesus Christ, the Father of compassion and the God of all comfort, who comforts us in *all* our troubles, so that we can comfort those in any trouble with the comfort we ourselves receive from God' (2 Corinthians 1:3-4, my emphasis).

Part of the blessing of an undesirable 'menu' is the opportunity to help others to tuck into their own, and to do so with understanding and empathy rather than just well-meaning epithets, which might otherwise sound trite and hollow. Our own 'feasting' gives weight and credibility to our declarations of God's goodness, and fosters faith and trust as we help others chew, swallow and embrace the 'dish' they have been served.

How we react to our own 'menu' is dependent on a number of factors. Since we are uniquely created, there is no one-size-fits-all textbook template for this. Our mental wiring, our DNA, our personalities, our learning styles, our maturity and how the nature/nurture themes have played out in our growth and development all play a part. Nevertheless, all of us, if we engage with the 'feast' set before us, can discover that the anvil of suffering is also, potentially, the table of feasting.

I remember the complicated parental administration of preventative travel sickness tablets when I was a child. Tiny as they were, they were thoroughly revolting, and in an effort to make sure that we didn't spit them out, we were made to swallow them crushed up and mixed with juice or milk. I'm not sure it helped much then, and it's certainly not what we need at this particular table. Self-help is of no consequence here and neither is a pseudo-psychobabble, mind-over-matter approach. God is not serving medicine at His banqueting table. He is meeting you where you are with kindness, grace, tenderness, lavish love and His very self. What more could we desire? Like King David in the Psalms, sometimes we will need to speak to our soul and remind ourselves of the things that are unfailingly true, and of God's faithfulness in the past.

In another story, told by C H Spurgeon, a minister was walking through the countryside one day and stopped at a farm where he gratefully accepted a drink of water and spoke with the farmer by the barn. Above it he saw a large weathervane on the roof swinging in the breeze; beneath it were inscribed the words: 'God is good'. The preacher was disturbed by this and thought it unseemly and inappropriate to have such declamatory words associated with something so variable as the direction of the wind. 'No,' the farmer replied, 'you have misunderstood the meaning. God is love no matter which way the wind blows.'[47] God's truth is not as capricious as the wind; thank goodness.

What do you know with the same certainty as that farmer? What has God said to you in the past that you can hold onto in the present? In the face of a 'menu' that turns your stomach and tempts you to push it away in loathing and disgust, you cannot 'feast' unless you trust the One who invited you in the first place. Neither can I. Knowing memory verses cognitively is of no value unless those words become 'flesh', with the same degree of substance that Jesus, 'The Word', did (John 1:14) – a living reality demonstrated in practice and the three dimensions of real life.

When Jesus was tempted in the desert, He rebuked Satan using words from the Scriptures; He was effectively wielding the 'sword of the Spirit' as depicted among the armour Paul talks about in Ephesians 6. Each time we handle this 'sword', it gives us spiritual 'muscle'; the more we use it, the more effective and skilled we will become and the more our faith is moved into action.

We have established that our faith is ignited, stirred and grown when we hear God's Word, in which case, it is wise for us to dwell on those words, allowing them to reach every part of us. Soaking, or marinating in His truths will be of inestimable

---

[47] Original source unknown.

value. Speaking these things out loud in declaration helps reinforce them in our minds and hearts. Clearly there is some connection between our hearing and our spirits; announcing God's Word verbally shifts unbelief, doubt and fears, which all lurk within us; hearing anew causes us to rise up in faith to take firm hold of those truths. Our eyes and heads then, inevitably, lift once more and we are ready, not just to 'soldier on', but to actively take ground for the kingdom of God. If we can 'feast' on His words and promises, learning to become one 'who correctly handles the word of truth' (2 Timothy 2:15), we will be well equipped for life at His table no matter what we are served.

The Bible is jam-packed with encouraging, meaty verses to nourish you in your faith. Whether you feel ambushed by doubts, anxieties and fears or isolated, aimless and distracted, there are plenty of counteracting words from God to displace such things. Again, this is not mind over matter, but an opportunity to dig into a 'banquet' of truths that will bring life and freedom. I urge you to seek them out and maybe opt to read them out loud to reinforce their impact; allow your spirit to engage with their faith-building truths. This 'course' could be a welcome 'palate cleanser', or perhaps an *amuse bouche*... To avoid spiritual indigestion (there are so many to choose from), it might be worth picking out one or two which are particularly relevant to you right now and placing them somewhere where you can read them daily until they are really part of you and become your new default.

What is true versus Truth

Paul wrote a letter to one early church which included instructions about how a husband needs to work out his responsibility to love his wife, in particular, 'to make her holy, cleansing her by the washing with water through the word' (Ephesians 5:26). The goal is to help her differentiate God's voice from all the others clamouring for her attention. Using this picture, my husband and I have coined the useful phrase, 'a darn good Word-washing' – much used over the years when we are seeking to remind ourselves of God's truth in the face of circumstances which sometimes appear counter to His kingdom values, or when I find it particularly difficult to see the wood for the trees. It's not just wives who need this!

We need to work hard to discern between what looks true with our human eyes, but which can send us off course, and what we know is The Truth as defined by Almighty God. This is the reality of spiritual warfare: battling to see His face, hear His voice, remember His promises and stay sensitive to His prods and promptings when the noise of our circumstances threatens to drown Him out.

It's important to remember who we are: children of God bought at great cost, and a dwelling place for the Holy Spirit. We are being trained here for the life to come, lived eternally in His presence. We are no longer 'ordinary', but the mark of God is on our hearts; we have been justified through Jesus and now walk clean, forgiven and holy.

Good news for all who long for significance: being a child of God comes with inherent significance; it's part of your birthright. We no longer belong to ourselves, but to the One who made, loved and called us. There are facts here that we know, but sometimes we forget that we know! Timely reminders keep us on track and actively stirred in our faith. That confidence is not presumption, neither is it misplaced. Trusting that God means everything He has said and that He cannot go back on His word brings us a gritty conviction and tenacity that banishes anxiety.

Repeating God's promises is not a magic mantra, but a reassertion of the certainty of those promises and the unshakeable nature of His words which supply us with fresh life, strength, courage and determination, even in the worst of circumstances, because those words, and God Himself, will not and cannot change. This is the place from which we can 'enter his gates with thanksgiving and his courts with praise' (Psalm 100:4).

Thanksgiving forces our eyes back on Him, so we are in correct alignment with Him; it compels our souls once again to acknowledge His lordship and His goodness in our lives. From this springs praise: proclaiming the qualities and character of God; reminding ourselves who He is – Lord and King, Holy, Creator, Omnipotent, Worthy One, Father, Mercy-bringer, Hope-giver, Death-defeater – and as many of His attributes as we can describe in our limited vocabulary, or in the prayer language given to us by the Holy Spirit.

Worship is the natural progression of thanksgiving and praise. David tells us this is the place where God lives – inhabiting the praise of His people.[48] So, where there is true thanksgiving, praise and worship, God's presence will be apparent; there will be no room for Satan and his demons. Worship is warfare!

Making such declarations is a challenge to our own emotions because their truths often fly in the face of how we feel. I'm not talking about proclaiming fiction or wishes as fact; that's foolishness at best, delusional at worst. However, replacing what we feel with what we truly know takes grit and discipline, but it is an important and worthwhile practice.

This is another way of speaking to our souls and encouraging ourselves to press forward in God. So, for instance, it may be true that we feel weak, but God says His 'power is made perfect in weakness' (2 Corinthians 12:9); which will you choose to believe? His truth trumps our feeling of what's true every time; but we must choose to embrace it, stand on it and live it out in faith, or we will be bullied by the enemy and fall prey to every fear that blows around us.

The Israelites wasted forty years tramping around the Judean desert until the original generation that left Egypt had died, all because they chose to shrink away from the promise of God to

---

[48] Psalm 22:3, WEB.

give them the land in the light of the report which ten out of twelve research spies brought back about the size of the opposition they would meet there. It was true that the giants who occupied the land were tall, strong and fierce to the point that the spies saw themselves as insects that would be crushed by them. However, The Truth was that God had already said, 'Send some men to explore the land of Canaan, *which I am giving to the Israelites*' (Numbers 13:2, my emphasis). In the light of God's intentions, it should have been a done deal. Tragically, only Joshua and Caleb out of the twelve explorers heard and recognised God's promise as such. His truth could only be seen by those whose eyes were fixed firmly on God and His faithful promises. Only those two trusted that God would do exactly as He had said. Their only addendum was a caution not to ignore God or give way to fear; they were convinced God was with them and were ready to go (Numbers 14:9). Disastrously, the unbelief of the other ten became a stumbling block for the whole nation; that generation perished in the desert and never set foot in the Promised Land.

Feasting in the mundane

One of the keys to 'feasting' is to nurture a spirit that 'feasts' on, or connects with, the greatness and character of God despite the circumstances. I first stumbled across this, pretty much by accident, in the two summers I spent between my years as a degree student, working at a busy guest house/conference centre in Kent.

My job was to be part of a team of chambermaids/waitresses doing whatever was required. It wasn't a demanding job mentally, and while I enjoyed interacting with the guests, most of the tasks were repetitive and dull. This is where I found that my mind could be happily employed in deliberate communion with God while my hands got on with the menial demands of sweeping three flights of stairs. There was no one else around, the acoustics were interesting, and I could sing. So I sang – a repertoire of old choruses and hymns that I had learned as a child. As I began to worship, I found that not only did the cleaning feel less arduous, but I had inadvertently discovered the same gentle delights of easy companionship with God that Brother Lawrence enjoyed during the twenty-five years he served as a Carmelite monk in France almost 300 years earlier. When people came to mind, I prayed for them; but in choosing to declare the characteristics of God in the lyrics of my songs, the chores became times of intimacy with Him. I had unearthed the valuable truth that even times of dullness which require perseverance can be a means of building up spiritual muscle.

We don't grow much during the mountaintop glory times of victory or ease; but we don't live on the mountains either. Tangible growth happens in the dry deserts where real life is worked out and where faith can thrive when we resolve to keep pushing determinedly into God – His words and His presence. When space is created – voluntarily or through circumstance – to hear His voice in a fresh way, we can see boredom banished and have a fresh understanding of God's purposes for us. Such a season actually lends itself to new discoveries of faith. It may not look spectacular but it is supernatural. That's exactly what I found, and it was so pleasant that I sometimes lingered longer than was strictly necessary on the stairs in order to spin out the special moments before returning to other duties.

Fast-forward almost thirty years to a grey afternoon alone in our rental apartment overlooking the Atlantic Ocean in Cape Town. There, feeling rather melancholy and homesick, I felt God drop a thought into my head so clearly that I knew it was truly Him speaking to me. 'There are days you have endured which I had planned for you to enjoy, because I had purposed that you press into Me.' I stood stock still and hoped it was a word for someone else… It wasn't. I was the only one there.

A rebuke is never pleasant and one direct from heaven even less so, but the words resonated in my heart like a vibrating tuning fork. The joy I used to seek out while sweeping the stairs as a student all those years ago, had withered to become, at times, little more than a grim and dogged determination to simply plod through the days despite my circumstances, rather than choosing to pursue His face and company in them. I had missed out.

More distressing than that, God's heart was somehow bruised by the choices I had made; apparently, amazingly, He had missed out too. I had been robbed of His presence and delight, but more remarkably, He had wanted to enjoy the time with me, so was also robbed. What a sobering revelation.

I knew the verse: 'Come near to God and he will come near to you' (James 4:8); but in that season I had forgotten the truth of another: 'The LORD your God is with you, he is mighty to save. He will take great delight in you, he will quiet you with his love, he will rejoice over you with singing' (Zephaniah 3:17, NIV 1984). That's a song I want to hear more often. The lyrics must be fantastic, but I may have to wait for heaven to really hear them clearly.

I don't know about you, but I still find it extraordinary that God should want to be in our company. The kindness of His rebuke made me squirm but brought me both to my knees and to my senses. I had inadvertently grieved the Holy Spirit. I needed to repent. How could I have been so foolish as to miss beautiful opportunities to 'feast' with Him and resort to simply 'getting through' or 'getting by'? I don't know, except to say that we all need our wits about us. Our old enemy is still on his scheduled programme to 'steal ... kill and destroy' (John 10:10), just as he has always been.

Jesus recognised Satan as a source of lies, and experience confirms that he still whispers destructive untruths to us about our past, present and future if we allow him access. Satan has no 'feast' to offer us, just a paltry 'menu' of heartache, bitterness, misery and despair meted out in tiny deceptive portions, disguised under headings such as 'my rights', 'personal fulfilment' or 'speaking my mind'. They will all prove sour in the end compared with the 'dishes' God has prepared for us.

Reminders and memorials

Over the past few years I have found the huge benefit of keeping a journal in order to remind me of the things I have felt God saying to me. For years I resisted doing it as the legalist in me knew I couldn't keep up a daily commitment of writing. However, with a new measure of grace, I have found that I can dip in and out of it as I please; it has been a huge benefit. Years down the road, these are now 'feasts' in their own right, allowing me to look back and trace the paths along which God has brought me. These journals serve as a written memorial to the goodness and faithfulness of God.

In the Old Testament, setting up memorials was an effective visual method of keeping history alive for the Hebrew people, in a similar way to the cycle of annual feasts. Altars of stone marked points along their journey which, years later, could be explained to generations who didn't have first-hand knowledge of the events they depicted.

Jacob set one up at Bethel, where he had his dream of the angels ascending and descending a ladder to heaven. He set up the exact stone (Genesis 28:18) which he had been using as a not-very-comfortable pillow, as a memorial pillar. Moses erected an altar at the place where Aaron and his companion, Hur, had held up his arms in prayer while the Amalekites and Israelites fought in the valley below. God gave His people victory and Moses called his prayer memorial, 'The LORD is my Banner' (Exodus 17:15).

Later, Joshua built a commemorative altar on the border of Jericho using twelve stones (one for each tribe), which had been carried from the dry bed of the River Jordan over which they miraculously crossed, to mark how God had fulfilled His promise of bringing the Israelites safely to the land of Canaan (Joshua 4:20). These memorials represented the community's pilgrimage out of a place of slavery and into one of freedom;

they made it deliberately hard to forget God's hand in their history and His presence in their present.

My personal favourite, if I'm allowed such a thing, is the one that Samuel set up as a reminder that the Israelites had pledged themselves to God after yet another season of rebellion. When God graciously delivered the Philistines into their hands, 'Samuel took a stone and set it up … He named it Ebenezer, saying, "Thus far the LORD has helped us"' (1 Samuel 7:12). What a wonderful name; the connotations here are much more positive than those we associate with that other literary Ebenezer: Charles Dickens' Scrooge! Stopping along the journey or, to keep our metaphor consistent, pausing between 'courses', to recall the many and various ways God has come to our aid, rescued us from harm, walked with us through the valleys, comforted us in the dark places and championed us through muddle and confusion, is a worthwhile exercise.

I would be able to point to numerous 'Ebenezers' in my life; countless times He has made His presence known to guide, rebuke, discipline, encourage, strengthen, teach and refresh me. In fact, Samuel's story so captured my imagination that, as a child, I procured a small quartz rock from a Devon beach one summer holiday which I duly called 'Ebenezer'. Over the years I have used it as both a bookend and a doorstop, but it still makes me smile when I see it; it's an effective visual prompt to remember God's faithfulness to me.

Conquering

In the much-quoted passage from Romans 8, Paul reflects on the way he has suffered through many trials which he deems inconsequential in the light of all the things that he anticipates God has for Him. Most people would relish the opportunity to recount the stories of hazardous adventures and brushes with death, probably embellishing them for the benefit of their audience and enjoying the attention. Not so Paul. Dismissing them as irrelevant and refusing to dwell on them, he chooses instead to focus on his Deliverer and boldly states, 'in all these things we are more than conquerors through him who loved us' (Romans 8:37). If we could get to grips with these truths in the same way as Paul, we would have some serious spiritual muscle.

For many of us, the reality is that in all our 'things', we might be more accurately described as 'barely survivors', 'hanging by a thread' or 'desperately trying to keep our heads above water'. Conquering can feel as unfamiliar to us as space walking. All too often, we express ourselves as being *under* our circumstances when the Bible expressly tells us that we are *over* them. 'And God raised us up with Christ and seated us with him in the heavenly realms in Christ Jesus' (Ephesians 2:6). There are currently numerous stories on the Christian circuit of individuals 'visiting the heavenly courts'. Whatever you make of those is irrelevant here, but don't be dazzled; God says that's already where we live and sit, if we are *'in Christ'* (Galatians 3:28; Colossians 2:10, my emphasis).

As you look at your life today, it might look less than heavenly, but spiritually, that's our residential address. Don't let the enemy or anyone else persuade you any differently. God has declared it to be so, Himself. If you need some extra encouragement, seek out relevant Bible passages and allow yourself time and space to enjoy a delightful 'banquet' bursting with living truths about the promises God has made you. Let yourself 'feed' on the richness of His words and the extraordinary dimensions of His unfailing love, and allow yourself to be satisfied.

Remaining hungry and thirsty for Him is irresistible to Him, for He longs to reveal Himself to us at the 'feasting table'. Like the crowds by the Sea of Galilee, your faith will be renewed so you too can say, 'He has done everything well' (Mark 7:37).

Palate-cleanser questions

- Which specific aspects of the nature and character of God have kept you walking with Him during times of trial?

- 'There are days you have endured which I had planned for you to enjoy, because I had purposed that you press into Me.' Consider whether this might also be something God is saying to you today.

- What memorials have you set up, real or metaphorical, at those places of encounter?

13. In the Presence of My Enemies

Your foes roared in the place where you met with us ...
(Psalm 74:4)

I wonder if David's talk of enemies in Psalm 23 puzzles you. What can it mean to feast 'in the presence of [our] enemies' (Psalm 23:5)? Who are they, and where do they come from? Surely enemies are to be avoided? If we do inadvertently acquire some along life's journey, we have instructions to love them, turn the other cheek and pray for them, don't we?[49]

You don't need to have been following Jesus very long to appreciate that you are in a battle. I find it wryly amusing that there is still a view which sees Christians as weak, fear-filled, insipid losers in need of either a good psychiatrist or an emotional crutch. My experience is that the real-deal Jesus-followers are far more likely to be seasoned warriors who have borne the knocks and blows of life with a weathered tenacity, humour and tested faith that would probably leave many others curled up in a foetal ball of defeat.

---

[49] Matthew 5:38-48.

Armour for the battle

We've established that the reality of a relationship with Him is not one long vacation, or an offer to glide through life without a care in the world. Indeed, Paul describes, in Ephesians 6, an entire set of spiritual armour which believers need to strap on, so that they can engage effectively in the business of each day. If there are no enemies to fight, then this would obviously be unnecessary. There would be no point in having our characters shaped and our faith matured if it were not going to be required in the course of life. Why train a warrior if they are going to stay at home for the rest of their lives?

Spiritual warfare is more than a turn of phrase; there is a reality to the ongoing battle the enemy wages and by surrendering to God and His plans we find ourselves in the crosshairs of the enemy, a tangible threat to his schemes for world destruction and domination. Let's not shrink back from that; rather, let's be the threat ourselves, boldly taking back what belongs to our King.

We live in a world which does not yet acknowledge Jesus as Sovereign, which marches to the beat of a different, and increasingly secular, drum. You don't have to be a full-time minister to be in ministry; followers of Jesus are *all* priests (1 Peter 2:9), kings (Revelation 1:6, KJV) and ambassadors (2 Corinthians 5:20) of Christ's kingdom on earth and therefore, by definition, under attack from majority values and contemporary spirits most of the time. There is good news too: you only need to read the New Testament to be assured that this war has already been won. There was never any doubt of that; it is not an equal struggle between God and Satan – remember, Satan is a created being; God is not.

However, we do live in that twilight time between the now and the not-yet of God winding up history, where the heat is still very much on. Once we discover our true identity as children of God, reflecting His image and walking in His ways, we become a potential threat to the kingdom of darkness which seeks to discredit God in every way it can. Satan wants us to fail. He plots and plans for our downfall and laughs in glee during the times we feel God has abandoned us, or let us down; when we fail; when we are confused, doubt-filled and questioning the reality of God's goodness, purposes and/or power in our lives. He is relentless in looking for opportunities to blindside us, to cause us to stumble, and then heap guilt and shame on us.

If he can destroy us completely, then he will; if he can simply steal our joy, dismantle our hope, unsettle our conviction, wreck our focus or shatter our resolve, then he will. Don't panic. This is far from inevitable; simply a recognition of the spiritual backdrop to our daily lives and a reminder of the world beyond the physical one in front of us, alerting us not to be naïve. It does, however, remind us that we are involved in a serious endeavour for which we must depend on Jesus alone for our resource and strength. None of us can stand up to our enemy in our own strength.

The world, the flesh and the devil

I hope you haven't made enemies of any sort in the course of your life, but here we are focusing specifically on spiritual enemies. In old-fashioned language, this triumvirate of foes is known as: 'the world, the flesh and the devil'.

Let's examine them in reverse order.

The devil
The devil has become a mythical figure in the modern era. Many people in Western culture no longer believe in him at all, which suits him just fine. Caricature and cartoons have reduced the idea of such a being to a benign joke on a par with the tooth fairy or the Easter bunny. In fact, there is nothing funny about our enemy, whether we call him Lucifer, Beelzebub or Belial; the Bible presents him as a real and formidable foe who perpetually accuses, tempts and schemes to sabotage our faith.

Satan is a fallen angel – Lucifer – who was once 'the seal of perfection, full of wisdom and perfect in beauty' (Ezekiel 28:12). Becoming dissatisfied with just being part of the heavenly host, he coveted God's omnipotence and this colossal pride led to an insatiable desire to receive worship himself. The battle lines were drawn. He, and the minions who had supported his attempted coup in heaven, were banished forever. Consequently, he was banished from heaven and fell to the earth where, thanks to the decision of Adam and Eve to choose something other than God as their source, all the good things God had designed for them fell forfeit to Satan.[50]

Satan is the antithesis of everything God is. God lives in Trinitarian relationship with the Son and the Holy Spirit; Satan is an individual. God is eternal; Satan is temporal, doomed to destruction. God is Spirit; Satan, as has already been pointed out, is a created being – the battle is not on an equal footing, despite what the devil so often suggests to us. He is not all-present, all-knowing or all-powerful as God is. Throughout history, the foremost desire of his rebellious heart has been to dislodge Jesus from His throne in any way he can. His entire mission is to discredit, mar, deceive and destroy anything and everything that bears any hint of the stamp of God; that not only includes us as part of humanity but, being adopted into His family – loved, saved and serving Him – puts us at the top of his hit-list. Because we are made in God's image, we draw the enemy's attention to ourselves. We have what he longed for; it was given to us at creation but he tried in vain to gain it by his deception, arrogance and sedition. Now the devil is mad as hell about it and, in his unbridled rage, seeks to destroy anyone who bears that image or reflects God's glory.

Let's not be naïve; this enemy wants to destroy you just as much as he wants to destroy me, whether by a single all-out blow, by the entrapment of addiction or oppression, or by the persistent attrition of smaller, attractive temptations which will

---

[50] Ezekiel 28:12-19; Luke 10:18; Revelation 12:4.

bring about the slow suffocation of our faith, like a python with a rabbit. He doesn't care which it is; the end result is the same. His whole unflagging strategy is to distort, warp or besmirch the image of God in us so that he brings continual dishonour to the pinnacle of creation – us – and therefore, more pertinently, to the One who created us. He still defies the order of heaven. Any behaviour he can stimulate, provoke, or encourage in us by thought, word or deed to serve his diabolical purpose is a temporary win for him.

Alternatively, he will work hard to render us ineffective as pursuers and extenders of God's kingdom; apathy works just as well for him as outright rebellion and, in fact, its very subtlety can seduce us into a state of dangerous unawareness. While we are no threat to him or his dark kingdom, he is less inclined to waste his attention on us. As we have already observed, he is, and will be until history wraps up, the ultimate thief who 'comes to steal and kill and destroy' (John 10:10).

Since Jesus gave His life for our salvation, the devil no longer has ownership of us in the way he did before we handed the keys of our lives over to Jesus. He was defeated at the cross, when Jesus laid down His life, disarming all the powers and rulers of the spiritual realm, and demonstrating His triumph as victor over them (Colossians 2:15). Satan has been conquered; he is a vanquished foe. Neither death nor a hand-carved garden tomb could hold the powerful Prince of Peace. This was the crushing of Satan's head prophesied back in the Garden of Eden.[51] We now live in the good of that fulfilment, but often need reminding of its validity and of our authorised citizenship in the kingdom of God.

So, while our enemy is 'down' he is not yet 'out', in the parlance of the boxing ring. The outcome of the battle has been decided by the events on a hill outside Jerusalem more than 2,000 years ago; but there are still a few rounds to go.

---

[51] Genesis 3:15.

The victory is still contested although it can never be overturned. Satan hasn't given up yet; he won't acknowledge his legal defeat until the end of time, and gives up ground reluctantly until then. We are no longer 'easy prey', but the devil will still try his luck to inveigle a way into our lives from time to time, often sowing seeds of doubt about the character of God, just as he did in Eden,[52] or the certainty of our salvation. He continually probes for our weak spots with a view to exploiting them for his own ends while God refines and delights in our growing faith.

Since we belong to Jesus, our foe cannot stand when we are truly walking in step with Him. To resist the enemy's onslaughts or seductions, we must be well anchored in God our rock. Without Him and His resources, we are as vulnerable to attack as a buck on the open plains of Africa. Obstinate faith that refuses to back down in the face of disappointments and discouragements is faith that can move mountains.

The flesh

Our *flesh* refers to our old sinful way of life, the nature that operated in us before we transitioned from outside God's family to inside it. This old nature is dead and yet because we are in a continual process of sanctification, or becoming more like Jesus, those old defaults can still raise their ugly heads from time to time. Our well-worn thought patterns and paths are not eradicated overnight into perfection; you and I become transformed in behaviour by having them regenerated.

This type of transformation means replacing old thoughts with new ones; it requires training so that our attitudes and behaviours fall into line with God's kingdom: faith-filled ways, rather than our old selfish, fleshly ways. This is how we learn new ways of approaching and dealing with life. We exchange grumbling for thanksgiving, anger for peace, bitterness for

---

[52] Genesis 3:1.

forgiveness, despair for hope, stinginess for generosity, lying for truth, fear of the future for trust in God's perfect plan, etc.

Leaving an empty space or vacuum and hoping for the best would be a disaster. We must replace one thing with its life-bringing opposite, and can break out from that old life because it doesn't have mastery over us any more; we have a new Master. We are no longer sinners as such, but saints who occasionally sin. As and when, and if, that may happen, we can quickly put it right, leaning into God's mercy and His provision of repentance.

Repentance is the wonderful means by which we can remain in open, clean, uncluttered relationship with Him. The word refers not just to sorrow or regret for particular behaviour, but a turning away from it accompanied by a change of mind and heart. It requires deliberate steps towards God's way and His standards for kingdom life. This is so much more than simply turning over a new leaf – a practice doomed to failure as demonstrated in the broken resolutions of every New Year. Once again, this is not merely mind over matter, but an inner revolution; a heart change; a realignment. Forgiveness flows freely from this place, because of Jesus. We need to truly grasp that.

We are forgiven, clean, pure and righteous before God. Jesus made sure of that. Our old nature is gone forever; the Holy Spirit lives in us. You might not feel as though that is true when life's demands impinge on your certainty, and you may struggle with living in the good of that – even Paul did;[53] but it doesn't change the facts. It's imperative that we keep coming back to this theological truth, reminding ourselves of what God says, until every fibre of our being has determinedly grasped, absorbed and manifested it.

The Holy Spirit is our constant companion, and the (only) source of dynamic power which can sustain this radical transformation; He helps us walk consistently in the life of

---

[53] Romans 7:7-25.

holiness to which we have been called. Our own resources of self-effort or self-will alone will not be able to effect such a change but the life, death, resurrection and ascension of Jesus can and do. It's really a load off our shoulders; the terrible pressure to 'be good' is gone because in Him we are just that in the eyes of God. Sin is no longer inevitable; our flesh no longer dictates our behaviour.

The world
The world simply means our societal culture which is intrinsically and inevitably opposed to God's ways. In other words, the trends and desires that most of our contemporaries run after but which are usually temporary, transient and often the opposite of Jesus' kingdom culture. This would include unfettered consumerism, materialism, self-gratification, self-promotion, insularism, individualism, forms of political correctness which fail to value the truth of Jesus, sexual promiscuity, gloating at the misfortune of others, ignoring the poor and marginalised and so on.

The devil can use any or all of these, as well as a thousand others, to give us excuses to justify certain behaviours which are contrary to God's best for us. Alternatively, he may try to dazzle us with the benefits these things claim to offer us: acceptance, admiration, prosperity, health, removal from adversity, fulfilment, etc. There is something appealing and alluring about these things, and the modern world of social media is constantly thrusting this sort of lie in our faces. It is frequently in the spotlight for the unnerving implications it has in contributing to degenerating mental health, particularly so in adolescents who have been encouraged to construct a counterfeit world based on distorted values – primarily image – and who then tend to derive their value from the ephemeral number of 'likes' or 'hits' they may or may not receive for each posting. Cyber bullying has become such a scourge in the West that some have even been driven to suicide. Such tragedies have Satan laughing all the way back to hell.[54]

Facing your enemies

While your enemies may not have recognisable names, I'm sure you will know some of those who regularly nip at your heels: anxiety, jealousy, pride, dishonesty, rage, wounding words, discontent, unprofitable comparison with others, ugly talk, resentment, bad language, unhelpful images, greed, gossip, impatience, fear, doubt, unrestrained appetites, meanness, self-pity… Doubtless you can enhance the list. However, when we stand up against these things and choose an opposite spirit, we are making a stand for the kingdom of God and attesting to the lordship of Christ in our lives. We declare His goodness, faithfulness, righteousness and peace, and enjoy the privilege and abundance of blessings that are ours by the simple virtue of being part of His family. This is not just a confession or declaration of things which are undoubtedly true; it becomes a battle cry to defy our spiritual enemies.

It's fairly easy to quietly agree that God is good, but I have an increasing desire to strap on that Ephesians 6 armour, yell that truth into the face of the enemy and see him limp away with a whimper, making him think twice about suggesting anything less certain to me.

Laying hold of all God's promises to us reminds both us and our enemies of who we are, as well as *whose* we are. Once again, faith rises as we hear the Word of God, the One who is already the vanquishing conqueror of all enemies. We too can take a strong stand against every onslaught and ambush they may throw at us. There is an intrinsic power in words, so speaking out God's promises and truth is an effective, powerful way of

---

[54] https://inews.co.uk/news/health/suicide-rates-teenagers-young-people-social-media-141803 (accessed 8th February 2020). Further statistics can be obtained from the Office for National Statistics.

massaging those unchanging biblical accuracies into our souls. We've seen that Jesus faced down Satan in the desert using the written Scriptures as His weapon of choice. For every thrust that the devil made, Jesus parried with a biblical quote.

Spiritual weapons

Paul told one New Testament church, 'The weapons we fight with are not the weapons of the world. On the contrary, they have divine power to demolish strongholds' (2 Corinthians 10:4). They were living in a city where maritime trade was the foundation of the economy and where the Greek deity of beauty, love, pleasure and fertility, Aphrodite, was worshipped. Here new believers were steeped in alternative influences which extolled wisdom and promiscuity, revered beatific utterances and scoffed at the idea of bodily resurrection as well as indulging in spiritual idolatry. Discipleship was not an abstract idea in this city; there was a lot of ungodliness to deal with, but Paul was pointing out that the tools for the job were, and still are, available from heaven.

Anything that claims to have a strong hold on you, be it past sin or things that harass, torment, defile, compel, deceive, weaken, enslave or entice you, will not, cannot, flourish where God's kingdom rule is established. All this makes our 'feasting' an act of war against the forces of darkness and the kingdom of the enemy.

Every time we give glory to God in word or worship, or consider the attributes of Jesus and proclaim His pre-eminence, the enemy trembles. Such declarations are part of us as members of the Church – the bride of Christ – expressing His unmatched beauty and wisdom to every spirit and power throughout the realms of heaven, hell and earth. In speaking or singing them out, we are not only articulating truths to ourselves, but declaring war 'against the rulers, against the authorities, against the powers of this dark world and against the spiritual forces of evil in the heavenly realms' (Ephesians 6:12).

Intimacy at the 'table'

None of these enemies is included in the invitation to our 'feast'. Thank goodness! However, it seems that they are allowed to watch. 'In the presence of ...' (Psalm 23:5) means in the vicinity of; or, we might say, 'within spitting distance'. We can see them, or at least the temptations they offer, and they can see us. However, it is the ultimate rebuke for them that they are allowed to observe and see the degree of intimacy we have with our divine Host which has been denied them ever since Lucifer fell, and which they want to deny us.

Imagine how shocked the hordes of hell must be. They expected God to accuse us just as they do, to point out our failures, flaws and falls, and watch us tumble into eternal desolation. Instead they are paralysed into inaction while they watch the Saviour welcome us, usher us to our personally assigned and prepared seats, then serve us, feed us, embrace us and laugh with us, wrapping His garment of acceptance and unconditional love around us. The enemies must quake and cringe, falling back in confused alarm as God celebrates over us and rejoices with singing.[55] What an excruciating punishment for them to know that they are forever separated from any positive relationship with their Maker; the offer of salvation does not extend to them. To be corralled as observers only must be torture; more so as it is compounded by the wonderful bill of fare we are poised to enjoy – love, joy, peace and grace in generous measure. Here there is a lavish, abundant overflow of a nature and dimension they will never understand or experience; it's for invited guests only.

The enemies are unable to cross the divine threshold without permission. It's as though they are on a leash which allows them

---

[55] Zephaniah 3:17.

so far, but no further. They cannot stand in the presence of our holy, righteous God, where mercy and forgiveness flow, and He will not allow them to gloat over us.

So, our 'feasting' takes on two dimensions: as both warfare and intimacy. All the resources of heaven are ours to enjoy as we 'feast', taking up not just our citizenship, but our sonship in God's family.[56] Even daughters can be sons in this context because this isn't about gender but about inheritance, and the daughters are included – something that was not a cultural norm in biblical times. This would have been another huge mental leap in understanding for the early Church.

All the fruits of the Spirit: 'love, joy, peace, patience, kindness, goodness, faithfulness, gentleness and self-control',[57] which are by definition characteristics of God and therefore reflections of His glory, are also ours, though they will need time and space to grow in our lives. In reality, much of God's shaping of us and conforming us to the image of Jesus[58] involves nurturing the growth of these characteristics through the rough and tumble of daily life. It's not glamorous but it is divine in its source and intent.

We 'feast' on these aspects of Jesus so they become part of our own character, and because of who we 'eat' with, we are also able to choose to 'feast' on the 'menu' of our circumstances. Without the accompanying servings of grace, love, joy and peace, we would find some of our 'dishes' very hard to swallow. Indeed, when life overwhelms us with challenge, or sorrow, or heartache, or stress, I truly believe that like any good parent, God takes a few mouthfuls Himself to help us finish the meal.

If you've ever endured a painful meal with an overtired toddler, then you probably slipped the occasional spoonful into your own mouth from time to time to speed up the process and get through the serving. (I wish someone had helped me out

---

56 Romans 8:16-17; 9:26
57 Galatians 5:22-23, NIV 1984.
58 Romans 8:29.

with that infernal liver!) Those were meals that you shared, not just in a literal, physical sense, but emotionally too. Hebrews says that Jesus is not 'unable to feel sympathy for our weaknesses, but we have one who has been tempted in every way, just as we are – yet he did not sin' (Hebrews 4:15). He understands our situations and is all too aware of the constraints of humanity and the difficulties we face. After all, He Himself was just as human as He was God, so has first-hand knowledge of an earthly life. In living here with the same restrictions for thirty-three years, Jesus knows exactly what that entails in all its inherent weakness.

On His own journey to Golgotha, Simon of Cyrene helped Jesus to bear the burden of the timber crossbeam which would be used at His crucifixion. At that moment, the humanity of Jesus was suffering; He needed and received help when it was required. I read that and breathe a sigh of relief; Jesus understands my weakness too. In identifying with us so completely as a human being, Jesus is well positioned to empathise with each obstacle, each triumph as well as with each tragedy that comes our way.

Choose your focus

The stark choice before us is to either focus on those enemies arrayed around us, or to be so taken up with the face and company of our host that we either ignore their shadowy, peripheral presence, or learn to forget about them completely. While they lurk beyond the borders of the invited circle, they cannot harm us or influence us unless we choose to regain eye contact with them and fall prey again to their influence to draw us away from our 'feast' and back into their miserable company.

With God on our side we are poised to trample our enemies underfoot. Heaven forbid that we invite them to come and sit with us too… But be on your guard, for we cannot be sitting in both places.

I remember hearing about the faith of radical evangelist Smith Wigglesworth whose ministry was consistently marked by remarkable outbreaks of the supernatural. One night, the story goes, he woke from a deep sleep to find an evil presence and shadowy satanic figure lurking near his bed. 'Oh,' said the drowsy man, dismissively. 'It's only you.' He promptly turned over and, quite nonplussed, went back to sleep.[59] Wigglesworth knew that although the enemy is very real, he is also very defeated! His own intimacy with Christ – something which he nurtured and attended to assiduously – kept him focused on the Lover of his soul to the exclusion of all other influences, including the insidious schemes of hell.

To be so hungry, so thirsty for Jesus' company, to be so taken up with His person that our enemies become as irrelevant as they were to Smith Wigglesworth, is not some self-generated, saccharine-soaked, holier-than-thou sentimental whimsy or delusional emotionalism. No; it is to be as consumed with passion, focus and pure delight as lovers who share their space with such intimacy that they are unfazed by anything else that is going on around them. Their lack of general awareness draws a smile from observers but indicates a very specific, concentrated focal point; a nucleus of attention around which everything else orbits. That is the kind of delightful relationship we are talking about: to be so engaged with Jesus that we are oblivious to all else. It means that we no longer just want the things God can give us, fix for us or provide for us; we just want Him. Should He choose to withdraw those other blessings, our desire for Him alone would remain undiminished.

What will it take to get you to such a place of hunger, of thirst and of trust?

Not so long ago, we were presented with a similarly provocative challenge. In a particularly difficult period when financial resources seemed to be drying up rapidly, we were

---

[59] www.charismamag.com/spirit/spiritual-warfare/21781-good-news-bad-news-about-spiritual-warfare (accessed 6th February 2018).

asking God, 'How long must this go on?' A faithful, praying friend who has walked with us for many years suggested that instead of asking God, 'How long?', we might surrender our wills and say, 'Father, feel free to take as long as You like.' I think it's accurate to say that our initial reaction was to flinch; the alternative reaction seemed impossible, but the words hit home; we knew that he was right. Our spirits wanted to protest, but were silenced in the presence of such profound truth. This was exactly the attitude God was consistently seeking to cultivate in our hearts: being satisfied with Him alone. It was time to stop resisting. It wasn't an easy word to swallow, but I will always be grateful for this revelation as well as for a friendship solid and strong enough to present such a raw challenge to us and call us on to something deeper in God. Surrendering to God's timing did not suddenly make everything easy, but it did bring a supernatural freedom of far greater value than an instant windfall. It was also a reminder that true, inner joy is peace and confidence in God during any trial, rather than the removal of all trials.

I love the perspective of Isobel Kuhn, reflecting on her days as a missionary working with her husband during the 1930s–50s. It reminds me, firstly, that our experiences are never quite as unique as we sometimes imagine. She compared her challenges, in mission and at home, with those of the gladiators facing their opponents in the Colosseum. Daily, she recognised 'giants' who tried to derail and destroy the peace of her heart and mind. The biggest fight of all she called 'the gladiatorial struggle with self-pity, a most unglamorous opponent'.[60] This is a 'giant' I have encountered myself many times and so I valued her honest confession all the more; perhaps you are familiar with him yourself. He usually comes calling when my eyes have moved from Jesus, dallied too long on the irritations and the injustices – both real and perceived – of daily life, and I fall into

---

[60] Isobel Kuhn, *In the Arena* (Singapore: OMF Books, 1988).

the deadly comparison trap so carefully laid by the artfully calculating enemy.

My journal has an entry from 28th December 2014 in which I was trying to get to grips with this. It reads:

> Of course, I have focused way too much on the giants and become 'a grasshopper in my own eyes'.[61] The weapons of God are more mighty, more powerful, more effective than any man-made or hell-made weapon. It is laughable. The enemy will be overcome by 'the breath of his mouth'.[62] Courage! Don't be afraid! He is bigger than all the giants combined. Yes, they're real; but He is greater (bigger-er!)... So, like the Proverbs 31 lady, I will 'laugh at the days to come'![63]

We have to remember, as Isobel understood, that whatever combatants present themselves along our path, 'The purpose of the Arena experience is not for our punishment; it is that God might be revealed.'[64] Where He is revealed, His name is exalted and His kingdom comes. That assignment is entrusted to us as emissaries and children of God. It's just too important to allow the enemy to wheedle us away from God's 'feasting table'.

---

[61] See Numbers 13:33.
[62] 2 Thessalonians 2:8.
[63] Proverbs 31:25.
[64] Kuhn, *In the Arena*.

Palate-cleanser questions

- Read Ephesians 6; identify the pieces of spiritual armour Paul itemises and consider their purpose in your life.

- Which are 'the enemies', 'who regularly nip at your heels'?

- How can declaring truths about who you are in God 'nourish' your soul?

14. Enemy Tactics

...there is nothing new under the sun.
(Ecclesiastes 1:9)

The reality of our adversary

At the beginning of the book of Job, Satan appeared before God, who asked, "'Where have you come from?'" Satan answered the LORD, "From roaming throughout the earth, going to and fro on it'" (Job 1:7). His time is spent as a wily opportunist, searching for anyone who is open to his whispers and lies. His cronies, spirits and demons, do the same, wandering in desolate places looking for somewhere to claim as their own. No wonder Peter warns the believers to 'be alert', comparing the enemy's tactics with those of a lion who ravenously stalks their prey.[65] I once watched a lioness bring down a wildebeest a mere twenty metres from me, and trust me, it was neither fun nor harmless.

Satan has the same intention as that top predator. We can banish all those caricatures of a cheeky guy in a red jumpsuit, with horns and a toasting fork, stage-managing harmless mischief.

---

[65] 1 Peter 5:8.

Recognising the reality of the spiritual battle which goes on around us is as wise spiritually as it is in any military confrontation. Victory is not won by turning and running, nor by disengaging from the tough assignment ahead. This is an urgent, ongoing engagement, but we do not need to be frightened. We must be alert to its reality without being cowed by it. Believers need to be walking in community with other soldiers and confronting the enemy with warriors alongside us.

The disciple John wrote in one of his letters, 'the one who is in you is greater than the one who is in the world' (1 John 4:4). This makes all the difference, of course. We overcome the enemy in our spiritual walk because of the One who walks with us and lives in us; hence, we are aware, but also equipped to live confidently and unafraid.

To illustrate the reality and crafty machinations of our spiritual adversaries, we'll see how some of them tend to manifest. It is in no way an exhaustive list, but by shedding light on a few of these tactics I hope you find yourself more equipped to recognise them and, therefore, less likely to be ambushed.

Jesus called Satan out as a persistent liar in John 8:44, but he has a thousand other disguises and strategies to compel us to walk away from the safety and intimacy of the 'feasting table' and move within the reach of his dark influence.

Each enemy strategy works hard to lure us into agreements of regret, hatred, crippling sorrow, revenge, unforgiveness and/or bitterness. We might conclude that some of these choices are natural or justifiable given the circumstances that birth them, and without God's grace and strength they are practically unavoidable. But God offers a different path when we reject knee-jerk reactions to a 'dish' and, instead, embrace the 'menu' by pressing into the arms of Jesus, our 'feasting' companion.

1. Distraction
Peter wanted the early Church to be aware of the relentless enemy attacks on their faith and wrote two letters warning them

to look out for spiritual trip-hazards including ungodly thinking, allowing their physical appetites to control their choices, and dangerous false teaching, any of which could knock them off course. He was well placed to give advice, since that same enemy once made a request to unleash a personal onslaught on him. Indeed, the devil came very close to using Peter to distract Jesus from His crucial mission, attempting to use him as 'a stumbling block' which resulted in a stern, authoritative rebuke, 'Get behind me, Satan!' (Matthew 16:23). That's an incredibly strong reaction from Jesus; I imagine that Peter recoiled a little. It certainly reveals a part of the character of Jesus which jars sharply with the gentle, mild, loving, affirming Jesus on whom we prefer to focus.

Jesus' rebuke here is an indication of the seriousness of the devil's intent and perfectly consistent with the character of a holy God before whom Satan cannot stand (unless given permission to do so, as we see in the book of Job). We've acknowledged that sometimes God does rebuke us, which is not the same as a punishment; it serves to open our eyes to a better, safer behaviour as, when and if, we stray from His path. This is a sign of a good father – which is not the same as an indulgent father. We might equate discipline with abuse or unrestrained anger; sadly, some of us have experienced just that, but it's not the discipline the Bible speaks about. Love and godly discipline are two sides of the same coin. They are not opposites, despite what contemporary culture may tell you; both are required to produce well-adjusted, mature offspring.

Love without discipline is indulgence; discipline without love is abuse. 'Training in righteousness'[66] includes embracing both; it prepares and matures us to recognise every strategy and encounter with the enemy, equipping us with the same confidence and authority which Jesus wielded against the enemy when he tried to work through Peter that day.

---

[66] 2 Timothy 3:16.

2. Diversion and comparison

Comparing ourselves with others is a classic diversionary tactic which has real traction in an era of social media where the lives of others are relentlessly thrown in our faces. We know that the images are curated, airbrushed and Photoshopped, and yet they still have the power to make us see ourselves as lacking. If we're more occupied with what everyone else is doing than whether we are following Jesus closely, then we can't be focusing on Him.

We are easily, if temporarily, dazzled by the excitement and success of others, which can inevitably leave us feeling self-critical and sorry for ourselves. There will always be someone who is funnier, smarter, richer, fitter (you fill in the blanks) than ourselves. So what? The important truths are the ones God has spoken to us. If we believe that, then let's resolve to 'feast' on those and live in the empowerment and confidence they bring: loved, chosen, called, adopted, blessed, forgiven, free, cherished, etc. That's a much more nutritious 'meal' than comparing ourselves with anyone else.

3. Resentment

This unpleasant 'dish' naturally follows on from the first and harks back to that petulant protestation of yesteryear, 'It's not fair!' If we allow ourselves to be distracted from our own 'meal' in order to examine the 'menu' of others, we may dwell on that to the point that we become increasingly dissatisfied with our own 'dish'. When we perceive our own 'serving' to be disproportionately laden with unpleasant, difficult or bitter elements, then rather than decreasing the impact of their sharpness by focusing on the company of our Host, we easily revert to childish sulking or outright resentment. This can only be squashed down for so long. Sooner or later, unless it's dealt with, its poison is going to overflow into every aspect of life.

Resentment isolates us from our communities, family and 'fellow diners', convincing us that we are the only one having a hard time, and that no one else can possibly understand what we're going through. Another enemy lie. This usually sets the stage for throwing our 'meal' in God's face and accusing Him of no longer caring for us. We can begin to make all sorts of excuses for our attitude as we try to justify our ungodly response. However, God can't forgive an excuse; but He does run to meet us with His all-sufficient cleansing when we confess our sin. However much we might stutter over that word 'sin', recognising ungodly behaviours or attitudes for what they are and leaving them at the cross is the only way to deal with it and throw off its malevolent entanglement.

4. Subterfuge and compromise

St Augustine was acutely aware of the enemy devices frequently used to entice him away from his focus on God, not occasionally, but habitually. Rather than an obvious diversion, he found it was the old habits and sins of his past which would come murmuring into his mind, seductively presenting themselves as harmless and appealing to his flesh:

> It was my old 'mistresses', the most vain and trifling of things that held me back. They tugged gently at the sleeve of my flesh, and whispered softly in my ear: 'Can you really part from us? From this moment on shall we never be with you again?' What shameful things they suggested! And then I hardly heard them speaking, for they were not openly contradicting me face to face, but rather stood muttering softly behind my back and they slyly tugged at me from behind as I left them, trying to make me look back at them. In this way they held me back as I hesitated to shake them loose, snatch myself away and leap over to the place where you, Lord, were calling me.[67]

[67] St Augustine, *Confessions* (AD397-400) (London: Penguin Classics; New Impression edition, 2002).

The subterfuge of Augustine's enemies appealed to his vanity, but by not allowing his gaze to be distracted from his Saviour and refusing to compromise his faith, he was able to 'leap' away from them and return to the place of safety prepared and assigned for him at the table, in spite of their insistent tuggings and his own initial hesitation.

5. Regret

One of the most powerful missionary stories I've ever heard, and which still regularly provokes and inspires me, is that of Dr Helen Roseveare who served God as a doctor in the Congo in the 1950s and 1960s.[68] In most aspects of her life she was measured, regularly calculating whether something was worth her time, money or attention; but with the reckless enthusiasm of youth, she had told God that she would go anywhere and do anything for Him, regardless of the cost. Time showed that He took her words seriously.

Helen remained passionate about giving God her all, despite the demanding conditions and deprivations of Africa where she learned to 'feast'. Her resolve was tested to the limit when Belgium granted independence and Civil War broke out there in 1964. Soldiers vented their hatred and anger for every injustice and hardship they had ever endured under white rule.

One night, the government troops came through the hospital campus and into her bungalow. Soldiers wrecked her house, indiscriminately breaking things before they threw Helen on the floor, kicked, beat and abused her, finally raping her in her own home. Miraculously, she felt God's supernatural peace throughout the terrifying ordeal.

Finally, she was dragged outside and tied to a tree where her violators continued to mock her until one of them discovered a manuscript she had been writing about the things God had been

---

[68] Dr Helen Roseveare, *Give Me This Mountain* (Fearn, Scotland: Christian Focus Publications, 2010); *He Gave Us a Valley* (Fearn, Scotland: Christian Focus Publications, 2006).

doing in the Congo over the past eleven years. It was the only copy and it was burned in front of her as the men laughed. Visceral nausea must have gripped her as, surrounded by people who hated her, Helen wondered whether this was the end of life's road. All the years, all the sacrifice, all the hardship and slog, was this what it all came down to in the end? I think I would have asked the same question.

How could anyone possibly find an opportunity to 'feast' in the face of such violent vindictiveness? Helen's enemies were not just spiritual that night, but big, three-dimensional realities with faces twisted with hostility; why didn't God rescue her? Was it really worth it, after all?

> the minute I [asked] that, God's Holy Spirit settled over that terrible scene, and He began to speak to me … 'Helen, my daughter Helen, you've been asking the wrong question all your life. Helen, the question is not, "Is it worth it?" The question is: "Am I worthy?" Am I, the Lord Jesus who gave His life for you, worthy for you to make this kind of sacrifice for me?' And God broke [my] heart …[69]

In a blink, Helen's focus shifted from the pain and trauma of a nightmare experience to the loving eyes of the One who had first called her there; she bent her will to His, and acquiesced. Her testimony was always that despite the pain and humiliation of that night, it faded into a sense of privilege in the light of all Jesus had done for her. Banishing regret about her ordeal, or even about being in Africa, she felt honoured to have been given a glimpse of the sufferings of Jesus and the opportunity to somehow share in them a little.

---

[69] From a talk by Dr George Murray: *A Mission Driven by Worship of Christ, WAM* (USA, 1999): ryanlee.org/wam/wam-1999-session-1.adp (accessed 27th March 2018). Also: www.bible.com/en-GB/reading-plans/3550-finding-forgiveness/day/16. (accessed 18th November 2019).

Regret would have been an understandable response. 'Why did I ever bother?' might well have passed my own lips. In many ways Helen was a victim of the circumstances of a nation in uproar, undergoing a vortex of violent transition in which she was unwittingly caught. And yet, she never saw herself as a victim. Here is the power of overcoming, intimate 'feasting', eclipsing even the cruellest trial and deepest wounds, resisting the promptings of regret.

Do you see why I find her story so powerful?

6. Revenge

The theme of a thousand movies, Satan feeds this desire in hearts which look for payback after injustices have been done. Revenge goes beyond justice, though; it takes us to a place where we give our verdict on people and circumstances, cutting God out of the picture.

Another missionary, Elisabeth Elliot, could have fallen prey to this enemy assault. Her husband Jim and four of his friends were killed by Auca, or Huaorani, Indians in Ecuador, an unreached people group at the time.[70] Their passion to share the good news of Jesus Christ was not without risk, but their commitment to Christ and His cause were paramount. Tragically, several weeks after first making contact and delivering friendly gifts to this group, Jim and his four friends were murdered on the sandy spit of ground where they had landed their plane.

Wouldn't you think that Elisabeth would have been justified in wanting revenge on those who robbed her of her husband and her young daughter of a father? The old adage that 'hurt people, hurt people' is a truism. Conversely, it's possible that 'forgiven people, forgive people'. You can't rationalise forgiveness.

---

[70] Elisabeth Elliot, *Through Gates of Splendour* (Milton Keynes: Authentic, 2005).

Elisabeth, her daughter, Valerie, and Rachel Saint (whose father, Nate, was one of the five men killed), all later went to live among that tribe. Literally living 'in the presence of [her] enemies' (Psalm 23:5), she demonstrated the revolutionary power of forgiveness by her own undimmed passion for Jesus. Rejecting any desire for revenge and refusing to wallow in unmitigated sorrow, she 'feasted' through horrendous circumstances, just as Uncle Robin did, as we saw earlier. Effectively, she declared war on the satanic swarm swirling around her, and not only stood her ground, but took territory for the Kingdom of God as, one by one, members of the tribe bowed their knees and made Jesus Christ their Lord. Elisabeth understood that we are not responsible for the events that unfold in our lives, only for our response to them and our obedience to Him.

Sometimes we will be 'feasting' with tears streaming down our faces, and Jesus will be right there weeping with us; then He will dry our tears, mend our broken hearts and put us back together more aware than ever of His immeasurable love. Her story reminds me that it is inappropriate for me to harbour grudges and hurts against others when God's forgiveness is so full and freeing.

7. Accusation

Satan has long been known as an accuser of God's people.[71] This tactic takes particular advantage of those who are prone to introspection and reflective deliberation. Quickly exploiting the opportunity to slide through the doorway of our thoughts, the enemy weaves tales of our unworthiness and often resorts to dragging up images from our pre-Jesus lives to wave in our face as though they disqualify us from His grace. Slyly, he takes us on a path of condemnation from which he offers no way back.

Paul told the church in Rome that 'there is now no condemnation for those who are in Christ Jesus' (Romans 8:1).

---

[71] Revelation 12:10.

Many of us are prone to mentally beating ourselves up over one thing or another. Thus Paul's statement helps me evaluate the source of some of those thoughts. Yes, the Holy Spirit will convict us of sin but always with generous provision to repent and be forgiven, to enjoy God's mercy and restoration; it's a demonstration of divine kindness. The devil, however, does the opposite, driving home a message of defeat and overwhelming hopelessness – a cul-de-sac of his own making. So, forewarned is forearmed; consider the thought by all means, but use your God-given discernment to recognise its source, and act accordingly.

8. Gossip

There's an old Jewish morality tale about a notorious gossip who caused havoc in her town with her quick tongue and sly speech; she would spread a rumour without hesitation, never bothering to find out the truth of any matter. The exasperated villagers eventually appealed to the old rabbi to help them curb her thoughtless and occasionally vindictive behaviour. After some thought and prayer, the wise man took a dead chicken, gave it to the woman and told her to go home, plucking the feathers along the way. Bemused, the woman did so, scattering feathers into the air as she walked. Some time later, the rabbi caught up with her and instructed her that she must now retrace her steps and gather every single feather into a bag. Realising the futility of the task, since the wind had since blown the plumage who knows where, the woman saw the implications of her own behaviour and reformed her ways.[72] Gossip, lies and accusation tend to enjoy one another's company and at such moments, the advice to tuck in close to Jesus and keep our gaze locked on His, is paramount.

---

[72] Original source unknown.

9. Pride

This one comes in many forms. We all know about personal pride which tends to puff us up with the value born of our own achievements, whether we parade it in public or cosset ourselves in it in private. More subtle is corporate pride, fuelled by allegiance to a nation, family name or tribe – collectives that are not recognised by Jesus' Kingdom.[73] Persuading us that our particular group or denomination is The Place where God is funnelling blessing is particularly insidious. His blessing is evident across the global spectrum of believers, but there's often a little part of us which, if we're honest, would like the monopoly on cutting-edge kingdom action. In that case, have a care for all the unnamed heroes of the faith labouring in countries closed to the gospel, where underground churches thrive in secret and persecution is a painful reality. Let's say 'No!' to perpetuating ungodly competition or jostling for a position or a 'name' wherever we worship.

Jesus' attitude was the polar opposite; He 'made Himself of no reputation' (Philippians 2:7 NKJV). That's an active verb: *made* – He took deliberate, intentional steps towards staying hidden, out of sight, in the background. It's also the absolute antithesis of the mentality which believes that the size of the building, the pizazz of presentation and volume of band is what it's all about. Going big does not necessarily equate with going deep. Nouveau Christian celebrities may garner crowds and acclaim but may not necessarily be reflecting the attitude of Jesus. It must be a tricky line to hold. The Bible demonstrates over and over again that God is more interested in what happens in stables than in stadiums.

10. Fear

Paul reminded his young disciple, 'For God has not given us a spirit of fear, but of power and of love and of a sound mind' (2 Timothy 1:7, NKJV). He identifies fear not as an abstract

---

[73] Galatians 3:28.

feeling, but as a spirit which doesn't come from God; its origin is demonic. That's a sobering observation. We live in a world which is increasingly ruled by fears of every variety: fear for your children, of the future, of financial crash, of climatic disasters, of governmental failures, of loneliness, dementia... the list is long, depressing and fed by a culture which exploits those fears for its own ends, usually financial. Of course, there are legitimate concerns for all of us, but fear is not to be the drumbeat of our life.

We were made to walk in step with our Creator, trusting Him with our whole self. That's not the equivalent of carrying a lucky amulet to protect ourselves. You've already read testimonies in this book of a number of God's children who knew disaster all too personally. The point is not that we're immune from it, but that God promises to walk with us faithfully through all of it. He will never abandon us,[74] so we do not need to give way to fear. His 'perfect love drives out fear' (1 John 4:18). Surely then, if we stay full to the brim with God's love by consistently receiving it from Him, there will simply be no space left in our hearts or minds for fear to enter, let alone occupy. Have a healthy fear of fire, but don't allow any enemy-induced fears to dictate how you are living.

Psalm 91 has been particularly relevant for me over the past twenty years or so, since we began to spend more time in South Africa as we responded to God's call. This is a country where life is cheap, violence is frequent, political corruption is the order of the day, malaria is a reality, high unemployment feeds discontent and AIDS has ravaged the population. Given the chance, fear can have a field day here. Time after time, I have felt God drawing me back to His promises:

> He who dwells in the shelter of the Most High
> will rest in the shadow of the Almighty.
> I will say of the LORD, 'He is my refuge and my fortress,

---

[74] Hebrews 13:5.

my God, in whom I trust.'
Surely He will save you from the fowler's snare
and from the deadly pestilence ...
You will not fear the terror of night,
nor the arrow that flies by day,
nor the pestilence that stalks in the darkness,
nor the plague that destroys at midday ... it will not
come near you ...
If you make the Most High your dwelling –
even the LORD, who is my refuge –
then no harm will befall you,
no disaster will come near your tent.
(Psalm 91:1-3,5-7,9-10, NIV 1984)

That doesn't make me reckless, but it does make me confident in the goodness of God, reduces my vulnerability to the insidious spirit of fear and allows me to know His peace in my heart and mind. Sometimes we need to fight to keep fear permanently outside our circle of 'feasting'.

11. Doubt

I think this is one of the sneakiest weapons in the enemy arsenal. Whoever said that a half-truth is more powerful than an outright lie was correct. Anything that raises a question about the goodness of God needs to be faced and rebuked very quickly.

Satan used this artful device of doubt back in Eden when he cunningly suggested to Eve that God wasn't quite as good as she had been led to believe. In four little words he set up a trip wire which sent her and Adam sprawling to destruction. 'Did God really say ...?' (Genesis 3:1). Sowing seeds of doubt in her mind set a trajectory for Eve down a slippery slope of deception and death, and he uses the same furtive trick with us. Has God really forbidden certain things? Did He truly deny us the pleasure of so many attractive pursuits?

The devil pushes us to the choice between binary right and wrong when God designed us to lean into Him and towards His consistent directions towards life rather than death. Be alert for things that can have a detrimental effect on your quality of 'feasting', even though they may not be wrong in and of themselves. Don't play this game with the devil; don't engage with the enemy's nonsense. We all wobble in our faith journey; some slip badly. If that's your story, then just ask Jesus to help you up, clean you up and keep pushing against the tide of lies to sit in that place next to Him at His 'table' where you can 'feast' again.

How enemies stumble and fall

A failsafe strategy for countering Satan remains, 'Submit … to God. Resist the devil, and he will flee from you' (James 4:7). That double strand piece of advice will always and unfailingly stand you in good stead when facing your enemy. He would like you to think that he still has authority over you as he either pelts or tosses temptations across your path; but as you stand firm, he has no option but to retreat. Don't be like the foolish person blindly falling into the pattern illustrated in Psalm 1, who walks, then stands, and subsequently sits with the type of company which doesn't uphold the things of God. That gradual and subtle seduction lulls us slowly, but effectively, into enemy territory. Let's be alert, aware and awake, without being neurotic or fearful.

Don't give Satan access to any part of your life either deliberately or inadvertently. Be wise about what you see and hear, where you go, who you spend time with and which influences you allow, or even welcome, into your mind and into your home. The Holy Spirit living in us is far more powerful than the evil which still influences so much of the world; we have no need to fear.

When lovers of Jesus are served 'dishes' to make the stoutest heart quail, the spiritual enemies get a front-row seat. Our intimacy with Jesus makes them scowl in vexation. Some of these enemies will be faced more than once, but as you grow in

Him you will be increasingly skilful in overcoming them and increasingly confident in the One who is by your side.

'Though I walk in the midst of trouble, you preserve my life; you stretch out your hand against the anger of my foes, with your right hand you save me. The LORD will fulfil His purpose for me' (Psalm 138:7-8, NIV 1984). That was David's testimony and it can be ours too. Digging deep into the resources of heaven we find joy, thanksgiving and a peace the world will never be able to fathom, all of which are beyond the reach of mortal ability.

We can also access the lavish grace of God, the rock-solid reality of His promises and find that these are still able to serve as protective armour for our hearts and minds. We don't need to abandon our faith, sulk, storm or give God ultimatums about changing the things which happen to us. No; we steadfastly refuse to blame God, claim He has abandoned us or assume He has been punishing us.

But we don't need to get weird either. It's never appropriate to thank God in some warped way for the behaviour of wicked or misguided people, to ask for persecution, for pain, suffering or loss itself. None of us needs to invite that or suggest to God that engaging with such a 'dish' will somehow prove our devotion to Him; as if anything we do could impress the One who calls light into existence with no more effort than speaking it.

Our thankfulness is always for His faithfulness, His presence and His grace through the trials. And then, my, how the enemies tremble. How they must quake in their collective boots as each syllable of God-honouring praise sucker-punches them full in the face! This is victorious 'feasting'.

Just imagine Jesus welcoming Helen Roseveare, or Elisabeth Elliot, to the spread He prepared for them, looking deeply into their eyes with arms opened wide in delight, and reminding them of His infinite, immeasurable love, even while the spiritual enemies are chattering with malevolence and grinding their teeth in frustration. In the words of another psalm: 'Though they plot evil against you and devise wicked schemes, they cannot succeed' (Psalm 21:11). In effect Jesus might say to them and to us, 'You don't need to worry, none of those you see ranged around you is able to touch so much as a hair on your head. I've got this. I've got you.'

Those who have chosen to 'feast' will agree with King David, 'You make known to me the path of life; you will fill me with joy in your presence, with eternal pleasures at your right hand' (Psalm 16:11). In the light of His presence, worship is our natural and appropriate response; declarations about God's truths rouse the warrior in our spirits.

These battles are real. David, a battle-scarred fighter himself, declares:

> When evil men advance against me …
> when my enemies and my foes attack me,
> they will stumble and fall …
> For in the day of trouble
> he will keep me safe in his dwelling;
> he will hide me in the shelter of his tabernacle
> and set me high upon a rock.
> Then my head will be exalted
> above the enemies who surround me;
> at His tabernacle will I sacrifice with shouts of joy;
> I will sing and make music to the LORD.
> (Psalm 27:2,5-6, NIV 1984)

We don't necessarily worship *because* of our troubles, but we surely can worship *in spite of* them; then we will find ourselves refreshed and replenished.

Victory

Every time we share the communion meal of bread and wine, in whatever format our tradition prefers, we are declaring God's ultimate victory over Satan. It's a symbolic reminder of how He overcomes every enemy, spirit, demon, stronghold, power and principality that sets itself up against Him. Paul tells us that a day will come when 'the Lord Jesus will overthrow [him] with the breath of his mouth' (2 Thessalonians 2:8); barely a cough, less than a sneeze, will banish him forever. Make no mistake, let's declare again, he is already a defeated foe, although he would have us believe otherwise and hold us bound in the paralysing fear that his lie can bring. Don't stand for it. Remind yourself of the truth once more; it bears frequent repetition.

Trust that God is not surprised by anything that finds its way onto your 'plate'. His 'table' is the one to stick at through thick and thin. He can make even the most monotonous selection of 'dishes' tasty. You'd think the manna God provided during the Exodus would have tasted pretty bland after forty years, but Moses took note of the taste of coriander and honey in it.[75] That's a detail that was important to God; His provision and blessing in the detail often goes beyond the basics. God can turn the ordinary, and even the distinctly unpalatable, into something exquisite.

Stories of overcomers remind me again that I need to be rooted in God's presence, rather than flitting from experience to experience or dipping in and out of my conscious, intentional walk with Him. God has a 'feast' for me whether I am in a dark place, a dry place or a place drenched with comfort, laughter and blessing. He does not change[76] and His abundant grace is poured out on me daily because of my position as a daughter of the King, not because of my performance. When the 'menu' is less appetising, that multifaceted grace can be known in greater measure.

I know that I may need to be careful what I ask for; God may choose to take me as seriously as He took Helen Roseveare. I must never play fast-and-loose with the things of God, and I

---

[75] Exodus 16:31.
[76] Malachi 3:6.

must certainly be sure to keep my gaze fixed on Him regardless of my circumstances.

Let's be clear: we don't need to 'eat' this banquet nervously, wondering whether those outlying, shadowy, shapeshifting figures we see will pounce on us at any second. Sheep graze safely when the shepherd watches over them, and we are 'feasting' right next to the ultimate Good Shepherd, Jesus.[77] There is no safer place to be. There is no room for fear here. Let's not give the enemy any space at all. In yet another of his psalms, David says, 'How abundant are the good things that you have stored up for those who fear you … In the shelter of your presence you hide them … you keep them safe in your dwelling' (Psalm 31:19-20). Thus guarded and secure, we can 'feast' without anxious misgivings and unease.

Adam and Eve engaged with the enemy, realised their blunder and consequently hid from God.[78] They could no longer bear His presence without being overwhelmed by their guilt and shame. Our challenge is to refute the enemy and instead of running from, run to, God – straight into His arms and onto the named chair at the 'table' set for us.

God's 'feasting table' is a place of unrestrained joy; it must be by definition, because it's where He is. If we don't fully know and revel in that, then the chances are that we are either focusing on those enemies, or at least engaging with them in some way. Where we fix our gaze will determine *where* we go, and *how* we go, into and through each day. What will you choose? Where will you 'feast'?

---

[77] See John 10:1-18.
[78] Genesis 3:8.

Palate-cleanser questions

- Of the eleven strategies listed, which one are you most alert for, and why?

- Which powerful truths about God, and about yourself as His child, do you habitually declare? How can you encourage yourself and nourish your soul more consistently with these certainties?

- Worship is a tried and tested weapon against the enemy. How do you make effective use of it?

Dessert

15. Intimacy: Feasting with the One I Love

The joy of the Father's house ruins us for the suburbs of religious mediocrity.[79]

If I were ever to get an invitation to one of those fancy Buckingham Palace-type dinners, it would be not only a massive surprise but, I suspect, a rather bittersweet experience. While I might enjoy the grandeur and dazzle of dressing up, and the inner buzz of being at such an exclusive banqueting affair, it would also be, I fear, formal, remote and more of a test of manners and etiquette than about my relationship with the Sovereign. While I see her image on coins and stamps most days, I have never met her. We don't write; we don't chat; we don't hang out in coffee shops, text, walk the countryside or watch movies together. She doesn't know me and I don't know her.

Recognition and revelation

There's a difference between knowing *about* your host and really *knowing* your host. If we are invited to feast with Jesus, then we can be quite sure that we are also invited to really, truly, deeply,

---

[79] Pete Greig, *Dirty Glory* (London: Hodder & Stoughton, 2016), p65.

actually, know Him. It has been said that the whole Bible is a love letter from God to us, intended to woo us, romance us and win us. Does that sound a bit sentimental?

The sort of relationship God had in mind for us to enjoy with Him, was one of closeness and transparency. It was not the relationship of a teacher and his students or a philosopher and his academic boffins; it was not that of service providers and clients, or even of pen pals. We were made in God's image[80] and, in community, to reflect the wonderful eternal dance (*perichoresis* is the magical-sounding word in the Greek) of the Trinity who exist in perfect unity based on mutual love and honour. In order to become all that God created us to be, we must find our place in that dance too.[81] This is not merely a philosophical or conceptual exercise; it requires so much more than a cognitive understanding. It requires both recognition and revelation.

We were created to share life with our Creator – to walk, talk, laugh, enjoy, discuss and share decisions and rule of the earth with Him. That's how it started, back in the garden where it all went so very wrong. We were also made with a God-ordained spiritual thirst which can only truly be quenched by God Himself. We are designed, one might say, with a God-shaped space at our very core, which requires Him and Him alone, to fill and satisfy us. We cannot be truly fulfilled by our own efforts at spirituality; that will only prove to be so much froth and bubble. Cultivating an ongoing, daily, spiritual hunger and thirst is the secret of spiritual maturity.

People whose heart and soul long and yearn for God for His own sake, rather than for what He can do for them, bring to them, provide for them or validate for them, are those who remain ever fervent in their desire for more of Him. Of course, because of His mercy, kindness and grace, He is well able to do

---

[80] Genesis 1:27.

[81] One of the reasons why I named my personal blog 'Dancing Through Chaos': dancingthroughchaos.wordpress.com/about/.

those things too, but He won't allow us to be truly satisfied with anything less than Himself. Without Him, we are as broken and bereft as Adam and Eve found themselves to be, banished from both their home and God's presence.

Sometimes we have to experience the profound misery of that crippling disconnection in order to realise that it's not where we should be living out our days. Like the prodigal in the parable[82] on realising that living with the pigs was not where he belonged, we need to repent, turn our faces and our feet to 'home', and start walking back to where we will be welcomed with open arms, forgiveness and a magnificent feast of celebration.

This is the place to which God's heart longs for us to return; an unfractured, uninterrupted intimacy. The whole unfurling of history is to this end. We tend to complicate it into something quite unrecognisable, full of busyness, good intentions, strivings, earnestness, attempts to impress God by self-sacrifice, attendance at meetings, even an abundance of 'ministry', all of which can lead to burnout and disappointment unless they are things God has actually asked of us.

'And what does the LORD require of you? To act justly and to love mercy and to *walk* humbly with your God' (Micah 6:8, my emphasis). Walking is not rushing; it implies rhythm, intention, action, engagement, direction and purpose.

Enoch was one of the few people who really grasped what it was to walk with God. In fact, for him it was such a reality that, the apocryphal story goes, it so happened that one day they were so much closer to God's house than Enoch's that God simply invited him to come in and stay forever. After a genealogical list of six generations who lived long lives, producing nothing of significant note except more sons to repeat the cycle, followed by dying, Genesis records Enoch's life and death as markedly different; Enoch simply walked off

---

[82] Luke 15:11-32.

into the distance with God and was never seen on earth again.[83] What an extraordinary passing. They had been talking together for 365 years already so presumably the temporal transitioned to the eternal with barely a blink for Enoch. This was a man who knew intimacy with his Maker at a deep level; he truly 'feasted'.

Three generations later, **Noah** had an intimacy with God which was also described in the same terms as someone who 'walked' with Him.[84]

Job thought he knew God, but it took myriad calamities and a maelstrom of sorrow and suffering (as we saw in Chapter 6) to take him beyond the confines of his own religious integrity, in which he had put so much trust, to the place where he could finally say, 'My ears had heard of you but now my eyes have seen you. Therefore ...' (Job 42:5-6). Not just education, but revelation at last!

Moses spoke to God face to face to the degree that he was physically altered by his proximity to the glory of God (Exodus 34:29-35). It freaked everyone else out – even his brother. No one else among the Israelites had that level of relationship with God, and it both disturbed and frightened them. God decreed that only Moses come and meet Him on top of Mount Sinai; neither the people nor the priests – even though they had consecrated themselves – were to be allowed to push their way up the mountain to see Him (Exodus 19:12-24). Mere curiosity was not enough to be allowed to follow Moses into God's presence.

Moses' heart was attuned to God and His presence in a way others apparently only wondered about. His longing and desperation to hear His Master's voice and see His face undoubtedly came from a place of understanding that in and of himself, he did not have the resources to provide what the multitude of escaped Hebrews needed, not just in terms of their

---

[83] Genesis 5:24.
[84] Genesis 6:9.

physical demands, but also in terms of leadership, governance and wisdom.

English author and evangelist Leonard Ravenhill publicly yearned for the same thing, and longed that all followers of Jesus would desire this kind of intimacy too. 'A daily glimpse at the Holy One would find us subdued by His omnipresence, staggered by his omnipotence, silenced by His omniscience and solemnised by His holiness. *His* holiness would become *our* holiness. Holiness teaching contradicted by unholy living is the bane of this hour.'[85] Strong words.

In times of pain it can feel as though God is shouting to us, calling to grab our attention through C S Lewis' megaphone. I would love to be so tuned in to God's voice that I can recognise Him in the smallest, quietest whisper too. This is how **Elijah** heard Him at Mount Horeb after a wind that splintered rocks, a devastating earthquake and a fierce fire. His was an encounter that also brought revelation.[86]

When it's difficult to hear God, the discipline of fasting is designed to sharpen our spiritual appetite while deliberately putting the physical desire for food to one side. That post-meal stupor that comes over us when we're replete tends to subsume our senses to all but sleep. By denying ourselves the physical satisfaction of food and using our time instead to nurture a conversation with our Father in prayer, study and intentional pursuit, we can often be more receptive to His voice.

Perhaps you think it's odd to talk about fasting when my subject is feasting, but by fasting from food we can focus on 'feasting' on the things and person of God. Remember that 'feasting' here is simply a metaphor for pushing into our vertical, spiritual relationship – a context in which the importance of recognition and revelation is often manifest.

---

85 Ravenhill, *Why Revival Tarries*, p34.
86 See 1 Kings 19.

'Who do you say I am?'[87]

Knowing who Jesus is, is key to 'feasting'. Even **John the Baptist** had a moment of uncertainty about Jesus' identity. He was the heralding prophet and relative of Jesus, who lived to prepare the way for the promised Messiah by announcing the coming of God's Kingdom and urging people to repent of their sins, change their mindsets, turn away from selfish living and get back on track with God. He even pointed Jesus out to his own followers as the One to follow, but when he was later languishing in prison, he began to waver in his conviction.[88] John needed a report from his friends to confirm that the works of Jesus were consistent with the kingdom life of the promised Messiah.

Likewise, **the disciples**, who lived in such close proximity to Jesus, needed to know this for sure. At a time when the crowds were saying that their rabbi must be a reincarnation of John the Baptist, Elijah or Jeremiah, Jesus asked them the question outright. It was Peter who spoke up and boldly stated his belief that Jesus was the Son of God; the true Messiah.[89] I wonder if the other eleven held their breath in surprise or nodded in heartfelt agreement, whether they would have said the same thing unprompted? Perhaps they had already come to this conclusion in the light of all they had seen and heard. Either way, it was a profoundly important moment for which Jesus commended Peter. Recognition and revelation.

Back in the boat, before **Peter** had his revelation, while being tossed about on the Sea of Galilee the disciples, you remember, were in fear for their lives. After Jesus had calmed that storm, they were all asking each other who He could be. Minutes later, when they landed on the far shore they were greeted by **Legion**, a seriously demonised man who roamed among the tombs, but

---

[87] Matthew 16:15.
[88] Matthew 11:2-3.
[89] Matthew 16:16; Mark 8:27-30.

who, somewhat ironically, knew exactly who Jesus was. 'What do you want with me, Jesus, Son of the Most High God?' (Mark 5:7). The evil spirits inside this tormented man recognised the approach of the One who had power to dethrone and eject them permanently from this poor soul, with just a word. In fact, they begged for mercy for they could not stand before Him; they were compelled to yield because of who they knew Jesus to be.

'Who do you say I am?' was effectively the same question Jesus asked **the Sanhedrin** during his illegal trial, and again, when He was taken before Pilate.[90] They had neither recognition nor revelation, and completely failed to understand who it was who stood in front of them. How calamitous, for it's the question on which all of history hangs.

Today, hundreds of years later, it is still the most important question anyone will ever answer.

Just as He has done through every generation, Jesus is still asking, 'Who do you say I am?' If you and I cannot say with Peter, 'You are the Messiah, the Son of the living God' (Matthew 16:16), then we will never know the joy of 'feasting' with the Saviour. We will not merely have made a serious mistake, but the most tragically foolish deduction of our lives, opting for a meaningless existence instead of the abundant life for which we were created. The consequences of our answer will be monumental.

The intimacy of the Marys

I love the passion of **Mary Magdalene,** who knew exactly who Jesus was. Her passion and courageous following of the itinerant rabbi was born out of her dramatic rescue from a life of torment, having been oppressed by not just one, but seven demons for part of her life (Luke 8:2). Her love and devotion for Jesus was the natural response of a grateful heart; she knew

---

[90] Mark 14:53-65; John 18:28-38.

the reality of His words of life, hope and healing. Whatever her previous life was, she left it to follow Jesus throughout His ministry, determined not to miss out, but to press in to His life-giving company. Her trust and faith in Him as both her liberator and as the promised Messiah is a provocation to me; an example of someone who has placed their entire being into His hands, who enjoyed the freedom of living in His sphere, and presumably who believed He was more than able to take care of the future.

Mary was last at the cross and first at the tomb, a witness of both the crucifixion and resurrection. Against all cultural norms, she was the one to whom Jesus chose to show Himself after His resurrection; a suitably unprecedented honour for an unprecedented occasion.

In contrast to the two disciples who walked the seven-mile road to Emmaus in Jesus' company without recognising Him (and despite inadvertently becoming part of what must have been one of the world's most compelling Bible studies ever), Mary, reluctant to leave the garden tomb, fell at His feet in recognition and worship on the basis of just one word from *her* Lord. That's how she referred to Him in reply to the angels who occupied the empty sepulchre and enquired after her distress. 'They have taken *my* Lord away … and I don't know where they have put him' (John 20:13, my emphasis). That personal pronoun reveals a subtle but material difference, and it unveils the depth of Mary's intimacy with Jesus. Her devotion was pure and personal; her joy on recognising Him, unrestrained and uninhibited.

It was Mary who was entrusted with delivering the message of Jesus' victory over death to the fearful disciples – another remarkable choice since in Jewish culture, the testimony of women was disregarded as worthless, even in a court of law.

Martha's sister, another **Mary**, also had a special relationship with Jesus. She is well remembered for sitting at His feet, a place of humility but close proximity, listening to His teaching – illegal in that culture where women were forbidden from studying sacred texts. Yet, Mary chose to be there rather than bustling about discharging the domestic duties which so consumed the thoughts of Martha. When the hostess expressed her frustration in an ill-disguised disgruntled appeal to her guest, it was the sister who had picked relationship over task who was commended by Jesus, 'Martha, Martha … you are worried and upset about many things, but few things are needed – or indeed only one. Mary has chosen what is better, and it will not be taken away from her' (Luke 10:41-42). By investing in those moments of 'feasting' on Jesus and His teaching, Mary was feeding her soul with nourishment which no physical meal could provide. She remained seated quietly for the sheer pleasure of enjoying His company. She wasn't looking for a specific 'word' for herself or so that He could somehow give credibility to her own ministry.

This Mary's motivation was also pure: to see His face; to hear His voice; to be in His presence. That was enough for her. I truly want it to be enough for me; but I wonder whether, in their place, I would have made Mary or Martha's choice. The good news is that the choice presents itself to me freshly each day, and if I have made a poor one in the past, like Mary, I can make the 'better' one today.

John 11:2 tells us that it was this 'same' Mary who poured perfume on Jesus and wiped his feet with her hair. Mark 14 also recounts a similar event; the details are slightly different. One account sees Martha serving – so presumably at her house – the other, also in Bethany, is at the home of a man called Simon the Leper.

Here is a devoted woman whose act of sacrificial worship, as Jesus predicted, has been told 'wherever the gospel is preached throughout the world' (Mark 14:9). She 'feasted' in, with and on the Person of Jesus with unrestrained delight, unfettered by the manners of the day and unconcerned by the opinions of any other attendee. She only had eyes, and a heart, for Him; a heart that was exultant and revelling in the freedom of unmerited forgiveness.

There is a similar story in Luke 7, of a meal in a Pharisee's house, during which an unnamed woman, notorious for her lifestyle, also poured expensive perfume from an alabaster jar over Jesus' feet.

The crucial part of the Luke story is the cultural audacity of a woman unwrapping her hair in public, lavishing shockingly expensive fragrance on the rabbi's skin-hardened feet and apparently not caring who was watching. Kissing Jesus' feet in an act of humble devotion, intimacy and self-abasement speaks of a parched soul who has found the one person who could assuage that thirst. Whatever burdens of shame, guilt, regret or emptiness the woman in Luke 7 came with were left at His feet where grace and mercy still flow.

First love

John refers to himself several times in his Gospel as 'the disciple whom Jesus loved' (John 13:23; 21:7,20). That's not arrogance or superiority, rather it's the declaration of a man who has understood how Jesus sees him; his use of repetition underlines his conviction of the fact. In our flailing modern culture, where relationships are so frequently sexualised regardless of gender, regrettably, some people have lost the joyful aspects, values and attractions of deep, honourable, same-sex friendships where integrity, dignity, adventure, intimacy, real heart-level communication, connection and laughter are foundational and pure. Whether we are aware of it or not, Western culture is being robbed of something precious.

Either Jesus and John had a closer friendship than some of the other men in the group, or John simply understood himself and/or Jesus better, and was at peace rather than discomforted by the unconditional nature of His affection. It would seem that the former fisherman connected with his emotions in a most unusual way. Clearly, they were relaxed in one another's company, but we shouldn't superimpose anachronistic, revisionist interpretations of our own. It was, after all, John who wrote three very challenging letters to his various friends concentrating primarily and provocatively on the subject of love.

The Greek language has four words for different types of love: *storge* (instinctual love such as between a parent and child); *philia* (brotherly affection); *eros* (romantic love and physical desire) and *agape* (unconditional and sacrificial). God's love for us is of the *agape* type; He absolutely wants the best for us. This is the love which flowed from Jesus to all those around Him as He helped His friends and listeners to understand their identity and purpose as designed by God.

Love was the topic Jesus highlighted in a letter written in heaven for the benefit of the Ephesian believers and entrusted to John through a revelatory vision he received in his old age, while exiled on the island of Patmos. The risen and ascended Jesus told him to write down what he saw, including seven fairly blistering letters to specific churches. Ephesus (in modern Turkey), was once a centre for trade and commerce as well as a religious centre where the goddess Artemis was worshipped, and where Paul's teaching caused the level of disquiet which led to rioting in the streets.[91]

In this missive, the church was praised for enduring and persevering through difficult times without giving up or becoming disheartened. This had been noted with approval in heaven; but then came a rebuke: 'Yet I hold this against you: You have forsaken your first love' (Revelation 2:4, NIV 1984). Jesus is grieved; God is distressed; the Holy Spirit is bruised. Those who once sought Him above all else, who prioritised their relationship and who reflected and responded to His passionate love had grown cold, passive, apathetic and lazy in nurturing their faith, and in pursuing Him.

First love is fiery, all-consuming and giddy; it makes everything glow and the simplest things special; it transforms both you and your circumstances, eclipsing your problems and

---

[91] See Acts 19.

transforming your perspective; it injects excited anticipation into the prospects and possibilities of the days that lie ahead. As sweethearts long to escape a crowd and share their time and company exclusively with one another, so Jesus longs that our hearts beat faster for Him; for a focused, undivided connection where companionship and rapport feed affection, and fond attachment gives way to a profound, life-enhancing, unbreakable bond. We cannot hide this kind of affinity; it overflows into our whole demeanour.

It was the loss of this kind of relationship that, as far as the Ephesian church was concerned, was being mourned in heaven. It is all too probably still a cause of sorrow over many others today. Since God does not regard churches as buildings, but as communities made up of individuals, we cannot escape the painful likelihood that Jesus' letter to the church at Ephesus might just as pertinently bear our own name.

It has taken me many years and some painful paths to begin to learn the art of savouring God, and so discover the reality and satisfaction of His company. There is so much more to still be discovered and I want to be vigilant about stoking the fire of first love. It's been a long road.

Palate-cleanser questions

- Recall the moment or season in which you answered Jesus' question, 'Who do you say I am?'

- Mary poured perfume on Jesus and broke all sorts of cultural protocols to express her devotion in a public place. Can you identify things which hold you back from unrestrained adoration and worship?

- How can you rekindle first love?

16. My Story

Where love sets the table the food tastes best.
(French Proverb)

An unquenched thirst

In 1986 I went to my first 'charismatic' Bible week after completing my degree. It was a week of camping with a church group I had only recently joined, and by going I forfeited my fledgling television career. My London agent was unimpressed that I had chosen some kind of religious festival over an opportunity to present *The Boat Show*. Understandable; but I absolutely knew that I had to be in the environs of a couple of marquees in East Sussex for a few days, although I didn't know why. Part of my conviction came through having very recently been filled with the Holy Spirit in a new way; a way I had been brought up to believe was dodgy at best, and quite possibly demonic. It was very perplexing.

My walk with Jesus throughout my student years had not been as close as I would have liked. I never resolved the conundrum I found between the fun I had with my non-Christian friends, and the downright dullness or, at the other end of the spectrum, the outright weirdness, of so many who eagerly bustled off to the Christian Union every week. You could say that I had tasted and seen the goodness of God,[92] but in truth, I had never 'feasted' with Him. While I couldn't shake off the realities of the gospel message or the relationship I had with God, there was a divine dissatisfaction within me. What I knew and had experienced so far in my life just didn't seem to be enough.

At the end of my tether and feeling pulled in two opposing directions, I finally sat on my squeaky bed and, feeling slightly embarrassed, said, 'Sorry, God; if this is as good as it gets, it's just not good enough.' No lightning struck. No audible voice came. I sat dejected, wondering how long the straining rope of my faith would hold out; unwilling to walk away and reluctant to tell anyone about my dilemma.

Not long before, in a state of befuddled desperation, I had sent off two letters to the only Christians I knew of who were working in television at that time. Since my entire family are of medical persuasion and employment, they could offer very little help in navigating the choppy waters of the media ocean which lay ahead of me. Somewhat surprisingly, both recipients sent replies which landed on the doormat soon after that rather combative prayer. One wrote back succinctly – and I paraphrase: 'Have a nice life.' Well, more or less. The other invited me to visit her.

So it was, a few weeks later, I found myself rather bemused, and then extremely surprised, to be sitting in her local pub having lunch with her when she asked me if I had been 'baptised in the Holy Spirit'?[93] Excuse me? My theological hackles raised a few inches. Wasn't this the flaky stuff I had been warned about as a teenager? Besides, I was here to talk about holding onto faith in the arena of a career in television, not to dissect doctrine.

In reality, I had become so thirsty for something more in my spiritual life that her excellent explanations of what and who the Holy Spirit is seemed not only logical, but had the ring of truth

---

[92] Psalm 34:8.
[93] Acts 2:1-4.

and the resonance of reality to them. Too much of my faith had been abstract and cognitive; too little had involved truly knowing, understanding grace or allowing God's love to liberate every part of me. On returning to her home, my new friend prayed for me and sat me in her garden to reflect and enjoy this new experience which, she assured me, would include speaking in a new prayer language. I'm not sure what I expected, but I felt absolutely nothing; I did not start leaping round the garden; no speaking in tongues ensued, nor did I burst onto the streets of Sussex preaching boldly and laying hands on the sick. I hope she wasn't too discouraged.

Hope

The train journey home was a mixture of relief that there was a possibility of more… something… anything… to be discovered in my spiritual life, yet disappointment that everything felt and looked exactly the same. Back in my room I still had questions. Why hadn't I spoken in tongues, if it was such a big deal? I even summoned the temerity to call God out on it. Pretty much waving Matthew 7:11 in His face, I prayed, 'Come on, God; You say you'll give good gifts to those who ask because You're a good Father. I believe that without question. If this really is a good gift and not made-up gobbledygook, then I want it, even if I don't understand it; please. Don't hold out on me.'

Over the next few weeks, I tentatively tried to formulate some words that went beyond English and which would express the longings of my troubled heart. Truth to tell, I was frightened that I would indeed make something up and thereby give God full permission to wipe me out. Aaron's sons in the Old Testament were burned up when they used unauthorised incense in worship,[94] weren't they? Eli's sons took liberties with their position as priests and God literally, permanently, removed

---

[94] Leviticus 10:1-2.

243

them.[95] God would be well within His rights to do the same to anyone who foolishly or flippantly messed about with holy things, including me. I knew the verse: 'Do not be deceived: God cannot be mocked' (Galatians 6:7); I didn't want to end up on that road.

While I was still grasping for something I felt was way beyond me, I was very aware that God could see every corner of my still thirsty, transparent soul. My feeble efforts gave me a hesitant vocabulary of five possible words which may or may not have meant anything, but I kept quietly returning to them knowing there was no magic involved, but hoping that somehow I could open the door to a more meaningful connection with God. The good news was that He opened the door to me.

The Bible week came around and I found that I had very mixed feelings about it. I'm not sure quite what I anticipated. Camping wasn't a big attraction; barely knowing anyone felt odd, but it was the Holy Spirit aspect of the teaching that had me on my guard. In my ears rang the warnings of my well-intentioned father, cautioning me not to 'jump on any bandwagons'. He seemed to imagine that I might be swept up in a wave of emotion-induced hysteria, followed by an inevitable and irreparable crash onto the rocks of biblical error. As someone who grew up in the 1930s, he was all too aware of the influence a leader of compelling charisma can have on a crowd; it had, after all, happened in Germany during his own childhood. As a boy, he had heard extracts of the powerful speeches of the Third Reich gatherings on the wireless, manipulating the crowds to their diabolical will. His current reluctance to attend anything remotely resembling a large gathering addressed by a single person was, therefore, understandable.

But God was kind to me in those few days in an English field. Still feeling very much out of my depth, I held on to the

---

[95] See 1 Samuel 2–4.

conviction that if I had asked God for the gift of the Holy Spirit in a new way, then He had, unequivocally, given me that gift. My feelings were neither here nor there. The evidence wasn't overly encouraging; but it must be so. That's how clear I was. I couldn't find any biblical back-up for my own response to receiving this gift, but there was plenty of proof to demonstrate that God does what He says He will do. Was I naïve? Probably. Fortunately, that's not a problem for Him.

I can't tell you how delighted and relieved I was when, during a morning worship meeting, I heard someone in the row in front of me use one of those paltry five words I had been whispering in my room. Unmistakably, it was one of 'mine' – hallelujah! Relief flooded me; I wasn't making it up after all. God wasn't going to destroy me for stepping out of line and He had come to meet me in my searching with just the reassurance I needed.

My spirit lifted and the weight of uncertainty slipped away. With it came the realisation over the coming weeks that I had spent much of my Christian life living in what amounted to second gear. No wonder there had been so many times when everything seemed like a joyless, burdensome effort. Too much of my Christian walk had been unfortunately marked by law rather than by grace. I felt as though I had been looking through the right camera lens all along, but suddenly, someone had come along and tweaked the focus button. All I had been taught, all I had known, learned, experienced and valued, was true; but in reality, it was even more true – if that's possible – than I had ever realised. It was like having the colour injected into a black and white photograph or a two-dimensional picture morphing into a three-dimensional one. It was life! My thirst really was being quenched. I was as relieved as I was grateful. God was greater, bigger, more powerful, more present and more knowable than I had understood or known previously.

While I came from an understanding of God's grace demonstrated in salvation, I became increasingly aware that I hadn't seen that demonstrated in very much else. With some notable exceptions, I saw that law, duty, unquestioning obedience and judgementalism had been the order of the day. Please understand that this was only my perception rather than necessarily the whole truth. I absolutely honour the long-standing faith of my parents who patiently built God's truth into my life from the word go, and who introduced me to the things of God in every way they knew how. I am inexpressibly grateful for that. In retrospect, I can easily identify Spirit-filled believers of my youth, who genuinely knew Him, loved Him and were infectious in their joyful following of Him. I am so thankful for the Bible-filled teaching and training I was given as a child and a teenager; I have the rich heritage of a third-generation Jesus-lover who was prayed for by name, daily, by faithful grandparents. The Sunday school teachers who invested so many hours of their time in me, and others, furnished me with a deep love for the Bible and a thorough acquaintance with its contents. They are all partying with the angels these days, but I am indebted to them all for this deposit of treasure, and continue to trust that the seeds they sowed in so many are still bearing healthy fruit.

Discovering intimacy

Moving on in time to the early 1990s, I met a new friend who talked about Jesus with a passion I found quite curious. When I saw her in worship it was obvious that she was completely taken up with Jesus. It wasn't an act; she wasn't going through the motions; her eyes sparkled when she spoke about Him and she described looking into His face and holding His gaze. Frankly, it made me distinctly uncomfortable, but the truth was simply that she was truly, madly, genuinely, deeply in love with Him. This was not a visualisation exercise or an emotionally induced fanaticism; she just knew Jesus in a way I was still to discover. Her undisguised passion was a provocation to me to seek Him yet again. In spite of my new-found Holy-Spirit-invigorated life, there were layers of relationship with Jesus which I still needed to unwrap.

Worship became a new opportunity to meet with Him. The challenge now was to seek His face, not just His hand; to connect with the Provider, not just the provision. That meant taking a deep breath, putting aside my personal preferences and looking into His eyes, like she did, without breaking gaze. This was no abstract intellectual assent; it wasn't just an exercise for a vivid imagination; it was a heart-shift.

I am so grateful that in this season I had two special friends to pray with every week. With them I learned to pray properly, seriously, effectively, confidently and joyously as my relationship with Jesus moved from simply brushing past His 'table' every now and again to enjoy a sumptuous treat, to finding a specific place assigned for me where I was invited to stop, sit, stay and 'eat' and 'drink' with Him. All three of us were hungry and thirsty for Him and, my word, we 'feasted' well!

This was during what is often referred to as the 'Toronto Blessing' season around 1994, in which the Holy Spirit began to move all around the world, in powerful demonstrations of His presence. We had enjoyed both His power and His presence in a new way in the church we led in Hampshire, after Bernard and a fellow leader had visited the Argentine revival together in 1993. Other friends who had visited the Toronto Airport church[96] also prayed with and for us. As with every move of God throughout history, I'm sure there were some supposed encounters across the national and international churches which were more fleshly than godly, some counterfeits and some plain silliness, but that will never detract from the authentic move of God which changed many of us and brought us into a deeper and more intimate joy-filled relationship with Him. Our authentic longing for Him was being met in new ways, refreshing our weary souls and more than satisfying our hunger and thirst for Him.

---

[96] Now called Catch the Fire Church.

An appetite diminished

Fast-forward a few more years, and I found myself back again at another Bible week with my young family. By this time we were juggling the demands of small children, and stretched across three church plants and an international team who worked globally. I was simultaneously trying to manage the demands of repetitive domesticity as well as leading parenting classes and women's ministry, discipling various people and hosting whichever house guests blew so frequently through our ever-open door.

In all honesty, I didn't anticipate a week of camping with unfettered enthusiasm. On this occasion, a gathering had been arranged for 'leaders' wives' (some of whom were, without doubt, leaders themselves). One of the featured speakers that year was a well-known pastor and Bible teacher who worked in Kenya, whose wife had been invited to speak to us. One of my praying friends will tell you I came back to the campsite from that meeting slightly dazed and deeply disturbed. To this day, I have no idea what our guest said, but I was not just disquieted; I was truly undone. It took quite some time before I realised the source of my distress. Simply put, this lady knew God in a way I knew that I did not. Clearly, there was a depth to her relationship – 'weight below the waterline', if you will – which was evidenced through the way she spoke. It threw me.

Perhaps I had become spread too thinly in the hurly-burly of family life; perhaps I had neglected my quiet times; perhaps this lady was just older and wiser and more anointed than me. I didn't know, and I have never spoken to her either then or since, but that encounter forced me to pause and reflect on where I found myself. One of the great disadvantages of full-time church leadership is how life can take on a momentum of its own and subsume every part of you into keeping the 'ship' on course, as it were. You can be so busy giving out to others and helping them access God's grace and purposes that your own resources are slowly depleted without you necessarily noticing.

I didn't like the revelation, but it gave me a welcome opportunity to realise my ongoing hunger to press in to God, and the impetus to pursue Him again.

Perhaps the core realisation for me was that while I knew a great deal about God, had a raft of Bible verses at my fingertips that were applicable to most circumstances that cropped up, enjoyed a measure of the fullness of life lived in and for Him, and met with Him regularly and meaningfully in times of worship, I had not yet grappled fully with the biblical kind of 'knowing'.

Older Bible translations speak of intimacy as 'knowing'; thus, 'Elkanah knew Hannah his wife' (1 Samuel 1:19, KJV). It doesn't mean they just recognised one another or were acquainted; no – they had intercourse; you can't get more intimate than that. As a result, baby Samuel was born. Likewise, Abraham 'knew' Sarah, and the fruitful result was new life in the form of baby Isaac. This kind of talk in the context of my spiritual life was extremely uncomfortable. It required a vulnerability towards God that was deeply unnerving. I am, by nature, quite a private person, and while I recognised that God knows me inside and out in every facet and detail, I think that had still been more of an intellectual fact rather than a heartfelt reality. I am also fairly suspicious of spiritual 'experiences', since I am convinced that not only is God looking for a habitation rather than a visitation but (and I realise this is very subjective) I haven't often found personally that the effusively told experiences of the majority have very much ongoing effect in the lives or character of the narrators.

However, determined not to slide into cynicism, and prompted by what I had perceived in the guest speaker that day, I began to pray in a different way.

I finally realised that I didn't need to know more *about* Jesus; I actually needed to *know Him* more. I didn't need to ask for things, solutions, clarity, wisdom, gifts or a thousand other things; I just needed Him. Like Jacob, I needed to engage to the point of wrestling, if that's what it took. Everything in me rose up to shout that desire down, wanting to file it under sentimentalism; soppy, schmaltzy froth; unfettered emotionalism; insubstantial feelings over conviction; hormonal weakness; or the very real temptation to just dismiss it with well-regulated European scepticism. I had a whole list of excuses for banishing this route; but I had seen something in that older lady that wouldn't let me rest on my spiritual laurels. All too aware that I didn't want to force something and couldn't make a deeper connection by my own will alone, I began to actively pursue God for His own sake.

This brings me to yet another stepping stone in my personal story of 'feasting'. Up until this point I had had some wonderful times with Jesus, soaking in His presence, and had been invigorated by His watertight promises and enlivened in my daily life. But I had not yet been 'undone'.

The unravelling

It began innocuously enough, with me sitting in a Sunday morning service in the East End of London, minding my own business and enjoying the worship. Then, as so often happens when people quieten themselves in the presence of God, someone shared what they felt He was saying. I remember the words verbatim because they landed with such a mighty 'thud' in my heart:

> When was the last time you were undone? How long has it been since your world unravelled? How long is it since everything you depended on fell away? How long since I was the only one left to cling to? I declare my intention today, that I will unravel you until there is nothing left for you to lean on but Me. That is what I built you for.

The words were left hanging in the air, resonating with authority. No one moved for a second or two, and then, inexplicably, the service carried on. I was puzzled. 'What are they doing?' I whispered to Bernard. 'That was weighty; we can't move on. It needs attention. Isn't anyone going to follow through on it? Who's facilitating this? It's like God was right in the room. Didn't anyone else notice that?'

Silly me.

In the coming years – not just days – the resonance that I felt in that London school hall reverberated through my life. Yes, God had been speaking and, whoever else may have found the words relevant, there was absolutely no doubt that He was definitely, specifically speaking to me. Without citing all the events, I can tell you with great certainty that I was 'unravelled', or rather began a process of 'unravelling'; and I didn't enjoy it. Not. One. Bit. Life seemed to be coming apart at the seams; it was just one pressing thing after another. Our children faced a variety of painful challenges which stretched all of us beyond our perceived limits; Jo, our lovely lodger, who was like a daughter to us, was killed in a traffic accident; we had two geographical moves, one across counties and another across the world; our finances were virtually non-existent but our commitments high; people still came to us with their pressing problems, often when they could find no solutions elsewhere and, consequently, were in desperate straits; our expectations of what awaited us relationally on both moves were brutally dashed for reasons we still don't fully understand. Logic, reason and common sense seemed to have evaporated completely; my busy head often felt as though it was going to explode as anxiety and imagination ran riot, effectively chasing peace out of the door.

Here's what I wrote in my journal just short of one year after that Sunday in London:

> [I am confronted by] my own horror at the self-revelation to find I am not the fighting warrior, the 'bring it on' fighter, the 'persevering to the end', 'keep-standing' person I thought. Attrition brings brokenness just as one major blow can do. The 'Peter spirit' in me has quietly said, 'Everyone else may

give up/stop fighting/fall away/compromise/opt out... etc, etc but not me; I never will.' Brokenness shows me I am no different. How often I want to hide under the duvet and sign out ... Suddenly, I am small and helpless.

Yes; I was truly unravelled.

Like my friends, like yourself, I faced the stark insistence of the choices before me. I could make the cold-blooded decision to press on, to press in and to 'feast', or I could take the attractive duvet option and surrender myself to depression and despair. On closer investigation, our choices aren't usually as binary as that. To be honest, I often reverted to the going-through-the-motions, automatic pilot approach to each day, deferring reflective thought by distraction to ease my pain. There are a lot of distractions out there, which in the short term seem to work fairly effectively for the rest of the world; you've probably tried some of them yourself. I think busyness was my drug of choice for a while, but it was not a viable long-term solution.

The chinks of light God gave me as I crawled onwards bear testimony to His amazing grace. It was certainly not my own efforts that brought me through and which keep me walking, talking, laughing and 'feasting' with Him today. While I could not see beyond the end of my nose; while I did not understand what was going on, nor why God would allow it to continue, I kept praying, though not at all eloquently.

In one of those private, sacred, moments I felt the reality of God coming to me as a loving father comes to his child. While I stood helplessly before Him, 'ugly' crying (you know what I mean – not quiet, ladylike weeping, but more gulping, snotty sobbing), pouring out my heart to Him with my head down and hair all over the place, I felt Him come and so, so gently hook my hair behind my ear and tip my chin up to look Him full in the face. Then His reassuring words: 'Did you think I didn't know?'

Yes, I have been unravelled, undone and broken beyond all recognition ever since, but God's words are true: 100 per cent dependency on Him is everything. That is what I was built for; so were you. That's not just cognitive; it's a painful but totally worthwhile revelation.

The original blueprint for Adam and Eve was to press into their Creator, to walk and talk with Him openly, fully, without secrets and without shame. He was to be their source and resource for every decision, every breath and every moment of their lives. What an extraordinary privilege! This season showed me how far from that original design I had lived much of my life. God has called us to intimacy with Him on a scale and at a level we have barely imagined. This is not supposed to be a one-off experience, but the place where we live consistently.

Abiding

During my childhood summer holidays, my family were fortunate to enjoy regular high tea with some old farming friends in Devon. This couple had no children of their own, and perhaps that's why they enjoyed the opportunity of providing this lavish annual treat for us. The table practically groaned under the weight of all the appealing goodies that were spread out for us to enjoy; it felt as though I'd fallen through the pages of a storybook for a few hours filled with abundant farmhouse delicacies. On the wall, above our heads, hung a framed Victorian relic of intricate, gilded calligraphy which read:

> Abide with us, Lord Jesus,
> Let this home circle be
> Thy resting place among us
> Another Bethany;
> That in your love our love may grow
> And make this home a heaven below.[97]

---

[97] Original source unknown.

I liked the simple, lyrical rhythm of the poem; at some point I must have learned it off by heart since it's still in my memory now. What I relished though, was that first word: 'Abide'. A seldom used, rich word; it fascinated me. It's really just another word for 'live', but somehow its assonance underlines the permanency of the meaning. Like the word 'dwell', you have to say it slowly. Try reading it out loud to yourself now. There's a longevity even in its pronunciation.

This is what our feasting at God's table is supposed to be like: not somewhere that we visit, but somewhere that we stay and live. This is a spiritual place where we linger, commune, gaze, rest and enjoy like-minded interaction, not because we have to, but because we want to; and our Host wants that too. It is truly home. Why would you want to be anywhere else?

We will learn, like Brother Lawrence, to abide when we are daily practising the reality of living in God's presence. 'The more we know Him, the more we will desire to know Him. As love increases with knowledge, the more we know God, the more we will truly love Him. We will learn to love Him equally in times of distress or in times of great joy.'[98] That dynamic of spiritual supply and demand which the brother discovered, in which our yearning for more of God will be satisfied as He reveals more and more of Himself to us, will not just be the murky background of our life, but in the spotlight or centre of our life all day, every day.

We can 'feast', therefore, regardless of our circumstances.

In truth, it makes sense that the more we love Jesus, the more we will want to obey Him. The more time we spend in His presence, at His 'feasting table', the more contented, the more peaceful and the more fruitful our lives will be. We will truly live; not just exist. Since we become like whatever, or whoever, we focus on, we will reflect God's glory more consistently and accurately when we keep our gaze on Him.

---

[98] Brother Lawrence, *The Practice of the Presence of God* (New Kensington, PA: Whitaker House, 1982), p55. Used with permission.

At this banqueting table we have the desire, the invitation and the opportunity to be completely taken up with the One our soul loves: Jesus. This type of abiding does not reduce us to an observational, passive thing – like a glove, which is only animated because of the living hand inside it. No, our mind, heart, will, feelings and passions, spirit and soul can be thoroughly engaged with Him. We don't have to work this up by our own efforts to be only a passing experience or fantasy; neither do we need to generate a fictional narrative in order to try to fit in. There is something liberatingly natural about living each day in the company of our Creator, which removes frenetic activity, persistent anxiety and the perpetual urge to surrender to the values, filters and perspectives of the rest of the world. That is not to make us superior or removed from our spheres of influence and circumstantial contexts; rather, it ensures that we are grounded and rooted according to the plumb line of God's Word and His kingdom – a rich 'feasting' table!

Jesus calls Himself a vine in John 15; the picture illustrates the function of believers as branches who bear fruit and so need pruning, but also notes that branches which don't bear any grapes need to be cut off. Painful either way! Older translations of the passage use that lovely word 'abide' in instructing us to stay and live in that vine. Importantly, the vine is indistinguishable from the branches; the whole thing bears fruit and it's the entire plant which is referred to as the vine, indicating how we are to be so thoroughly bound up in Him that we can't be recognised apart from Him. The separation is nigh on impossible to discern – '[my] life is now hidden with Christ in God' (Colossians 3:3). That's real 'abiding'; remaining, staying, being part of; making our home here.

God's relentless pursuit of His loved ones

God loves us too much to leave us where we are and how we are. We've seen how His unprecedented pursuit of us is relentless. Yes, He will woo us and romance us, but because He is a jealous God who will not tolerate rivals for His affection, He will also rebuke us. We spent some time exploring this in Chapter 14, referring to the time when Jesus rebuked Peter and recognising that love and discipline are two sides of the same coin. It may not be a very popular doctrine right now, but the fact remains that our heavenly Father doesn't bow to fads and fashion either. God disciplines us, not because He is harsh, but because any loving father worth his salt gets angry when he sees his children flirt with danger or teeter on the brink of harm, destruction or ruin. His aim is not to bring division or disconnection, but to strengthen the parent–child relationship for the benefit of the recipient.

I mentioned in Chapter 12 that particular day when God lovingly yet sternly rebuked me. I couldn't have mistaken His voice for anyone else's. In the upheaval of increased travel, leaving a stable home for a more nomadic lifestyle, which included being far from my children, I did not always live from a place of 'feasting'. Slowly and subtly, I discovered that rather than embracing the adventure with expectant faith, I was sometimes gritting my teeth like a good Brit, and reluctantly enduring. There was more resignation than rejoicing. That afternoon had been a wake-up call for me. Not only had I not been 'feasting', but that element of choice stood out starkly for me. God was not reluctant to 'feast' with me... the responsibility for my absence at His table was mine, and mine alone. I had been missing the opportunity to spend time alone with Him, pursuing Him with all my heart, and had allowed the old enemy to sneak in with his own infernal tri-point programme. Giving him room to steal my joy, kill my contentment and destroy my peace meant I was missing out on 'feasting' at the table God had so abundantly set for me. How foolish. I broke down in repentant tears and drastically changed the way I used my time, all the while immensely grateful that He broke into my myopic lethargy.

When we abide at the feasting table, we can know the unfettered companionship and enjoyment of Jesus. It's an activity which simply requires a clean heart which leans into Him and keeps our desire for Him active. Now we know that 'he will give you the desires of your heart' (Psalm 37:4), but before we get carried away with an extensive wish-list, we must understand that this does not necessarily mean your heart's desires.

There's a subtle difference here which long-term 'diners' will recognise. When we press into Him, God will, gradually or swiftly, change our old, selfish desires to be in line with His own will, because His passion for you, as for me, is that we discover the fullness of who He made us to be. In all probability it is, at best, unlikely that our natural earth-bound inclinations will coincide with those of heaven. Indeed, our own desires tend to be small, feeble and insipid compared with what God has in mind for us. We are too easily satisfied with short-term solutions to our immediate needs, distracted by popular culture and its alluring pastimes, when God intends something much more substantial, relationally satisfying and purpose-filled for us.

God's desires for us are fixed; He longs for us to enjoy everything that was in the original creation blueprint: freedom (from sin, shame, burdens, wounds, the past, death, hell), openness, forgiveness, joy, intimacy, willingness, trust, peace, obedience, continuous communion, radical worship, embracing His will above our own and submitting to His 'menu', all evidenced in all aspects of our everyday lives, as well as healthy fruits of His Spirit, which grow and bear the seeds for reproduction in the lives of others. In short, we are to replicate Jesus – no small thing. His desires include us successfully meeting the challenges of accepting with joy the 'menu' in front of us, bearing the cost of the sacrifice it will require to follow Him fully, consecrating ourselves for His lordship, and enjoying the journey, even when the view is dismal or the path rocky.

'Deeper' feasting

I am persuaded that there are new 'levels' of 'feasting' yet to be discovered, some of which will be unearthed in worship. I know that I can 'feast' continually; my whole life, after all, is to be 'a sacrifice of praise' (Hebrews 13:15) and a life of worship; but there are highlights in life, special places, precious moments of particular significance. For me, these often, but not exclusively, happen in designated times of worship when I can join the throngs of heaven praising Jesus, the King of glory. Whether I fall on my face, kneel, dance, lift my hands or sit in reflective silence, in my heart I make space to meet the immensity of God in His utter holiness, where countless angelic beings, heroes of the faith and all of history's believers join to celebrate the Champion of heaven through whom salvation has been purchased. All too soon I run out of words to adequately express the wonder and glory of who He is.

Just as there are new depths to be plumbed in my relationship with my husband, so it is with the divine Bridegroom. We've enjoyed more than thirty years of marriage, but that doesn't mean that Bernard and I can call it a day and disengage; we have promised to continue walking together, finding out new things about one another, and enjoying the contentment of being in the company of one another's unconditional love. We have had quite a journey through the years, and I'm quite sure there are still fresh things to discover together. It's rather like exploring the layers of an onion from the inside out, yet somehow going deeper: the reverse of diminishing our relationship. Each layer will reveal something new and enriching, while actually increasing the dimensions of our 'knowing'. Doubtless there are more adventures ahead, and there's no one with whom I'd rather face them. Our shared history, shared memories and shared battle scars unite us in a unique and unbreakable way within God's powerful grace.

In the same way, spiritually, I believe Jesus has many 'courses' for me to eat that I haven't been served yet. Some will taste sweet, some may be bitter; not all will be easy to swallow, but when the 'menu' leaves much to be desired He will, I know, change my desires if I remain surrendered to Him. When my gaze is fixed on Him, the 'menu' will be secondary. He will be seated next to me, giving me His full attention, encouragement and grace for every morsel. He knows me fully and – I am so grateful – isn't put off by my faults and foibles; He is never surprised by me and is fully present in every aspect of my life, unstinting in His love and affection for me.

The more we are able to enjoy true spiritual 'feasting' in our temporal life, the more prepared we will be to take up our invitation to the heavenly Wedding Feast of the Lamb. Like any bride, we have a responsibility to undertake some serious self-reflection and preparation in order to meet our Bridegroom in a way that is worthy of Him. At the same time, let's recognise that perfection is not for this life, so self-obsession is inappropriate; the Bridegroom must always be our reference point. A Church that doesn't understand this will miss Him and forfeit so much.

At that final feast, all enemies and their influence will be banished forever. For all eternity we will be wrapped up in the arms of our Friend, Lover, Saviour and King. He will never tire of our company, just as we will never tire of His. Everything we have known here will seem like a shadow or a dream; a pale, two-dimensional suggestion of something insubstantial will become a vivid, three-dimensional living reality. Finally, 'I shall know fully, even as I am fully known' (1 Corinthians 13:12); perfect intimacy at last.

Palate-cleanser questions

- Who are the people who spur you on to dig deeper into Jesus? What are the qualities you see in them?

- How has God ever unravelled you?

- Which heart desires has God changed in you, and with what were they replaced?

Coffee & Petits Fours

17. Conclusion

Behold, I stand at the door and knock. If anyone hears my voice and opens the door, I will come in to him and eat with him, and he with me.
(Revelation 3:20, ESVUK)

Jesus is still knocking

When Holman Hunt, inspired by this verse, completed his famous work, *The Light of the World*, in 1853, he was unaware of the impact it would subsequently have on Victorian society in England and beyond. The painting was a response to some of the spiritual questions he had, and he used specific techniques in his composition which were out of step with the accepted religious iconography of art at the time. For a start, his figure of Christ was painted as a solid individual, emphasising the real, risen, eternal person of Jesus, rather than the ethereal phantasms of contemporary works. The light from His lantern suggests an illumination of truth, drawing the viewer into the picture. You won't have to look too closely to realise that the painting is packed full of symbolism. What you will also notice, however, is the complete absence of a handle on the weed-strewn door at which Jesus stands and knocks; this portal must be – can only be – opened from within.

For years this well-loved painting hung in homes, churches and public buildings as a provocation to 'open the door' for Jesus to enter. As a child, I had an illustrated bookmark of this painting in my own Bible and was frequently encouraged to 'open the door and invite Jesus into [my] heart'.

It's a classic work of art; but the problem with our interpretation of Hunt's picture is that it takes the Revelation verse completely out of context.

This is Jesus speaking to the church at Laodicea in one of the letters recorded by John. If you read the whole passage, you'll find that Jesus says their lack of either hot zeal or cold indifference has left them with only a lukewarm mediocrity which actually makes Him sick. He would rather they were 'one or the other' (Revelation 3:15); He can't abide tepid, insipid, lacklustre faith. Granted, it's a painful, emotive, sharply challenging word for that church; but it's definitely not a rebuke to the unsaved. Jesus doesn't speak those words either in the context of evangelism, nor as a means to galvanise the 'lost' to wake up and take hold of the salvation that can be theirs in Him. The clarion call to repentance and renewed commitment of relationship and intimacy with God is directed at the bride of Christ; at the worldwide Christian community; at the Church; at me; at you.

The verse immediately before is pertinent: 'Those whom I love I rebuke and discipline. So be earnest and repent' (Revelation 3:19, NIV 1984).

This is a wake-up call. A critique not a criticism.

A timely spiritual health-check

It's no secret that the Church in all its many forms has had its problems, pressures, heresies, compromises and distractions throughout history, mostly since it became 'respectable' during the time of the Emperor Constantine. In the twenty-first century, Jesus might observe a palpable loss of passion in many places of worship and note the increase in the number of chapels and churches now used as art galleries, restaurants and residential dwellings.

What would Jesus say, I wonder, about prayer meetings which are ditched in favour of personal prophecy and self-centred blessing, or Bible studies that are replaced by feel-good, pithy, self-help maxims? I surmise that He might question why fasting is seldom mentioned, why personal holiness is often viewed subjectively, or why repentance sometimes gets skirted around in favour of popular short cuts for lifestyle-enhancement. It pains me to find places where 'church' has become institutionalised, programme based, agenda driven, hierarchical, introverted, business orientated, platform led and production centred, with decisions made on the basis of finance and personal preference rather than what God may, or may not, have said; how must it make Jesus feel? Sometimes I think He will have to build His Church[99] in spite of us rather than because of us.

Would Jesus weep if He were to see worshipping 'in … Spirit and in truth' (John 4:24) bypassed for manufactured atmosphere, or even polished performances which are more about the expertise of the musicians than about glorifying Him? In trying to emulate the success of secular concerts with their mandatory smoke machines, complex lighting and thumping bass lines – exciting as they can be – there's a distinct possibility that we may find the real Jesus obscured.

I think we need that wake-up call just as much as the Laodicean church did. Can we measure how far we may have moved away from God's original idea of families of believers living life in relationship together, towards our current school or business models of 'church'? With a culture of Christian celebrities and pop-style interaction, my observation would be that Christendom sometimes seems to have reached only for a poor imitation of what the world offers. The world doesn't seem to have responded very positively so far, perhaps

---

[99] Matthew 16:18.

disconcerted by the seemingly unending and heartbreaking exposure of financial misconduct, sexual scandals and abuse that has come to light across denominations.

What on earth has happened to our 'sincere and pure devotion to Christ' (2 Corinthians 11:3)? We really do have to be prepared to do some serious self-examination and get back to the grass roots of what it means to walk with God authentically in a contemporary context. I wonder what letter Jesus would write to us today?

This is deeply uncomfortable, but it's not anti-church. I've been fortunate to have travelled across the world over the past few years and I've reluctantly discovered that the spiritual themes are much the same everywhere. Obviously, no one can say they genuinely love Jesus and dislike His 'wife'/bride; that would be nonsense. Nevertheless, it is appropriate to lament and to weep over things which have gone badly astray and which almost certainly bruise the heart of God.

Don't forget that Jesus Himself having just arrived in Jerusalem on Palm Sunday was so horrified by what He saw going on in the courts of the temple that He broke up the market it had become, toppling tables, grieved that the place designed for prayer had become 'a den of robbers' (Matthew 21:13). There wasn't much sign of mildness on His part in that moment. Likewise, the letters Paul wrote to the New Testament churches contain the sort of admonishments that truly astonish me: someone sleeping with his father's wife; believers taking one another to court; heretical teachers and false apostles bringing unsound, divisive teaching into the family of God, and causing mayhem in the body of Christ, etc.[100]

Assuming that very few of God's people start their day with the intention of destroying His kingdom, it's probably fair to say that these tragedies don't suddenly happen overnight. Complacency, if not downright sin, creeps in slowly or wears a community down by attrition over time.

---

[100] 1 Corinthians 5-6; 2 Corinthians 11:13-15.

I know it's not difficult to find fault, poke holes and criticise the sometimes mud-stained bride of Christ. If you feel angry about it, then check yourself that it is a righteous anger – 'In your anger do not sin' (Ephesians 4:26) – which is truly seeking God's best for His beloved children. Like Paul, it can be the most loving thing to ask the same question he posed to the churches in Galatia: 'After beginning by means of the Spirit, are you now trying to finish by means of the flesh?' (Galatians 3:3). Clearly, he was deeply concerned for the purity and authenticity of the church, just as Jesus shows Himself to be in Revelation.

We cannot respond to the invitations of Jesus without changing, or being changed, both inside and out. As our hearts turn to Him in greater measure, with determined consistency, drenched in the grace of Jesus, the power of the Holy Spirit and increasing delight, our feet must turn that way as well. We will want to shake off the transient mediocrity of the ordinary in order to seek His face and sit in His company, with the eternal delights that are spread at the table set for us. We were not made only for this life and this world.

In the light of this, I am encouraged to notice that there is a righteous discontent starting to brew among many communities of believers. Some are indeed waking up from having gradually, inadvertently fallen into a semi-paralysing enchantment of mediocrity which, in some instances, has marred the glory of Christ and brought God's name into disrepute. In an echo of Hunt's painting, Pete Greig wrote in his provocative book: 'Sometimes … I wondered just how long the Lord had been standing on the church doorstep, ringing the bell, before we stopped doing Christianity long enough to let him in.'[101] Apparently others are wondering too, and consequently are making changes. This is good news!

'Doing Christianity' can become just that: a task we are doing rather than a relationship we are living. Church has sometimes taken on a warped life of its own in which God's Word has been

---

[101] Greig, *Dirty Glory*, p16.

neglected, Jesus' radical demands have been relegated to options and the Holy Spirit has been squashed into a back seat. We might call such a hybrid 'Churchianity'.

So, while things may have looked grim for a season, while there have been multiple false starts and stumblings, Jesus' followers are being stirred and positively provoked to the reality of a relationship with Him which is truly more about Him than about them. Good news, indeed!

A new day?

Thankfully, Church has, to some degree, started to emerge from buildings in a welcome move to connect with local communities who would probably never step inside the doors of a religious building of any kind. Pioneers, evangelists, church planters and many with a call to address issues of social justice have weathered multiple setbacks in order to find a relevant connection with people in their towns and cities, without watering down the gospel or the message of salvation.

News of miraculous healings, divine encounters, outbreaks of spiritual awakenings and radical conversions are reaching beyond national borders, each one bringing whispers of hope, renewal and life beyond our own circle of experience. Believers are breaking out of their church walls and are breathing the ripe air of a world which is desperate to be healed from its brokenness, and where the expanse of God's goodness needs to be seen and lived out every day.

The realities of self-sacrifice, servanthood and complete surrender are beginning to be taken seriously once more. It's time for all of us to consider the realities of Jesus again: His invitations and His demands as well as His immeasurable love and His unfathomable grace. I, for one, welcome an increasing awareness of the meta-narrative unfolding behind and beyond the scenes displayed on our news screens or in our suffocating echo chambers and bubbles. It's heartening too, for those imploring God to break into our world; He has already done so.

The salvation plan started in the heart of God, manifested itself in a rustic stable in Bethlehem, won the unequivocal victory over sin, death and hell at Calvary, broke out of a sealed tomb and hasn't stopped since. Heaven is not silent; God is on the move.

God has not made any of us for a 'second best' life. That truth bears repetition! He has the finest and best for us in His storehouse; it may not look as we might expect or prefer, and we may have a zillion questions along the way, but it will prove to be perfect if we meet and abide with God in it and through it, as He desires.

Radical Jesus

Episcopal priest Robert Capon asked the following pertinent questions:

> What happened to radical Christianity, the un-nice brand of Christianity that turned the world upside down? What happened to the category-smashing, life-threatening, anti-institutional Gospel that spread through the first century like wildfire and was considered (by those in power) dangerous? What happened to the kind of Christians whose hearts were on fire, who had no fear, who spoke the truth no matter what the consequence, who made the world uncomfortable, who were willing to follow Jesus wherever He went? What happened to the kind of Christians who were filled with passion and gratitude, and who every day were unable to get over the grace of God?[102]

I have a feeling that at least some of the answer is that they got distracted by all the 'doing' they felt was required by their faith,

---

[102] Original source uncertain.

and forgot there was a compelling, but unopened, invitation to joyful 'feasting' lying on their spiritual doormat the whole time.

Both John and Jesus were taken to task by rampant legalists. The religious elite of the day condemned John the Baptist although he lived an austere life without partying or wine-drinking; they assumed he was demonised. But when 'the Son of Man came eating and drinking … they [said], "Here is a glutton and a drunkard…"' (Matthew 11:18-19). The Pharisees were so determined to reject the messages and persons of both John and Jesus that they contradicted themselves in their expectations of what they had decided was, or was not, appropriate for these young rabbis. When was the last time you were rebuked for the passionate nature of your relationship with Jesus, I wonder? Have you ever been reined in for taking Jesus too seriously? I know I haven't.

In my introduction, I said that I don't think it will be possible for Jesus-followers to flourish in our peculiar and demanding times unless we can learn to 'feast' on the things God has entrusted us with currently.

We have to grow up; it's not an option any more, it's a requirement. We have to take Jesus a whole lot more seriously and ourselves far less so if we are to stand firm and rightly represent our King at the crossroads of history where we have been placed. None of us knows what lies ahead as around us nations crumble, leaders fall, disasters of social, financial, natural and physical hues assail our ailing world in new and more terrifying ways. Wisdom calls for us to avoid the thermometer-like lurching swings of emotional reaction to external conditions, but rather to keep ourselves steady, like a fixed thermostat, in tune with something – or Someone – less arbitrary.

Continual, consistent, habitual, glorious 'feasting' with Jesus is our true purpose in life. It's the only pursuit which will bring us the satisfying love, peace and joy we all yearn for, when we sit at the table prepared for us in union and fellowship with Him, sharing our hearts as we 'eat' in the presence, but beyond the reach of, our enemies. 'Feasting' with Jesus needs to become our goal, our priority, our raison d'être.

I hope you've grasped it now; this is what we were made for! We urgently, diligently, unwaveringly need to seek it out, like the valuable treasure that intimacy with our Creator is, regardless of the cost. Let's not settle for anything else.

'Come!'

This book began with an exploration of the seven biblical feasts and a number of invitations. Here's another invitation, from Isaiah – a call to press into the company and character of our generous Host and partake of the lavish banquet He provides:

> Come, all you who are thirsty,
> come to the waters;
> and you who have no money,
> come, buy and eat!
> Come, buy wine and milk
> without money and without cost.
> Why spend money on what is not bread,
> and your labour on what does not satisfy?
> Listen, listen to me, and eat what is good,
> and you will delight in the richest of fare.
> Give ear and come to me;
> listen, that you may live.
> (Isaiah 55:1-3a)

Our souls were made to truly live; to reverberate with the presence, person and power of God; to be satisfied with nothing less. So why would we bother looking elsewhere? The prodigal tried that, but there was nothing the world had to offer which gave him the peace and fulfilment he was looking for.

Again, Isaiah, in another multilayered prophecy, looks forward to the day when, 'the LORD Almighty will prepare a feast of rich food for all peoples, a banquet of aged wine – the best of meats and the finest of wines' (Isaiah 25:6). The prodigal discovered that the best of everything was all back at 'home', in his father's house. We have a living God who deals in superlatives and abundance, and He continues to invite us to come to Him.

There is a Jewish tradition that epitomises the nature of God's blessings when the Sabbath *kiddush* cup is filled with wine until it overflows. David used exactly that image in Psalm 23. It's a powerful picture of the life of God in us. Any vessel is only truly full when it overflows. If we aren't spilling the life of God into those around us – if it doesn't show – then maybe we just aren't full.

It's almost inevitable that we may have to wait for heaven to make sense of all the confusing threads of our life and to finally appreciate the completed tapestry as God does. But, there, when we are face to face with our Maker and Redeemer, all our questions will be swallowed up in extravagant worship as we realise He is the answer to them all. Then they will fade into a world of shadows as we press on into the life for which we were truly made: to see the face of God Himself – a privilege which, according to the Beatitudes, is only granted to 'the pure in heart' (Matthew 5:8).

We know that only Jesus' blood can make our hearts pure. For all in His family this is the greatest miracle of all: that we can be clean before Him because, and only because, of His sacrifice. Our finite minds and temporal hearts will never fathom the eternal dimensions of His love and His passion for us this side of heaven.

Finally, our days of hungering and thirsting for Him will be completely sated; Truth personified will stand before us with His arms of love outstretched to welcome us. What a thrilling prospect!

What do you want?

My journal has an entry for 3rd October 2013, a time when I was in a dark valley, when 'feasting' was elusive and had to be fought for with every fibre of my spiritual being. I should have been excited by the new adventure ahead, confident that God would come through for us as He had faithfully done over so many years. Instead, I was exhausted physically, emotionally and spiritually, nervous about the lack of a secure home base and overwhelmed by the prospect and logistics of living between two hemispheres, as we ministered between Europe and Africa, far from my adult children. I didn't have a dream or vision, but I began to wonder how I would respond if, at this moment, God were to make the same offer to me as He made to Solomon (1 Kings 3:5). If I could ask God for anything, what would it be…? I didn't choose wisdom – perhaps I should have done. I chose courage. It seemed the most elusive commodity at the time; I felt I needed it for even the smallest of tasks, like getting out of bed in the morning, let alone for embracing the 'menu' that lay before me. So, I reflected that I would ask for courage for six specific challenges.

Courage:
- to face the storms, the battles, the giants, the fears, even the 'little foxes that ruin the vineyards'[103]

- to keep on keeping on with hope; to trudge over the next hill, the next hill and the one after that

- to implement wisdom; to find the treasures in the darkness;[104] to see the light ahead, and push on

---

[103] Song of Solomon 2:15.
[104] See Isaiah 45:3, ESVUK.

- to trust and obey; to declare truth; to speak up, and stand up and grow up

- to forget the past and press onward to the goal; to keep my scars clean and my spirit sweet

- to finish well; to be a 'good and faithful servant';[105] to sing in the rain, laugh at the days to come and enjoy the journey.

If I were to respond again, I would add that I desire the courage to continually 'feast' well at the 'table' that is so lavishly spread for me – no matter what is served – 'in the presence of my enemies' (Psalm 23:5).

I need courage to take up my assigned place, to trust the One who knows my 'menu', to grasp my spiritual 'knife and fork' as an act of warfare, and revel in the company of my host – the One who my heart loves – as my cup surely overflows. I want to live in that place where 'goodness and mercy' are both chasing behind me, and are naturally left in my 'wake' to flow over others, as I have a taste of what it will mean to 'dwell in the house of the LORD for ever' (Psalm 23:6, ESVUK).

Next time you read Psalm 23, dispense with any sentimental overfamiliarity that may have subtly crept in; resist the urge to race through it so it's little more than a mindless mantra. With me, take David's words as a declaration and a battle cry; a warrior's heartfelt response from our assigned place at His banqueting table, beneath His wonderful banner of love.[106] That's where my heart longs to be: entranced by His company, focused on the One my heart loves, taken up with His majesty, overflowing with gratitude, continually praising and 'feasting' at His beautiful table.

May it be your faith-filled battle cry too, and let's 'feast'!

---

[105] Matthew 25:21,23.
[106] Song of Solomon 2:4.

18. Babette's Feast

People take refuge in the shadow of your wings. They feast in the abundance of your house; you give them drink from your river of delights.
(Psalm 36:7-8)

In August 1987, a Dutch film directed by Gabriel Axel was released, based on a short story by Karen Blixen of *Out of Africa* fame; it was called *Babette's Feast*.[107] The narrative depicts the austere life of two spinster sisters who exist under the legalistic roof of their father, a strict pastor, where pleasures, colour, luxuries and anything considered worldly, has been foresworn. Life is wearisome, quiet, bleak and drab in this desolate corner of Jutland until the arrival of a Parisian refugee, Babette, who is sent to be the family cook. It's a pitiful job since approved supplies are meagre, and eating constitutes little more than a miserable chore. Slowly she loses her spark; loses her heart; loses her hope.

One day a communication arrives which tells Babette she has unexpectedly won the colossal sum of 100,000 francs. Unbeknown to the family, in her former occupation, Babette was the head chef at the famous Café Anglais in the capital,

---

[107] Astrablu Media, Inc. Used with permission.

where her extravagant and superior dinner for twelve cost exactly this amount.

Here and now, in this pitiful, joyless house and without revealing much detail, she pleads to be allowed to embark on the task of reproducing a special meal for her employer and his friends with this largesse, and before her creative spirit shrivels up altogether from lack of use. With permission reluctantly granted, she begins with what she has in the confines of their rustic kitchen and with limited utensils.

Soon Babette is ordering delicacies from afar, seeking out and preparing fresh ingredients, artfully combining flavours and mixing specialities and delights for this remarkable occasion, relishing it all, just as she used to do in Paris.

Finally, the day of the feast arrives. The table is laid, the marinading, sifting, stirring, folding, baking and roasting is completed. Babette tastes the food so she is satisfied the quality is up to her exacting standard, and the last garnish is arranged. The guests take their places and with seductive smells emerging from the kitchen, they wonder what could possibly lie ahead.

As the feast is served, the dozen stiff, unsmiling, emotionally cold and shut-down members of the pastor's dwindling congregation begin to discover the astonishing physical and emotional effects of good food and wine. It's a complete revelation to them. Babette's culinary creations have them revelling in textures, fragrances and flavours they have never encountered before, apart from one guest who begins to recall a meal he once enjoyed, years ago, at the Café Anglais in Paris...

Eyes light up in wonder, cautious smiles creep across lined and weary faces; a new world is opening up in front of them. Gradually, conversation begins, tentatively at first, ushering in unfamiliar conviviality and, rarest of all, laughter. The meal awakens latent memories, evokes long-forgotten impressions, revives dormant sensations, and thaws icy hearts. Babette's true passion erupts in her preparation, planning and serving of a sumptuous feast, including the famous Clos de Vougeot 1845 wine, resulting in an extraordinary meal which appeals to all the tired, crippled senses of her employers. She comes truly alive in this, her arena of expertise; the place where she was clearly designed to flourish. That life spills out and embraces every guest who partakes around the table.

Babette's Feast is a vivid portrayal of the uniquely life-giving relationship between people and their food. As a viewer, you can almost smell the complex layers of each fascinating and extraordinary dish, and undoubtedly appreciate the supreme artisanal craftsmanship and detailed care that went into each separate one. It's a compelling scene which draws the viewer in to be at the table too; to vicariously indulge and feast with the invited diners.

I hope that reading this book has opened your eyes in a new way to understand that Jesus has His own banqueting table spread for us, bearing dishes and delights that have been carefully prepared for us to eat with Him. Like Babette, it cost Him all that He had to make such a feast possible and like the diners, we will come truly alive when we take our own place as an invited guest at that table. But unlike those guests, for whom this was a once-in-a-lifetime experience, we have the enormous privilege of a permanent invitation, a designated seat and the uninterrupted gaze of the One who loves us more than our finite hearts and minds can fathom.

As we feast we will find nourishment, solace, intimacy, healing, strength and equipping for everything that lies ahead, as well as the maturity and hope we need to engage with a needy world.

Let's not be reluctant to 'feast' at the table set before us.

Bon appétit!

Postscript

While this manuscript was in the final stages of editing, I found myself served two contrasting, but related, 'dishes'.

First of all, I was privileged to speak at an event where we focused on the words of Lamentations 3:22: 'The steadfast love of the LORD never ceases, his mercies never come to an end' (RSV). Exploring the unchanging, dependable nature of God's character was a celebration of His goodness, faithfulness and unwavering love for His children. We followed biblical stories to remind ourselves that He is the God who sees (Genesis 16:13), hears (Genesis 21:17), knows (Psalm 139:13-18), loves (1 John 3:1), cares (1 Peter 5:7) and saves us (Psalm 88:1).[108] No wonder that we responded in worship together; that was a 'feast' indeed!

The second dish came less than a fortnight later when I was diagnosed with breast cancer. Would you believe me if I told you that I smiled wryly? I am not a masochist in any way and my pain threshold is not high, but I felt the irony of suddenly being served such an unpalatable 'dish' while having spent so many hours in writing and speaking, communicating the importance of 'feasting' at the table God has set for us in spite of the 'menu' that may be in front of us. Here is a fresh opportunity for me as I find myself facing what honestly feels like a double portion of liver!

---

[108] See chapter 6, page 112.

There is a brutal reality in the walk of faith. Either our relationship with God is real or it isn't. We face the same choices, the same decisions in all our varying, changing circumstances: will we trust Him in all things and follow wherever He takes us?

Will I do that now?

By His grace and in His strength, and though I may well have days when I wobble, I choose to say, 'Yes.'

Once again I find I am asking for courage to 'feast' with Him as I navigate this unappetising serving. I am well aware that my place at God's table remains set aside for me specifically and His invitation to me is as compelling as ever. I want to 'feast' however I can, under His banner of love,[109] assured of His closeness and in the presence of my whispering enemies who would love nothing better than to steal my joy, hope and peace. By pressing in to Him, I know I can defy them regardless of the outcome. I am privileged to have praying friends and family committed to walking with me through this valley and would welcome your prayers too.

I look forward to journeying in His company and choose again to lock my gaze with His. He is still my refuge, my strength,[110] the Host of this feast, my all in all.

I've already reached for my napkin; now where did I put my cutlery?

9th February 2020
Bath, UK

---

[109] Song of Solomon 2:4.
[110] Psalm 59:16.